masters of movement

masters of movement

Portraits of America's Great Choreographers

Rose Eichenbaum | Photographs and Text

Clive Barnes | Foreword

SMITHSONIAN BOOKS

WASHINGTON

Photographs and text © 2004 by Rose Eichenbaum

Copy editor: Jan McInroy
Production editor: Joanne Reams
Designer: Kate McConnell

Library of Congress Cataloging-in-Publication data

Eichenbaum, Rose.
      Masters of movement : portraits of America's great choreographers /
      Rose Eichenbaum, photographs and text ; Clive Barnes, foreword.
          p. cm.
      Includes bibliographical references and index.
      ISBN 1-58834-185-2 (alk. paper)
          1. Choreographers—United States—Biography.
      2. Choreographers—United States—Portraits. I. Title.

      GV1785.A1E53 2004
      792.8'2'0922—dc22
      [B]

                              2004048246

A paperback reissue ISBN 978-1-58834-248-5 of the original cloth edition
First Smithsonian Books paperback edition published 2007

British Library Cataloging-in-Publication Data are available

Printed in China, not at government expense.

11 10 09 08 07   1 2 3 4 5

*I dedicate this book to my parents, Adela and Wolf Manheimer,
who raised me to believe that honesty, integrity, and respect
were virtues I should live by.*

CONTENTS

AUTHOR'S NOTE
. . . . xiii

FOREWORD by Clive Barnes
. . . . ix

Donald McKayle
Dance Aficionado. 1

Carmen de Lavallade
Vision of Loveliness 5

Fayard Nicholas
Acrobat of God. 9

Graciela Daniele
Adventurer 13

Edward Villella
Prodigal Son 17

Susan Stroman
Belle of Broadway. 21

Eliot Feld
Dance Engineer 25

Bella Lewitzky
Kinetic Thinker 29

Helgi Tomasson
Classic Visionary. 33

Onna White
Tough Bird. 37

Gregory Hines
Tap Dancer. 41

Michael Kidd
Man with the Midas Touch 45

Toni Basil
Improviser. 49

David Parsons
Risk Taker 53

Pilobolus
Dance Organism 57

Anna Sokolow
Rebellious One. 61

Mark Morris
Bad Boy of Dance 65

Ann Reinking
Jazz Dancer 69

Vincent Paterson
Director 73

Debbie Allen
Bold and Brave 77

Dee Dee Wood and Marc Breaux
Dynamic Duo 81

Katherine Dunham
Anthropologist 85

Gus Solomons Jr.
Dance Architect 89

Patricia Birch
Little Giant 93

Rob Marshall
Dance Environmentalist 97

Sophie Maslow
Communicator 101

José Greco
Ambassador of Spanish Dance 105

Tommy Tune
Tall Talent 109

Luigi
Jazz Master 113

Judith Jamison
On the Path 117

Dwight Rhoden
Emissary of the Dance .121

Garth Fagan
Caribbean Man 125

Meredith Monk
Singing Body 129

Moses Pendleton
Choreographer Incognito 133

Lar Lubovitch
Dance Painter 137

Murray Louis
Movement Maven 141

Mary Anthony
Servant of the Dance 145

Bill T. Jones
Socrates of Dance 149

Elizabeth Streb
Action Hero 153

Rennie Harris
Messenger 157

Cholly Atkins
Man with the Moves 161

Alex Romero
Assistant 165

Kenny Ortega
Soul Man 169

Paul Taylor
Reporter 173

Lynne Taylor Corbett
Triple Threat 177

Eleo Pomare
Radical 181

Christopher Wheeldon
Balletomane 185

Grover Dale
Man of Means 189

Mia Michaels
Blond Bombshell 193

Alonzo King
Dance Mystic 197

Cleo Parker Robinson
Ambassador of Love 201

Donald Byrd
Tough Guy 205

Alan Johnson
Guardian of the Tradition 209

Glen Tetley
Connoisseur 213

Doug Varone
Man of Emotion 217

Ronald K. Brown
Storyteller 221

Daniel Ezralow
Free Spirit 225

Anna Halprin
Forest Nymph 229

Russell Clark
Artist/Alchemist 233

BIOGRAPHIES 236

ACKNOWLEDGMENTS 261

BIBLIOGRAPHY 262

INDEX 263

FOREWORD

Dance and photography would seem to be arts made for one another—both are visual, both can suggest undertones of an often ambiguous drama, and both rely on shape, line, and balance to achieve their fullest impact. Yet in fact comparatively few photographs and even fewer photographers can begin to capture the kinetic impact of dance. Even cinematography, which can certainly suggest dance movement and its interplay with music, lacks both a third dimension and the instant impact of reality.

In *Masters of Movement,* Rose Eichenbaum very adroitly makes no overt attempt at capturing the movement—she simply focuses in on its masters. Yet, yet, yet . . . these portraits are so skillfully drawn that somehow a vital essence of dance emerges that is usually so peculiarly absent in action photographs of dance itself.

The book is a collection of faces and bodies—people whose almost coincidental connection with one another is that they have chosen, some have virtually been selected, to make a professional career in theatrical dance. It could be a portrait collection of generals, politicians, or couturiers. But these are the people who have made America's dances—choreographers who have become legends. And somehow these people as a group have been brilliantly scrutinized by the camera as dancers. You look at them and feel they could be nothing but and nothing else.

With some it is a gesture—Gregory Hines joyously hugging tap shoes; José Greco, patriarchal in sombrero, looking flamenco under a garden trellis; Patricia Birch flinging wide her arms in front of the Lincoln Center Plaza fountain; David Parsons balancing crazily but res-olutely on the branches of a tree in Central Park. With others it's simply a movement—an aged Anna Sokolow holding her arms in an unconscious but eerie echo of her own young photograph on the wall behind her; Murray Louis, eyes closed, hand to forehead, seemingly remembering times lost; Anna Halprin, clad only in strategic sylvan undergrowth, suggesting Lilith basking in the sun. With many others it's just a look—Bill T. Jones, aware and wary; Bella Lewitsky, weathered with time, hardened with purpose; a very young Christopher Wheeldon, hugging his mirror image, searching for self-discovery.

A photographic portrait—unlike a candid, unposed snap—is always a special interaction between the photographed and the photographer. The subjects being photographed are always expressing their view of themselves to the world. The photographer is always trying to reach beneath that literally subjective view to a perhaps more truthful objective reality. The photographer has the last word, not only in the lighting, setting, even the ambience and tone of the meeting, but also in selecting from all the negatives that vital final print, the signature portrait.

In virtually all of these portraits Eichenbaum has, I feel, caught wonderfully the character and vitality of the individual's artistic spark and identity. These are loving dance portraits, yet blindingly revealing—look at any of them and you get a shrewd glimpse of the artist beneath the skin—while with their simplicity and zest they themselves emulate the elusive spirit of the very art of dance itself. These people, the photographs make us feel, were born to dance and to make dances.

—*Clive Barnes*

author's note

In the fall of 1998 I set out to profile America's most celebrated choreographers.

With my Hasselblad, a pair of Minoltas, and a cassette tape recorder, I aimed to capture something of their essence through photographic portrait and probing interview.

What I discovered immediately was that the source of dance knowledge resides not in the process of dancemaking, or even in the finished work, but in the humanity of the creators. To gain access to this accumulated wisdom, I needed to penetrate their public personas through conversation combined with the intimate encounter between photographer and subject. Most embraced me like a long-lost relative, perhaps because I was once a dancer. My questions sometimes elicited laughter and sometimes a somber confession. On more than one occasion the interviewees confided their worst fear—that devoid of dance their lives would be without meaning and purpose. Some recounted the pivotal moments in their development as creators, as well as the influences and experiences that defined them as dancemakers.

Each portrait is the product of a collaboration, an artistic negotiation. I invited the choreographers to inform the conceptual design of their photograph. In this way, each portrait would emerge from a spontaneous interaction following no predetermined formula.

In the course of this work, I learned that dancers and dancemakers are links in a chain. They have inherited the muscle memory, idiosyncrasies, and movement vocabulary of their mentors. They stand on the backs of such greats as George Balanchine, Jerome Robbins, Martha Graham, Doris Humphrey, Charles Weidman, Hanya Holm, Agnes de Mille, Alvin Ailey, Gene Kelly, and many others. They perpetuate the legacy, but not before infusing it with their own artistic vision and sensibility.

Dance is more than steps. In the hands of a master choreographer, it frames popular culture, speaks to the issues of our times, reflects and gives shape to cultural trends, and explores the most intimate of human emotions. At their best, choreographers give us pleasure, inspiration, and insight into ourselves. Their kinetic commentaries and stories, even their abstract art pieces, mirror who we are and who we want to become.

While *Masters of Movement* is an exploration of dance from the concert stage and Broadway to film, television, and music video, it is by its very nature an incomplete work. It does not, and cannot possibly, include all choreographic points of view. A very small number of leading choreographers declined to participate in this project. Others, whose contributions to the art of choreography are no less significant than those included, are absent because every book can have but a finite number of pages.

To those choreographers who stepped out in front of the curtain to reveal themselves to us—I extend my heartfelt thanks.

Dance Aficionado

donald mckayle

"You've been making dances for more than fifty years now, with no signs of letting up. What drives you so?"

Donald leaned back on the sofa cushion in my living room and said simply, "That's the way I live. My dreams are larger than my memories. I'm always looking for things and ideas that will excite me. If something I see or hear interests me, I tuck it away. That breathtaking sunset, that beautiful woman, all get filed away in the back of my mind. When I need it, I pull it up. Nothing in life is ever wasted. Those visuals can one day be the key to something extraordinary."

"How did it all begin for you? Was there some event or experience that drew you to dance?"

"Yes, seeing Pearl Primus dance on the stage. I was fourteen years old when a friend who was studying dance took me to her concert. Seeing Primus dance caused a chemical reaction in me. It changed the focus and direction of my life. I wanted to do what she was doing even though I had no knowledge of what dance was. After the concert we went back to my friend's house, and her parents let us move the furniture so we had space to move around. It was then that I began to explore the first inklings of making dances."

"You fell in love with the process of dancemaking before you even knew how to dance?"

"Yes. I didn't realize that you needed to learn a movement vocabulary before you could choreograph. I made my first dance before I had ever taken a dance lesson. I just started putting things together. Later I'd get people together and start telling them what to do. 'You go over there and you do that.' That kind of innocence was invaluable."

"I suppose you had leadership quality?"

"Oh, yes. I always had it from the time I was a little tyke. I'd have people doing creative things based on a vision I wanted to see. I remember I couldn't have been more than nine or ten years old and managed to get the kids in the neighborhood to build an ice sculpture."

"What was greater—the need to create or the need to move?"

"The need to create was greater. I loved to move and I think I was a fine performer, but when I only choreographed, I found that I didn't miss it. That showed me that I was not a dyed-in-the-wool dancer for whom taking that away is like cutting your heart out. Shifting to the role of choreographer was very natural for me."

"You've created a huge body of work. Can you recognize your choreographic evolution when comparing your early work with your most recent work?"

"Yes, several of my dances are constantly being revived. I'm finding that they are just as contemporary now as when I first created them. If you watch an old film clip of *Rainbow 'Round My Shoulder* taped in 1959 and compare it with a more current performance done by the Alvin Ailey American Dance Theater in the 1980s, it's the same dance but very different. It has evolved. Anything that is going to remain alive must be communicative and relevant to its time. If it becomes transfixed, it becomes heavy and hardened with sediment. You have to rinse it off and regenerate it in order for it to live. Dances change when performers embellish or add something to them. Quite often their imprint remains, and it becomes part of the canon. I look at these more contemporary versions and say to myself, 'It wasn't originally created this way, but let's keep that in.' If the work is strong, it will survive its various permutations."

"*Rainbow 'Round My Shoulder* is one of your signature pieces and has been performed all over the world. How did foreign audiences relate to a dance that deals with a prison chain gang in the American South?"

"The dance has strong social content and a potent message behind it. I did not have to translate it for the Russians or the Israelis; they knew exactly what it meant because they had lived their own version of it. In Buenos Aires, Argentina, many in the audience had lived through their own politically repressive regimes. They understood its message. The movement needed no explanation."

"When you create a dance, do you see it all in your mind first or do you have to go through the motions?"

"Oh, I can choreograph a whole dance in my mind."

"And you remember it all?"

"Oh, yes. I remember what I was thinking, who would be doing it and where it will be going. I always start with a concept. The concept can come from something I've seen and pulled from my memory, or be based purely on how a dancer moves or looks. Even if it's something fairly static, I look at it with a visual rhythm. Where it will be performed also affects how it turns out. If it's going to be seen on a proscenium stage, then I shape it specifically for that venue."

"Has it always been your intention to make statements in your movement?"

"I was never a choreographer who was just interested in creating movement. I always wanted the movement to convey something, a thought or a message. Communication is the key. Your creation should say something. I can really dislike a performance but still feel it had value because I felt something. If you have to ask, 'What was that?' then it was a waste of time. I think audiences should be moved or entertained. But they should not be bored. If you have nothing that you want to give people, then do it for yourself. Don't put it on the stage."

"I would imagine that you look for very expressive dancers to perform your work."

"Yes, I look for dancers who have a spark and are deeply committed and passionate. Just being a vessel won't do it. Facility can get boring if there is nothing deep behind it. Many young dancers want to achieve a greater level but lack the deep inner voice that guides their choices. They are distracted by outside limits like 'Oh, if I could get that leg a little bit higher or turn that leg out a little more, then I'd be satisfied.' But if that little bit higher adds nothing to the performance, then it's an exercise in futility. Usually those are the dancers who have much shorter careers. You can only do that so long if you haven't honed and developed a deeper sense of self. You simply have nothing to say."

"The bar keeps rising in terms of what dancers can do with their bodies. Their jumps keep getting higher, and their bodies are more flexible. Have today's dancers lost some of the spirit of dance in their quest to be more technically adept?"

"If you live long enough in this profession, you see that the body is capable of doing pretty amazing things. When I watch young dancers today, I realize that they are much more highly skilled. We had legs, arms, and muscles too, but the dancers of my day had such heart and soul. So I ask myself, 'Does virtuosity stand as a barrier to true human feeling and understanding? Can't we

*"Step out on those edges and ledges.
It's in that off-balance moment that you will
find what you are looking for."*

bring these two things together?' I don't know. It's a thought that goes through my head."

"It must be an incredible rush when you're inside the creative process and all is going well. What's it like when things are not working out?"

"You have to be secure enough in yourself to know that there will be days when things flow freely and days when they do not. Sometimes you have to say, 'Let me think about this.' You have to have the confidence to accept that there will be failures and that it is not the end of the world. This too will pass and something else will be there. Time has taught me this."

"And the secret to your success is . . . ?"

"Never use a formula, even though it can be very profitable. If you have an agenda you'll always stick to one thing and never grow as an artist. If you are open and ready to receive what comes your way, you will never run out of creative energy. Step out on those edges and ledges. It's in that off-balance moment that you will find what you are looking for."

"Is there something specific you'd like to see revealed about yourself in the photo we're about to create?"

"Well, that I enjoy my life today and am constantly excited about tomorrow. I don't know what I'm going to be doing or how it's going to be done or even who I'm going to meet, but the future is always filled with promise."

Donald followed me into my studio, carrying a garment bag of shirts and jackets he had brought along for the photo. While I loaded my cameras, he asked me who I studied dance with and where I had performed. I named some teachers who had most inspired me. He knew each and every one of them per-

sonally. As for performing, I told him that I did some dancing in college but never really had a performance career.

Donald posed like a pro. He looked natural and relaxed, and I could tell he enjoyed watching me compose the shots and adjust the lighting.

"Are you observing me?"

"I love to watch people create," he replied.

Before he left to drive back to Laguna Beach, more than two hours away through the afternoon traffic, I gave him a hug. I hated to see him leave.

That night I dreamed I was on the stage. I could feel the warm spotlight on my face and the smooth wood floor beneath my feet. I danced as if I were Isadora, free and triumphant. I floated through space, molding my body to shape and form while draped in sheer white fabric. Loud applause and shouts of "Bravo!" roared through the theater. I awakened with a start and looked at my bedside clock. It was 3:00 a.m. "Where did you perform?" Donald's question echoed in my head. I got up quietly, careful not to disturb my husband, put on a robe, and checked on my three sleeping children. By the time I got to the kitchen, I was sobbing uncontrollably. Donald's curiosity about my dancing had unlocked years of hidden sorrow over the performance career I had sacrificed for family. The emotions were as dramatic as a deep Graham contraction. I wept until the sun rose over the hill behind my house. I realized that if I was going to be honest in portraying these great dance artists, I would need to come to terms with my own unfulfilled dreams and regrets. I felt thankful to Donald for helping me take the first steps in the healing process.

Encino, California, 1998

3

Vision of Loveliness

carmen de lavallade

Sixty-six-year-old Carmen de Lavallade entered my LA studio dressed like a teenager, in blue jeans, T-shirt, and baseball cap.

"Don't worry. I brought some clothes for the photo," she said, handing me her garment bag. I hung it in the powder room and offered her a cup of tea and a homemade banana muffin. Once we were settled on the sofa, I began my probe into her remarkable dance career.

"How old were you when you first discovered dance?"

"I was exposed to dance when I was very young through my cousin Janet Collins, who was a professional dancer. In the 1950s she became the leading dancer for the Metropolitan Opera. Janet was my idol, and I wanted to be just like her. I began taking classes here in LA at the age of fourteen. My first teacher was Melissa Blake, who taught in a studio on Highland Avenue. A couple of years later I got a scholarship to study with Lester Horton, whose dance theater was the first established multiracial dance troupe in the country. Every day after school I'd take a ninety-minute streetcar ride to his theater at 7566 Melrose Avenue. They premiered their first concert in May of 1948. You know, I went back to visit the old place a couple of years ago. It looked like a souvenir shop. I entered and walked to the back of the store, looking for things I might recognize. The vaulted ceiling was still there. Suddenly I realized I was standing inside a porno shop. I tried to get out of there as quickly and as gracefully as possible. I edged my way to the front door, thinking, 'If only these walls could speak.' The place held so much history, and here were all these young people buying and

"Dance is transformation!

selling sex videos and paraphernalia. They had absolutely no idea what went on in here fifty years ago. I thought about sneaking in at night and hanging a commemorative plaque."

"What were some of the gifts that Lester gave you?"

"Lester gave me a sense of self and a love for the profession. He taught me to be generous to others and avoid feelings of jealousy. From a technical standpoint, he taught me everything you need to know about the profession. Lester's knowledge of dance, theater, music, and human nature was mind-blowing. He was incredibly creative and inventive. His technique was constantly changing because he was always searching and evolving his art. He had a way of giving you information so that you didn't feel that you were being taught. He made you do the brain work and inform yourself. In that little converted machine shop we learned how to perform on the stage, work the lights, operate backstage equipment, and make sets and costumes. Lester encouraged us to research our characters so we'd be able to perform them with greater depth. Our education was so comprehensive we even learned how to teach dance and theater techniques. What I learned from him fifty years ago is still with me."

"Who were some of the other dancers and students you worked with?"

"We were like this amazing family, and I learned from everyone. There was Bella Lewitsky, who cofounded the theater and was Lester's lead dancer. Other great artists included James Truitte, Joyce Trisler, Don Martin, Herman Boden, Carl Radcliff, Rudi Gernreich—who incidentally was the man who invented the topless bathing suit—and, of course, Alvin Ailey."

"You also studied with the famous ballet dancer Carmelita Marracci?"

"Yes. I was what you'd call an exchange student. Lester and Carmelita were great friends, and he arranged for me to study with her for free. I think one of her students came and studied with him. They did this sort of switch. I will never forget when he said to me, 'She can give you what I can't.' That type of generosity is rarely seen among dance teachers. Between the two of them I received the most incredible training a young dancer could get."

"What did she leave you with?"

"Carmelita taught me about being truthful in my presentation and technically precise. She was very stern and a total perfectionist. She'd say things like, 'You must have an attitude about your attitude.' She'd get furious if we did not approach our dancing musically. She played Beethoven, Schubert, and all the great composers in her class and was very particular about how we treated music. One day she was so angry with everyone, she stopped the class and yelled, 'Who do you think you are? When I ask you to pick your foot up on the count of one, I don't mean and one or one and. What makes you think you are incapable of being as precise as music? You are a musician and your body is your instrument.' Carmelita also used imagery to teach us ballet technique. For example, if she wanted to emphasize balance, she'd say something like, 'I want you to suspend in the air like an El Greco painting.' So, if you knew what an El Greco painting looked like, you'd get that image in your head and you'd just rise right up. When she taught the *rond de jambe*, she would instruct the girls to do the action as if they were kicking up a skirt, because originally ballerinas wore skirts. Men were told to show their calves, as was the case during Louis XIV's time. Her mental images and historical references helped us master the technique."

"You've been described by critics as a vision of loveliness. Was that because you were so highly accomplished technically?"

"I might have given the appearance that I was a great technician, but my dancing has always been motivated by content, what the dance was all about. When you find yourself truly immersed in the spirit of the dance, the technique takes care of itself. If you have a yearning feeling, your arabesque will reflect it. Technique is a means to an end. It allows you to get where you're going. The point is to transport yourself and your audience to another plane of existence. When I'm dancing, I don't want people to be aware of my physicality but feel what it is that I'm conveying. The idea is to transcend technique, not notice it."

"How do you connect with an audience? What do you have to do to reach them?"

You have an audience watching your work.

You spend your entire life trying to elevate them to

another level. You also spend your entire life afraid you might not!"

"You get out there and you do what you have to do. The people watching you have to become part of your experience. You spend your entire life trying to elevate them to another level. You also spend your entire life afraid you might not! That is, unless you are someone like Ethel Merman. She never worried about transforming an audience. I was never like her. I've always lived with trepidations. You never know who you're going to be once you get on the stage. You might feel like yourself, but your body might decide to act like someone else. You only know that you've reached an audience when it's silent in the house. It's silent because they've been transported somewhere else."

"So the dancer, actor, or musician can never really predict the outcome of a live performance?"

"No, they can't, because they never know what's going to distract them. When you perform live you are at the mercy of the moment. That's why live performance is not for everyone. It's really, really scary when you forget your lines or steps. You're basically living your own nightmare, and it happens to everyone sooner or later."

"You were one of Alvin Ailey's closest friends. Tell me a little bit about him."

"Alvin and I met in junior high and were good friends by the time we attended Jefferson High School. I remember that he majored in Spanish and was extremely shy. When Alvin saw me perform my own choreographed version of *Scheherazade* during a school assembly, he became absolutely enamored with dance. I took him with me to Lester's. It took him about six months of watching on the sidelines before he pulled up enough courage to take his first dance class. It was obvious to everyone from the start that Alvin was gifted. But no one knew he would grow up to have a name as famous as Coca-Cola."

"Are you still dancing and choreographing?"

"Yes. I'm performing now in a group called Paradigm with Gus Solomons Jr. and Dudley Williams. We go way back, a long way together. We're working up a repertory that fits our age and sensibility."

"What's it like dancing well into your sixties?"

"It's interesting. Every age has its story to tell. When you're young there is a tendency to overdance, because you're always trying to prove yourself. You throw your leg over your head because you can. But when you can no longer do that, you have to find other moves to say the same thing. And sometimes the dance is even stronger. My initial motivation for moving has not changed, only its outward appearance."

"Do you think the impulse to create is unstoppable?"

"Yes. I think it is one of the most powerful forces in the universe. It is an absolute physical and mental necessity. Why else would God throw creativity into the mix? All human beings are endowed with it to greater or lesser degrees. The imagination is extraordinary, and that's what continues to challenge and at the same time frighten us."

I retrieved Carmen's garment bag so she could change for the portrait and directed her to the powder room. When she emerged ten minutes later, I found myself staring at a vision. Her hair, previously hidden under the baseball cap, now cascaded around her face and down her back. She wore a hint of eye makeup and lipstick and long, dangly earrings that made her look like an exotic princess. Her black sweater and elegant pleated skirt accentuated her slender frame and delicate features. I invited her to take a seat on a chair covered in black velvet. She posed for me with a straight back and a Mona Lisa smile.

After the shoot, I drove Carmen back to her sister's house in a section of town called Silver Lake. She suggested we get off the freeway and take a shortcut through Griffith Park, one of LA's most beautiful landmarks, and so I turned onto a road flanked by tall trees and acres of sprawling green grass.

"Look up there—it's one of God's rare gifts," she said, pointing up at the sky.

There, high above us, soared a magnificent hawk, its wings outstretched as it curved and dipped through the sky. 'Yes,' I thought to myself, 'it takes one to know one.'

Los Angeles, 1999

Acrobat of God

fayard nicholas

The legendary hoofer waved to me, as if to say, "I'm coming, be patient."

I held up my hand and called out, "Take your time."

Dressed casually and sporting a baseball cap, Fayard Nicholas made his way across the lobby of the Motion Picture Retirement Hotel in Calabasas, California.

"Hello," he said, shaking my hand, his eyes sparkling. "I hope I didn't keep you waiting. I move a little slower these days since my stroke, but I intend to get rid of this walker very soon and shake a leg. I may be eighty-three, but I have a lot of living yet to do."

"Yes, I'm sure you do. This is a lovely place. I imagine you have many friends here."

"Yes, many of us have had very successful careers in Hollywood."

"And I've been told that you're pretty popular around here."

"Well, you see, I like to make all these old folks laugh, give them a little plea-sure. I tell them stories and jokes. Someone's got to liven up the place," he said with a giggle.

"Shall we go to your apartment for the interview?" I asked.

"No, my place is sort of a mess. I'm still sorting out my wife's things. She passed on not long ago. Over there is a nice spot." He pointed to a bench just outside the lobby entrance.

"Tell me, how did you and your brother become dancers?"

"We call ourselves entertainers. We do so many things. We sing, we dance, we act, we play the drums, and we tell jokes."

Fayard spoke in the present tense, as if he and his brother were working on a new Hollywood musical, amazing audiences with their synchronized back flips and splits. I asked Fayard about the beginnings of his show business career.

"We started entertaining professionally in 1930 in Philadelphia. I was about eleven years old. Our parents were vaudeville musicians. My mother played the piano and my father the drums. So my brother and sister and I practically grew up in the theater. I loved watching all those acts—the acrobats, the jugglers, the singers, the dancers. I knew at a young age that I wanted to be doing something like that, so I taught myself how to perform. Then I taught my younger brother and sister. One evening our parents came home from the theater and found us working on a routine. 'You have school tomorrow. What are you doing up so late?' my mother asked. 'We have something to show you,' I said. So we went through our routine. When we were finished, our parents looked at each other and said, 'Hey, we have something here.' The next day my father spoke to the manager of the Standard Theater in Philadelphia and asked if he'd take a look at us. We got up on the stage and did a little song and dance. After a few minutes the manager said, 'They're booked for next week.' Our parents resigned from the orchestra and began to manage us. Soon we were performing all over Philadelphia and New York City. We called ourselves the Nicholas Kids."

"You are completely self-taught?"

"Yes, that's right. I never took a professional lesson. If I had taken professional dance lessons, I wouldn't be dancing like me. I'd be dancing like that dance teacher. I never would have developed the Nicholas Brothers' style. You see, in the beginning I used to watch the other vaudeville dancers and take ideas from them, and then one day my father gave me some very important advice. He said, 'Son, you are very talented, so don't imitate the others. Do your own thing and develop your own style. I see you like to use your hands. Keep doing that.' He also told me, 'Don't look at your feet while you're dancing. Look at the audience, because you're entertaining them, not yourself.'"

I glanced down at Fayard's large hands and noticed how delicate and youthful they looked.

"The great dance director Nick Castle once said that I had the most expressive hands in show business. Fred Astaire was a close second, and then came Buddy Ebsen."

"How do you describe the Nicholas Brothers' style?"

"My brother, Harold, and I call our style of dancing 'classical tap.' It's not flash. We do those splits and things just to excite the audience, but we start every routine with classical tap dancing. We use the whole body from head to toe. We never concentrate solely on the feet but feel that the arms, hands, and even the head are of equal importance. We integrate the entire body when we dance. We always try to relate to our audience, even when we're dancing just for the camera. People have often told us that they feel our dancing is so intimate, they feel like they're on the stage with us. That's what we like to hear."

"How did you structure your dance routines?"

"When we first started out as children, we'd come back to the dressing room all huffing and puffing. We couldn't catch a breath from all that dancing. 'Man, we've got to do something about this,' I said one day. 'Yeah, I'm with you,' said Harold. So I told him this: 'We'll come out on the stage and do a little soft shoe, nothing too strenuous, something with a little class and style and grace. And then I'll go to the microphone and say to the audience, "Good evening, ladies and gentlemen. Glad to see you here to enjoy our show this evening. In a few minutes my brother is going to sing you a little song and I'm going to conduct the orchestra." 'Now we're catching our breath, you see.'"

"Ah, you devised a way of pacing yourselves."

"Exactly, and we'd take turns doing solos, so that while one was dancing the other one was catching his breath. But I thought that the one catching his breath should still be drawing attention to the soloist by presenting him with hand movements."

"Oh, yes, I remember seeing that in several of your films. Your hands are like magic. It looks like you are causing the dance to happen."

"That's right. I'd do like this or I'd do like that," he said, re-creating some of the hand gestures.

"It's almost like you're working a puppet."

"Oh, working a puppet. Oh, I like that!" he said, bursting into laughter.

"Fayard, even by today's standards some of your choreography was daring and a little dangerous. Those split jumps down a flight of stairs were spectacular."

"Young people are always coming up to me and asking how do the Nicholas Brothers do that. I always tell them, 'Very very carefully.'"

"Were you ever concerned about getting hurt?"

"We always warmed up and tried to be safe. Let me tell you a little story. I remember one time we performed live at the Roxy Theater in Manhattan. It held 6,000 people. The show's producers wanted us to re-create the dance we did in the film *Stormy Weather,* the one with the stairs. They built an extremely high staircase, and at the bottom sat a 100-piece orchestra. The producer came over to us during rehearsal and said, 'Fellas, when you get up there at the top of that platform, I want you to jump over the orchestra and land in the splits.' I turned to him and said, 'Holy Christmas, are you crazy? We'd have to be able to fly to do that.' I looked at my brother and said, 'What do you think?' Harold thought a minute and said, 'Let's try it.' I took a deep breath, and we went on the count of three. One, two, three. WOOOOOOOOOW! Over the orchestra we flew, down into the splits, and finished with a little soft shoe. But when we got to our dressing room I said, 'Harold, I hurt my heel on the landing. I can't do that jump again.' Harold said, 'Don't worry. I'll do it by myself. You do your hand gestures as if you're moving me up and down the steps.' So Harold climbs up to the platform. I bring him up with my hands, and while he does the jump, I bring him down with my hands." Fayard demonstrated the gesture. "I join Harold at the bottom of the stairs, and we dance off the stage. In the dressing room Harold says, 'Fayard, you were right. I hurt my heel on the landing. I'm not doing that again either.'"

"I read somewhere that you worked with George Balanchine on Broadway."

"Oh, yes. He was the choreographer of the 1937 Broadway show *Babes in Arms* at the Shubert Theater. We were headlining at the Cotton Club with Cab Calloway and his orchestra when we got a call to do a number in George Balanchine's show. He approached us in the theater and said he'd seen us in the movies. He asked if we could go on the stage and show him a few things. So Harold did the splits through my legs, and I jumped over his head into a splits when Mr. Balanchine yelled, 'Stop! Stop everything. I have an idea.' He lined up a couple of girls and had Harold do the splits through their legs and had me jump over them into the splits. Then he kept adding girls—two, then four, then six, and finally there were eight girls. In the end, Harold did the splits through the eight pairs of legs and I jumped over them, landing in a splits. Later he asked us if we had ever taken ballet. I told him we never did and just dance the way we feel. 'Sure does look like you've had ballet training,' he said."

"Was it more fun creating your routines or performing them?"

"Both. I loved them both. As a choreographer, I loved developing numbers and watching the progression of each dance. You say to yourself, 'Oh, wow, look at this. See what I have created.' We always tried to make each routine better than the last."

"When you were under contract at Twentieth Century Fox, did they let you do your own choreography?"

"I did the choreography for everything we ever did—every live show and every movie. But in 1940, when we were under contract at Twentieth Century Fox, Nick Castle was our dance director. The three of us would get together and

think up all these wonderful ideas for the movies. Two of our most popular movie numbers were 'Chattanooga Choo Choo' and 'The Girl from Kalamazoo.'"

"Did you anticipate that you would achieve world fame?"

"I didn't know that we would become so popular. I had no idea. Harold and I performed all over the world, in Las Vegas supper clubs and on television. We never did it for the fame or the money. We did it for the applause. That was music to our ears. The Nicholas Brothers were always in demand, even with all that propaganda about tap dancing being dead in America. It never stopped us from performing. Some people hung up their tap shoes, but not us."

"Did racial prejudice ever get in your way?"

"I became aware of racial prejudice when we opened at the Cotton Club in Harlem. We performed with great artists like Duke Ellington, Cab Calloway, and so many amazing black entertainers, but to white audiences. Black people couldn't come to see the show, even though they lived in Harlem. As a child I couldn't understand that. Our parents taught us right from wrong. We saw everyone as human beings. I always thought it was odd that when we went to church, the preacher was calling us sinners and saying we're all going to go to hell unless we straighten up and fly right. I wanted to hear about love, about how we're going to make this a better world for everybody to live in. I love all people, and I want them to love me."

I thanked Fayard for sharing his amazing stories and suggested that we begin the photo session. While I set up my lighting in the community room, Fayard went back to his apartment to get some old movie stills that I thought we could tape up on the wall as a historical backdrop. Once I had the lighting in place, Fayard stepped out in front of the camera, forgetting all about his walker, his balance steady. He immediately turned on the Hollywood charm, striking a new flashy pose after each shot, prominently displaying his famous hands. To Fayard's delight, a small crowd gathered to watch.

Four years later I ran into Fayard at an awards banquet in Beverly Hills. Since our meeting at the Motion Picture Retirement Hotel he had married Katherine Hopkins, a beautiful blond woman thirty-six years his junior. A handsome cane had replaced his walker.

"Fayard," I said, "you look wonderful. What's your secret?"

"Keep living, honey, and keep dancing."

Calabasas, California, 1998, 2002

Adventurer

graciela daniele

I must have looked a sight when Graciela opened her front door. There I stood, my lighting stands, umbrellas, power pack, camera equipment, and portfolio hanging off my arms and shoulders like Christmas ornaments.

"Oh, let me help you," she said. "How did you get here? How can you carry all that?"

"With tremendous difficulty," I said, sinking under the weight of my gear. "I took a taxi, and he dropped me off in front of your brownstone here. I didn't want to leave all this expensive equipment on the sidewalk while I came upstairs to ring your doorbell. This is New York, you know."

Graciela grabbed the stands and umbrellas, and together we hauled everything into the living room and piled it in a corner. After she served us coffee, we sat down in her cozy living room.

"Graciela, when did you start dancing and where?"

"I was born in Argentina and started my dance training at the Teatro Colón. It is Argentina's equivalent of Moscow's Bolshoi Theater—subsidized by the government and very strict in its approach. You would normally enter at the age of seven and graduate at fourteen, maybe," she said with a laugh. "After I graduated I had an offer to dance in a company in Rio de Janeiro, Brazil. So I went, chaperoned by my mother. But my real dream was to go to Paris to study with the great ballet teachers. Back in the 1950s that's what you did. My intention was to stay a couple of months, but I ended up dancing with the opera in Nice and stayed five years. One night in Paris I attended a live performance of *West Side Story*. The show changed my life. I remember coming out of the theater and just walking the streets in a daze. I thought to myself, 'I must go to New York City and learn how to tell stories through dance.'"

"But you tell stories in ballet."

"The difference here was that Jerome Robbins brought to the stage what was going on in the streets. I was struck by how one could tell stories in such topical ways. I worked hard and managed to scrape up enough money to go to Manhattan. I began studying jazz with Matt Mattox, a disciple of the great Jack Cole. Turned out he was choreographing a Broadway show called *What Makes Sammy Run?* and cast me in the show. I had only been in the country for a month."

"Wait a minute. You were in New York for only a month and landed a role on Broadway?"

"Yes, that's right. I barely spoke a word of English. I was so naive at the time—I didn't realize how difficult it was to get into a Broadway show or how competitive it was. That was 1963, and I'm still here!"

"Sounds like a fairy tale."

"When I look at my life, I always feel like I'm a kid and someone knocks on the door. I open the door, and the visitor says, 'Graciela, do you want to come out and play?' I say, 'Yes,' and I go. Before I realize it, I've been blessed with an extraordinary opportunity. I've always been ready for adventure and not afraid to try something new."

"You're obviously not afraid to fail. You jump right in."

"Failure is not to come out and play when you're invited."

"What happened next in your career?"

"I began training in modern dance with Martha Graham and Merce Cunningham and continued to study jazz with Matt Mattox. I danced in a number of shows, including *Here's Where I Belong* and *Promises, Promises* [1968], *Coco* [1969], *Follies* [1971], and *Chicago* [1974]. I also assisted many great choreographers, like Bob Fosse and Michael Bennett. I was particularly in awe of Michael Bennett, who opened my eyes to the creative process of dancemaking. I had spent my entire life as a dancer looking at myself in the mirror, trying to make myself perfect. Only when I turned my back to the mirror did I find myself looking at the world for the first time."

"That's extraordinary. In other words, when you stopped focusing on yourself, you saw the potential to create for others?"

"Yes. Once I began to assist other choreographers, my passion for performing was replaced by the passion to create dances and theater pieces. I fell in love with the preproduction work, the research, the getting into the studio and improvising with movement, and casting dancers. My eyes and ears had been wide open, soaking up volumes from these great choreographers. Only now do I realize how much they taught me. I was immersed in the world of creativity, and you know yourself, Rose, there's nothing like it."

"You must have a lot of confidence in yourself, in your skills."

"No, it's not that. I tremble before every new project. I just have the willingness and a natural curiosity to explore the unknown. I'm an adventurer. I'm drawn to the process of invention, but I know that you can't predict its outcome. I'm also excited because I know I'll always learn from the experience."

"Why is it often so daunting, so frightening, to start a new project? It's like jumping off a diving board into the deep."

"Like the writer's page or the painter's canvas, you have to fill the emptiness. It's even more difficult for the choreographer, because with dance it's three-dimensional. And from the point of motion, it's like designing an ephemeral painting that keeps erasing itself as you create it."

"Can you really teach someone how to choreograph?"

"In the beginning, you emulate other choreographers just to get going, but then you must find your own voice. The greater your vocabulary, the more eclectic you become, the more pieces you can serve. But there is no school you can go to. There are no books you can read to become a choreographer. It's nonacademic. It's about experience, and that is scary!"

"Why not play it safe by using proven formulas?"

"Well, I'm not against using formulas, but if you just think about pleasing people, you do Radio City Music Hall. The work tends to be repetitive and lacking in real imagination. You're not growing as an artist. That's not for me."

"What compels you?"

"My main impulse in dance is to tell a story. I admire abstract dancing, but I'm not about that. That's not what pushes me forward. I'm moved by musical theater."

"Maybe that's why *West Side Story* changed your life."

"Yes, exactly. Mr. Robbins not only managed to choreograph a brilliant work, he told a story through movement. How extraordinary is that? And . . . Agnes de Mille created *Oklahoma!* She came up with the idea for the dream

"I was always trying to make myself perfect;
only when I turned my back to the mirror did I
find myself looking at the world for the first time."

ballet. How extraordinary is that? My goal is to continue this tradition of telling stories through the language of dance."

"How do you create movement that audiences will understand?"

"In musical theater, if an audience recognizes the movement, they think it's good. If you give them something they're not familiar with, or can't identify with, then they get uncomfortable. You see, in my career I've learned to make a sep-aration between 'commercial' work, which is directed toward general audiences and is more formulaic, and my own personal work, which is more about my own personal expression. That's when the artist in me can go to the edge of the diving board and jump off."

"How do you create movement that your dancers will understand?"

"The choreographers who got the most out of me as a dancer were the ones who could draw me out emotionally. Agnes de Mille used to talk to the dancers. Her words made our dancing more meaningful. I learned the value of directing dancers as if they were actors. I sit them down and talk to them about the intention of the work. I ask my dancers to explore what they're feeling and what they're saying. If they don't feel anything, how can they be communicat-ing to an audience? I remind my dancers that when they have something to say, they should speak. When they don't, they should remain silent. If they have something to convey, they should move. If they don't, they stay still. In musical theater, dance has to move the story or character forward. I don't like to be a voyeur who is removed emotionally from what's there. Dance is the language of communication."

"Any lessons learned along the way?"

"I've learned not to get discouraged by the criticism of people I don't necessarily respect. Sometimes the critics beat you up, and it can be very painful. But I always try to give 100 percent. It's important for artists to believe in their work and serve it as best they can. But you can't please everyone."

For the photograph, we decided to use as our backdrop a display of old marquee letters hanging on the living room wall. Graciela looked natural and comfortable, and the shoot was finished in only minutes.

"Rose, how will you get back to your hotel with all the equipment?"

"Good question. I'll take a taxi."

Graciela helped me carry my gear down to the sidewalk and flag a cab. She thanked me for a lovely afternoon and wished me much success.

Moments later I was headed uptown, her parting words echoing in my mind: "Believe in your work, Rose, and you'll never go wrong."

New York City, spring 1999

15

Prodigal Son

edward villella

America's first male dance superstar greeted me at the door of his hotel suite, his face half covered in shaving cream.

"Oh, I'm sorry," I said. "Am I too early?"

"It's fine. Come in," he said, opening the door wide. "Please make yourself comfortable. I'll just be a minute."

I wheeled in a cart filled with lighting gear and began setting up. When he returned, clean-shaven, I could see years of strain etched into his face.

"Now, where would you like to begin?" he said, sitting down on the sofa.

"The interview," I replied, pulling out my notes. "In reading your autobiography, I was impressed by your candor. You held little back in describing your personal and professional life."

"If you've chosen to perform in the public arena, it's natural to seek the honesty, the poetry, and the truth of it all. The art of acting is not to act but to be. I had the challenge of a Balanchine and a Robbins. When you're dealing with those kinds of extraordinary minds, you realize that being open is what it's all about. I still seek this kind of ideal, this truth within the work that is presented to me."

"Not everyone is willing to reveal themselves or their process. They hide behind the art form."

"I received my dance training in New York City, where there were no windows. We were cloistered away to learn our craft. So when I started the Miami City Ballet sixteen years ago I housed our company in a mall. I left the windows

"Be guided.

Face what you don't know and allow those who do

to help you reach your full artistic potential."

and doors open all the time so that people could hear and see our process. Anyone could walk in at any given time. Also, I felt it was good training for young dancers who were not used to being watched. I want dancers to be touched by real people on an ongoing basis. Too often, dancers retreat into the profession and become reclusive and uncomfortable outside their own particular environment. Ballet has always been mysterious, particularly to those who haven't studied it, but even to those who have. I think it's incumbent upon artistic directors, choreographers, and teachers to reveal ballet's internal process and say, hey, this is how we do it."

"What do you look for when you choose dancers for your Miami City Ballet?"

"The truth is that most companies are reflective of their artistic director's manner and drive. My company has an attack. It has verve. Forgive me, but I was accused of that myself. I choose dancers very specifically for their ability to physicalize music and move beautifully and naturally."

"It is widely believed that you were one of those unique individuals with 'raw talent.' What does that term mean to you?"

"There are certain people who have beautiful, incredible natural talent. They feel so comfortable with the instinctive God-given aspects of who they are. For them, the technical approach, the investigation, and the development of student to dancer, dancer to performer, performer to artist is a wholly different kind of trip. In my case, I had people like George Balanchine, Jerome Robbins, Lincoln Kirstein, Igor Stravinsky, and Stanley Williams providing for me and guiding me. I did not have opportunity, if you will, to rely solely on my talent."

"Why did they invest so much in you?"

"First off, I was a guy. At that time, guys had an advantage in an area dominated by wonderful women. As Balanchine said, 'Ballet is woman.' But natu-

rally man has to present women, provide for women. Simply stated, they needed men."

"Yes, but you went way beyond providing for women."

"I had driving passions, and that's always convenient when you have talent. My drive was instinctive, but also neurotic. You see, I was pressured to dance as a young boy, but once I fell in love with it, I was forced to stop. After I had danced for six years, my father decided that I should attend military school. So I had four frustrating years as a cadet at New York State Maritime College. Once I'd made the decision to return to dance, my drive to catch up and excel was extreme and obsessive, and therein lie the neurotic aspects of my ambition. It took me a couple of years to slow myself down."

"How do you slow yourself down when your passion propels you with such intensity?"

"I had to learn that slower is faster. If you practice every day with patience and correctness, you will get there. It's like preparing for a jump. You can't rush it. You must summon the appropriate energy with split-second timing and have an understanding of purpose to get up in the air. It requires training, confidence, and mental effort. You can't have a vocabulary without the alphabet. Balanchine used to say, 'Do you want to be a poet of gesture or do you want to be a physical entity?'"

"You've described yourself as having a competitive nature and a fighting spirit. Do you think you would have risen to the top the way you did without those traits?"

"Not at all. I don't think I would have made it. I'm a very competitive, aggressive, and pugnacious kind of individual. I'm arrogant, and that's who I am. I don't mind telling some angelic thing to go to hell. It doesn't matter to me. What matters to me is honesty and truth. And if you don't like it, get the hell out of my way."

"What was your relationship with Balanchine like?"

"People think we had this terrible, rancorous relationship. No. We had a deep regard and respect for each other. He was my artistic father and my hero. He allowed me to be me. You see, after not having danced for four years, I found his classes not conducive to what I needed. My muscles were a disaster, and I suffered crippling pain in my joints. Injuries came quickly to me. When Stanley Williams, this wonderful teacher from the Royal Danish Ballet, began teaching at Balanchine's school, I chose to take his class exclusively. With this, I committed the worst sin imaginable. I stopped taking George Balanchine's class. I simply could not continue with his training. His classes were more involved with the tenets of ballet rather than the logical development of the body, which was what I needed."

"That took a lot of guts."

"Yes, but that decision saved my dancing life. I knew it was a tremendous risk. I was a mere mortal insulting a god. Mr. B was very displeased by what I was doing, but by the same token, I lasted longer and gave him almost twenty years of my life. My abilities became more sophisticated as I matured. I went from a brash, punchy, bravura athlete to an artist who could do the sophistication of a Stravinsky's *Pulcinella*, to create commedia dell'arte, to be the force that along with Patti McBride started *Dances at a Gathering,* and to be Jerry Robbins' choice to do *Watermill*, a work that is beyond technique, that takes background experience, thought, and artistry."

"So once you freed yourself of the physical pain with Mr. Williams's help, you were then able to really grow as an artist?"

"Well, I never lost the pain in my joints or the spasms, but I knew now how to deal with them and control them."

"Why were you having these physical problems?"

"It was from lack of knowledge, and the frustration of not having learned these methods earlier. I desperately wanted to make up for the four years I had missed. I can't begin to tell you the desperation I felt when I thought I'd never dance again. There are no sadder words than 'it might have been.' I acted out of neurotic motivations and overdanced everything. With Stanley Williams's help it took me two years to control my hands and fingers when I took a jump. I had to learn that the hands, the arms, the neck, and the head did not use the same force as the feet, the thighs, et cetera. Subdivision of time and energy is a very important aspect of training. You must assess whether to use full force, bring the throttle back a little bit, or shift into another gear. The only way to learn these things is to apply your natural ability with the help of people who have tremendous background, understanding, and experience."

"You wrote in your autobiography, 'Balanchine made me very uncomfortable because he was so sure of himself and his art, and I was not yet me.' What is the recipe for an artist to come into his or her own?"

"Be guided. Face what you don't know and allow those who do to help you reach your full artistic potential. There are no great talents out there who are fully evolved and developed without understanding the history, tradition, philosophy, behaviors, and relationships pertaining to their particular artistic expression. You can't just rely on the audience loving you because you do wonderful *tours* in the air. That's great, really great, but all of that has to be networked with all the other aspects of the art form. So often we have brilliant talents who show us their brilliance but never achieve the artistry."

Los Angeles, 2002

19

Belle of Broadway

susan stroman

Susan and I planned to meet in front of the Vivian Beaumont Theater at Lincoln Center.

I spotted her at a distance, in her signature black cap, climbing out of a taxi hurriedly. I knew that with *Contact* and *The Music Man* running successfully on Broadway, and *The Producers* in the works, she had little time to spare.

"You must be Rose," she said, approaching with a warm smile. "I'm sorry I'm late. We had some last-minute emergency with *The Music Man,* so I only have enough time for a quick photo. Can we do the interview on another day?"

"Yes, of course," I said, hiding my disappointment. I moved into overdrive, quickly loading my cameras and wracking my brain for composition ideas, determined not to come away with a mere snapshot. I used the posters of *Contact* lining the theater entrance as backdrop to my first couple of rolls. Susan was fun and contagiously playful, flashing a well-rehearsed smile for each exposure. When we moved inside the theater lobby, I staged her in all sorts of theatergoing situations—heading for the box office, purchasing tickets, handing out programs. She indulged my every request. Finally she looked at her watch and said she really had to be going.

"Please call my assistant later," she said. "He'll set up another time for us to get together for the interview. Oh, and I've arranged a ticket for you to see *Contact* tonight."

"Thank you!" I said with delight.

My interview with Susan would take place a year later, just after the explosive success of *The Producers*. She asked me to meet her at the St. James Theater on Broadway, around 3:00 p.m. As before, she was wearing her black cap and greeted me cheerfully. She gave me a hug and led me through the seats to the back row of the house, where I could see the stagehands preparing for that evening's performance.

"How's this?" she asked, nestling into one of the seats.

"Just fine," I said. "Here you are in the afterglow of yet another wonderful success. What does it feel like to be responsible for creating such an enormous hit?"

"Well, Rose, I never just work alone. I'm swimming in a sea of collaborators. I work very closely with designers, actors, writers, and composers. In theater, the work is story-, character-, and plot-driven. So the choreography must support the written word, the lyrics, the music, and the actors. You can do the most beautiful dance step in the world, but if it's not lit right or costumed right or doesn't fit with the music, it won't mean a thing."

"When looking for theatrical projects, like *The Producers*, what really turns you on?"

"I look for stories that deal with the human condition, human behavior, and the vulnerability of people. I'm not interested in doing anything with cartoon characters or animals. As a director, I am an observer of life and of people. I often sit and wonder about people I see in restaurants or clubs or in parks. I imagine short stories about them. Being curious inspires me."

"Do you need to prepare yourself to create, go through some sort of ritual?"

"Well, I don't need to meditate or have a cup of tea, if that's what you mean. I write things down and then in my mind explore that which would make them more interesting and more enticing. I immerse myself in music. Since I was a child, I've had the ability to visualize music. It didn't matter if it was classical or rock 'n' roll, I would imagine hordes of people dancing. Till this day, I don't listen to music to be calm. I hear music, and something starts to cook inside of me. I don't conjure anything up, ever. It's just present in me."

"What do you expect from the actors/dancers who perform your work?"

"For my choreography, the necessary elements require three things: The dancers need to be able to act, have great rhythm, and be fearless. If they have those qualities, then they can get into one of my shows."

"How can you tell if a dancer can act and is fearless?"

"I can tell immediately during the auditioning process. I ask them to repeat the combination many different ways. For example, I might say, 'Do that again as if you are really shy or just had six margaritas. Try it again aggressively or flirtatiously.' I toss out different emotions and character choices, and see what they do with it. Dancers need to be able to act in order to make the choreography rich.

"I can tell if dancers are fearless when I ask if they'd like to show me something of their own. I let their personalities have a moment to shine. Those who are unwilling to share their talent with me would most likely be unwilling to try new things in a rehearsal process."

"How do you invent the different moves for your characters? Do you internalize them first?"

"Yes, all the time. I imagine what they would do, how they would feel. That's how I make the actors dance. I have to become them in my own preproduction, but not when I'm working with them directly. I allow the actors to imagine they've made the whole thing up themselves."

"How do you do that?"

"A visual structure is set up very early on. I deal with designers and costumers before I deal with the dancers. We establish a style and a look that the dancers will need to conform to. Before anyone moves, or reads anything, I sit them down and discuss with them the nature of their characters. I guide them and give them clues about what serves the story line and character. They begin to feel the movement, as if it's coming out of their own being. It should be spontaneous for them, never as if it is imposed. I also use abstract imagery. For example, in *Contact,* I had the dancers spread themselves across the stage while spinning and hopping in place. The idea was that they become a human pinball machine. So when Michael, the main character, runs through them, he tries not to get smacked around like a ball in a pinball machine."

"Do you ever get stuck creatively?"

"You know, you're always stuck. It's really all about not giving up. In my case, I don't just choreograph, I revise the music, so when anyone sees my shows, the choreography is completely supported by the music. Even when I did *Oklahoma!* I changed the music, and that was a big deal for the Rodgers and Hammerstein estate. I rearranged the dream ballet so that the music supported the dance. I won't settle until I have the perfect harmony of music and dance. I spend most of my creative energy working it out so that the piece is as pleasing to the eye as it is to the ear."

"How important is it for you to do personal work versus commissioned projects?"

"I think one should do both, but I feel personal work is very important! Personal work forces you to stretch. Doing work for the Martha Graham Dance Company and the New York City Ballet only made my work in theater stronger. It forced me to explore other techniques and styles, as well as other rehearsal processes. The more you extend yourself, the more you grow in other fields.

"As far as personal projects, I have a lot of different stories to tell and ideas to convey. *Contact* was actually personal work that became commercial. Whatever project I'm involved in, I carry a piece of that previous show on into the next one. Like pebbles across a creek, each stone gives me strength to step onto the next one, and the next. Even if the show has been a financial failure, it's always been an artistic success for me because I will have taken something I've learned and applied it to the next show. For example, everything I've ever learned exists in *The Producers*."

"Is it possible for you to separate your personal life from your professional life?"

"For now, no. I only have a professional life. I have no desire to run off to an island. People's lives are just a series of short stories. This is the short story I'm living right now. It's either direct and choreograph or go insane. At some point it will change, and I'll find myself inside a new story."

"How does the work you do feed you, satisfy you?"

"Whether people are crying in *Contact* or laughing in *The Producers*, I derive great pleasure from watching how the work affects an audience. While watching *The Producers* the other night, I saw a man fall out of his chair because he was laughing so hard. In *The Music Man*, I noticed an elderly couple embrace because the musical brought back a special memory for them. I like to stand in the back of the house and see how what I've helped create moves people. This gives me great satisfaction, more satisfaction than I can get from anything else."

New York City, 2001

Dance Engineer

"The dances that you make owe you nothing.
  You owe them everything."

eliot feld

The petite, ponytailed choreographer led me to his office inside the famed American Ballet

Theater building at 890 Broadway. We walked through the lobby, passing a gallery of framed concert posters that chronicled his performance seasons all the way back to his first dance company, Feld Ballets/NY. When we arrived in his sunny office, he sat down, threw his legs on the desk, lit a cigarette, and stared at me. I could feel him sizing me up. I pulled a tape recorder from my bag and took a seat facing him.

"So what do you want to know?" he said, blowing smoke to the side.

"How do you sustain a dance career? You've lived and breathed dance practically your whole life as a dancer, choreographer, artistic director, and educator."

"Sheer stubbornness," he said with a laugh. "From the start, I tried to create an environment in which I was free of the imposition of other people's wishes, opinions, and desires about my work. It takes perseverance to continue making dances and sustain a company against all odds. It helps if you have your own studio to come to and a company of dancers you've been with for a long time. Unfortunately, you are never fully insulated; you have to work with your dancers, raise money, and endure critics. But to the extent possible, I wanted the work not to be answerable to anything but the imperative of the work. I've been striving toward this through my thirty years of dancemaking."

"Tell me about that impulse to create dances. How do you birth a ballet?"

"Once I find a piece of music that fills me with a mood, or something ineffable, I am compelled to find the best expression for that mood in the form of shape and motion. Then I must find the language that speaks to that music and that feeling. In its early stages it's fairly incoherent. I begin by imagining a dancer or several dancers. I then slowly start blending the dancers with the music. When I feel I have enough to go on, I work up the courage to call in the dancers, and we develop the first tentative movement ideas. It's not any different for me now than it was 110 ballets ago."

"Is it useful to refer to previous work while creating a new ballet?"

"I don't know how useful it is to refer to your own work. Picasso said, 'The biggest danger is to steal from yourself.' Besides, the ballet doesn't care what I've done in the past. It doesn't respect me. It has its own needs—blind, selfish needs. It's like an infant. It just wants to be fulfilled. The ballet is really just an objective expression of a subjective feeling, my subjective feeling. Each piece of music that intrigues me wants its own form of expression and independence."

"Sounds a little like parenthood. You decide to have a child, you birth him or her, and the next thing you know, they want to borrow the car."

"It's different when you birth a human being. The first thing you do is check to see if the baby has all his fingers and toes. The outcome is really out of your hands. But when you create a ballet, you are in a sense playing God. You have the power to shape it and change it, if you choose to. It's like developing a new form of engineering. You are directly responsible for its integrity and originality."

"If the ballet has its own identity and integrity, you eventually have to let it have its own life, don't you?"

"The whole idea of control over your art is complex. You want it to have its own life, and at the same time you want to control it. The artist finds himself in a tug-of-war over his art. Ultimately you find yourself a slave to it."

"Does the ballet idiom serve you well in your quest for self-expression?"

"Ballet is a lot like Latin in that it is the root of so many dance languages and, therefore, of transcendent importance. We don't use ballet in its eighteenth- or nineteenth-century forms, except that we are conversant with it. I'm not interested in a verbatim recapitulation of the ballet vocabulary, but I do acknowledge that it is a great way to train dancers. One can be bereft of ballet influence or compelled strictly by it and still find original ways of expressing oneself. In the end, I think, there is a certain amount of luck and synchronicity about the way things happen. We are not always in control of how things come together."

"Do you believe that one can be taught to be a successful choreographer?"

"No. Nor do I believe it should be taught. The ability to get people to follow you is at the heart of what makes a choreographer successful. It's so basic. If you don't demonstrate that first, what's the point of all the rest? All choreographers of significance have had the capacity to get people to follow them of their own free will. And how do they do that? Who knows? Jerome Robbins, Anthony Tudor, and George Balanchine demonstrated it, and it is so essential that without it you lack some aspect of DNA that could possibly enable you to be a choreographer."

"I find it curious that some choreographers who have that capacity are not very nice people."

"It's irrelevant whether they are nice or not. The work is the only thing that matters. People can be shits and do good work, and they can be nice and do lousy work. I worked for Anthony Tudor, whom I esteemed as highly as I esteem anybody, and he was a perfect shit. I've worked for nice choreographers who bored the hell out of me."

"When did you feel comfortable enough about what you were doing to call yourself a choreographer?"

"I made my first ballet in 1967 when I was twenty-four, but I think it took me fifty ballets to feel like I was a choreographer. There's no technique; you do it by the seat of your pants. As a dancer you need some evidence that you're a dancer. You go to class every day, you practice, you train your body. It's palpable. There is nothing palpable about choreography. Even now, I don't know if I'll ever do another ballet. When I go into the studio I feel a constriction around my throat—no doubt it's my own hand. All these questions come to mind. Can I find some movement that is not a recapitulation of something I've done or seen? Can I find something that matches the feeling of the music in some original way? Does the work have a reason for being? Does it have integrity?"

"It sounds a bit gut-wrenching. Ultimately what do you get out of it?"

"Out of the need to overcome despair, I've learned that it is unreasonable to expect rewards simply because you have given everything to make your dances. Dances don't exist so you can receive applause or critical acclaim. It's a one-way street. You owe them everything, and they owe you nothing. You commit seppuku [a Japanese form of suicide performed with a knife to the stomach] to fulfill what it is that they need. It's your job and that's what it takes.

Every time I make a new ballet I go into crisis. I have to face the disappointment that the ballet did not reward me, and that expectation goes on endlessly. The pleasure comes from the privilege of making the ballet, and the funny thing is that it stops the moment the work is complete."

"You must derive personal satisfaction and reward in knowing that you've helped perpetuate the art form over the last thirty years."

"I don't know how much I've perpetuated the art form. I believe that people, according to their talents and predilections, should have the opportunities to develop whatever talents, gifts, and impulses they might have. That should be the only criterion for the application of talent. I think it's ethically and morally correct to support this view."

"Is that why you've done so much work with children?"

"I derive great personal and professional reward from the development of talented children into full, wonderful dancers. Never mind that I may have found these kids in the third grade in Bedford-Stuyvesant or the Bronx and have known them since they were eight, nine, and ten years old. I don't look at the dancers with a paternal attitude. I'm not a parent. I'm a choreographer, and the ballets have needs."

"So your relationship as choreographer to dancer is practical and useful?"

"An audience sees choreography only through the dancers. These people are part of what makes choreography possible. The greater the intimacy of the collaboration between the dancer and the choreographer, the better the chance the choreographer has of a successful expression of his point of view. In the process we become equals with different responsibilities and are dependent on one another."

"Sounds to me like you're supplying dance with dancers, and that perpetuates the art form. That's admirable."

"Well, people are making babies. Some of them can dance. So, you still want to take my picture?"

"Yes, of course."

"Oh, shit! I hate being photographed."

"Come on, you'll be fine."

We moved into one of the dance studios for the portrait. I positioned him in front of a large window looking out onto rooftops crowned with barrellike water towers.

"You know what this scene reminds me of?" I said, waiting for my Polaroid to develop.

"No, what?"

"*West Side Story.* Do you ever think about having played Baby John in the movie?"

"Oh, come on, Rose. That was over forty years ago. It's ancient history. No, I don't ever think about it! I've moved on. Must everyone bring that up?"

"Oops, sorry," I said. "I didn't realize it's such a touchy subject."

He pretended to be annoyed with me, but I could tell it was just an act.

New York City, 1999

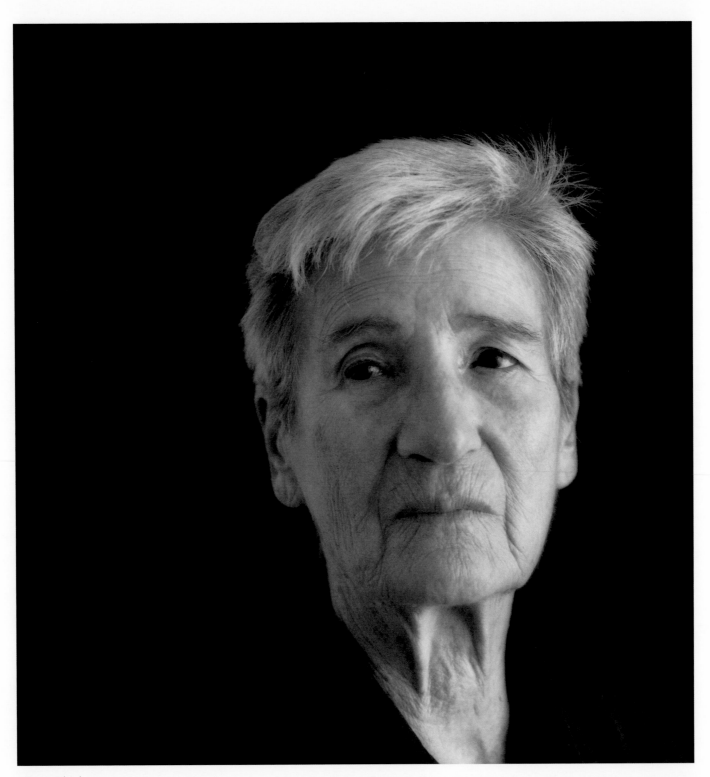

Kinetic Thinker

bella lewitzky

"This is not going to take long, is it? I hate having my photo taken,"

Bella said as she and her husband walked into my studio.

"No, not at all," I reassured her. "But I would like to spend a little time talking with you about your life in dance."

"That would be fine," Bella said, following me into the sitting area, where I had prepared a tape recorder and a bowl of fruit.

"Bella, when did you start creating dances?"

" I started creative work when I was very young. I made up my own dances and cast all the neighborhood kids in them. I simply took charge and told the others what to do. It was a natural role for me, and something I never got in trouble over."

"So you've been a dancemaker all your life?"

"Yes, I've had a tremendously supportive family, both my birth family and my immediate family. I've always been able to tend to the work that I love without having to make personal sacrifices. For me, it's been an easy path. I didn't have to waste time trying to find out what I wanted to do. I always knew. The impulse to create started with my early neighborhood dances and then just continued to develop. I knew very early on that I was going to be something that would later be called a choreographer. It was a path that I set out on, and I never felt the need to change. What that does is free you to do what you need to do. Only in looking back can you realize such a thing."

29

"Most people never find their true path, and yet you knew as a child. Were you guided in some way or influenced by anyone in particular?"

"Yes, I was very influenced by my father. He was a Sunday painter. That means he was an amateur painter. I learned a tremendously valuable lesson from him. He taught me that it didn't make a damn bit of difference what you did for a living, as long as you had something that rewarded your life. Every night he'd come home from his indifferent day job to something that made life worth living—his painting. He didn't care if anyone ever saw his paintings. It was the creative act that he loved. My sister and I would sneak into his room and steal his paintings because if we didn't, he'd paint right over them. We never discussed this, my father and I. There was never a need to."

"So for your father the act of creating was more valuable than the creation. Was it the same for you? How important was it to see your work performed on the stage?"

"My father's medium was private. I viewed dance as a public medium. So, yes, I needed to see the work on the stage, but that's not to say that the creative process was of any less importance to me. I liked the visual act of seeing the choreography both in my head and on the bodies of the dancers."

"When you created work for your dancers, where did it come from?"

"My first impetus always came from my own movement in my own body. I was kinetically stimulated. Still am. Even now I have to move before any truth passes my direction. All of my sensibilities were in the body knowledge first, foremost, and always. I got to a point where I could visualize movement. That came through experience. I learned if you did such and such, that would happen. The results became fairly predictable, but it took me a while to get this and understand it. If I have a new idea I have to move to it. It's got to come kinetically for me. I am a kinetic thinker. So, it's always there. It makes me a very good coach, I have found incidentally. I can tell on someone else's body where they're going right or wrong."

"Did you generally start with a concept or movement phrase?"

"It was not formula-ridden. It's of the moment. It's clearly a visual as much as a kinetic creation. That's what's so lovely about the creative process. You never know where it's going to come from or when. You can't depend on it at all. It has many origins and comes from any place and every place. Anything can be the impetus for a creative thought. It can come from someone running down a hallway or two dancers having a conversation. It can come by my establishing a sequence of movement, and it can go on from there. Most of the time I have no idea where it comes from."

"So you're really at the whim of some unpredictable force."

"I have discovered that when I'm at my best, I am the handmaiden of the art. I'm not leading it. It's leading me. Where it's going, I don't know, and if I wanted to change it, it would be hopeless for me to try. So I'm hanging on to the tail of this thing and making this happening thing happen. I wouldn't be able to tell you how it began or where it will end. It's an original every time. It's excit-

"When I'm at my best,

I am the handmaiden of the art. I'm not leading it. It's leading me."

ing, so exciting, because it's totally unpredictable. It's this that has kept me in dance my whole life."

"How is it for you now that you are retired and no longer have a company?"

"I face the next step in my life rather easily most of the time. I feel no need to repeat where I've been. I lived that life and now I'm in another place. I'm not dependent upon a dance company for fulfillment. You can always find new paths and avenues to explore and develop within yourself."

"Does that mean you are uninterested in preserving your work, sustaining it for the future? Many companies continue long after their namesakes have passed on. Take, for example, the companies of Alvin Ailey or Martha Graham."

"I had a wonderful career, but I'm not interested in being my own museum. I think that would be awfully self-indulgent. Lots of people can't let go, but I can."

"But what if my children want to experience your choreography? How will they be able to?"

"They won't. They'll be out of luck. My work was of the moment and had its time. I learned from Lester Horton that your work is reflective of who you are and where you are in your development. I'm not interested in its survival. My repertory lives on in the bodies of the dancers who performed it. I hope that my students take what they've learned and develop it. If there are people who gained something from the life I lived, then that's great. But I don't owe anyone anything. We don't dance to be rewarded. The dance is its own reward."

"You've been such an important presence in the world of dance. Do you miss the limelight of public life?"

"No, I don't. I discovered that when I was a well-known person, nobody really knew me. The public's perception of me had more to do with opinion than truth. I learned as a public figure to be graceful about it and accommodate it, but their truth had nothing to do with my own, not a thing."

"Where do you find fulfillment now?"

"Family has its definite rewards. And … I have the time to enjoy the things I never had time for before, like watching the sunrise. I never knew how exquisite it can be. I now have the time to partake of the beauty of nature. It is absolutely fulfilling."

"Bella, thank you so much," I said. "Why don't we take that picture now? The powder room is to the right if you'd like to fix your hair or put on some lipstick."

"No, I'm fine as I am," she said, dismissing any need to alter her appearance. I invited her to sit on a piano bench that was covered with black fabric. Behind her hung a black backdrop. I bounced my strobes off the wall, which bathed her in soft white light.

"Just be yourself," I said as I pointed the camera at her.

"I don't know how to be anyone else," she replied.

Los Angeles, 1998

Classic Visionary

helgi tomasson

As I faced the famous dancer-turned-choreographer, one word came to mind: "nobility."

Yet this Iceland-born dance legend was not only approachable, he was even down-to-earth. We were introduced in the hallway of the San Francisco Ballet School minutes before our scheduled shoot, and I thanked him for his time, then described my idea for his portrait.

"I thought you might sit on a stool with two or three of your students in the background, warming up at the barre. It provides us with a bit of context."

"Yes, we can do that."

He excused himself and asked one of his assistants to choose three dancers from the ballet class in the next studio. In a few minutes the young dancers walked in. I measured the distance from where Helgi would sit to the ballet barre at the wall and arranged the lights accordingly. I thanked the dancers for their participation and assigned a dance position to each.

"You do an arabesque. And you, why don't you port de bras, feet open in fourth, and perhaps you, in the middle, can look as if you're ready to do a *grand battement*, arms in fourth."

Helgi expressed surprise. "You know ballet?"

"Why, yes. I was a dancer."

"That's wonderful. It must be very helpful to you as one who photographs dancers."

"Oh, yes. I'm able to speak to the dancers in their own language."

After the shoot, Helgi and I sat down to talk.

"You've been described by many as a visionary," I began. "Is ballet in trouble as we head into the twenty-first century?"

"In the last couple of decades we've lost the great pillars of our art form—George Balanchine, Jerome Robbins, Frederick Ashton, Martha Graham, Alvin Ailey. What I'm trying to do is uphold the classical tradition of dance and, at the same time, find ways to expand it. I'd hate to see some of our most important full-length ballets become museum pieces. As artistic director of the San Francisco Ballet, I try to hire choreographers who have a strong working knowledge of classical ballet and a comprehensive understanding of women's point work. That's not to say that we don't also appreciate other choreographic voices. We have a Paul Taylor piece in the repertory, and he is not a ballet choreographer. I'm always thinking about the unlimited possibilities of classical ballet."

"Where do you place yourself on the choreographic continuum?"

"I fall into the category of disciple. I worked with George Balanchine and Jerome Robbins for fifteen years. I started to choreograph while I was with New York City Ballet. After Balanchine saw my first work—*Introduction, Theme, and Variation Polonaise*, op. 65—he encouraged me to continue to choreograph. Jerome Robbins was also a great mentor. In fact, I owe him my entire career. He discovered me and brought me to New York."

"Where did he discover you?"

"I met Jerome Robbins when I was seventeen while training at the Pantomime Theater in Copenhagen's Tivoli Gardens. He was very impressed with my dancing and arranged a scholarship for me to study at the School of American Ballet. I would later join the New York City Ballet as a principal dancer. Both Balanchine and Robbins created roles expressly for me."

"What are some of the biggest challenges facing ballet today?"

"Audiences have many choices when it comes to entertainment. They have movies and videos, theater, and everything else. I always ask, 'How are we going to survive?' The answer is by giving audiences really exciting dancing. One of the problems is that they hear 'classical' and say, 'I don't want to see that.' To a lot of people 'classical' means old-fashioned. They say, 'I'm into the beat. I need a beat.'" He snapped his fingers. "You have to show them that classical technique can be performed contemporarily."

"How do you go about doing that?"

"What I have been doing is using contemporary music in many of my new pieces. I'm finding that it's opened up a whole new creative side to me that I didn't know was there. I might go into the studio and put some things together and say, 'Where did that come from? I didn't know that was in me.' I'm also working on creating more contemporary movement but based on classical technique. Having a solid base in classical dance allows you to become very inventive and experimental. It's really exciting to see what the human body can do."

"What do you look for in the dancers you choose for your company?"

"That's a little tough for me to answer. I know what it is when I see it, but it's difficult for me to articulate. There are certain things that I like to see: speed and careful articulation, fluidity of movement and passion. I try to get that out of my dancers through teaching and coaching. The main thing is that they must be able to communicate their passion across the footlights. I look for dancers who are willing to give of themselves."

"Do you feel that your passion for dance was so great in you that you had to succumb to its power?"

"Oh, I feel I was destined to be a dancer. I performed on the stage for over twenty years. And I would do it all over again. Dance has brought me great joy and fulfillment. All those pliés and *tendus* have been worth it. It even brought my wife to me. I met Marlene when we danced together at the Joffrey Ballet. Today we have two sons, Erik and Kris."

"How do you get dancers to do what you want them to do?"

"I started out by showing them. I would perform the choreography. Then one day a male dancer came up to me and said, 'We can't really do what you do. It's too difficult for us.' I had never thought about it that way before. I was an accomplished dancer, and I sort of just did it. But this young man's comment made me realize that I can't make them imitate me. I started demonstrating a lot less. What I do now is talk to them about the feeling that I want and invite them to put more of themselves into their dancing. Besides, I don't think I can do that stuff anymore," he joked.

"How do you decide who is going to dance in one of your ballets?"

"When I start a new ballet and choose my cast, I do it the same way a painter might choose his colors. I look at my color palette and see who I think will bring my piece the right shades and tones. To this day, I have yet to have all the dancers that I started out with at the premier. Invariably some leave or have injuries, and what I thought I was creating based on the original cast has to be adjusted."

"What is your creative process in creating a ballet?"

"This is something I don't even know how to talk about. I walk into the studio after I've listened to the music at length. I have a vision—some sort of structure in my mind. I see a group of people coming from here and then there. Some days it just begins to flow and then suddenly you can't keep up. You get mad at yourself because you can't remember what just came into your head. And some days nothing seems to work."

"When you choreograph, do you perform all the roles, all the movement?"

"Not in the same way that I did when I was a dancer. But I do want to sense the feel of the movement. Sometimes it feels right to me but doesn't look right on the dancers. So then I have to change it. It's amazing that you walk into this big empty space with an idea of what you're going to do, and two hours later you have the makings of a ballet. You look at the clock, and you have only fifteen more minutes with the dancers, and you beg them to stay so you can continue the flow."

"Do you gravitate toward story ballets or conceptual pieces?"

"Most of my works are in the abstract, but all of them are music-driven. The music tells me what to do."

"Process or product—do they have equal weight?"

"For me the process is more rewarding, because when the work is done it's no longer yours. The dancers take it and put their own personalities on it. I'm always a little mournful. The ballet becomes detached from you."

"Even though your name is still on it?"

"Yes. But then you start thinking of your next work, and it takes some of the hurt away."

"When you revisit ballets you've choreographed in the past, do you see yourself in the work?"

"I see where I was back then and begin to contrast it with where I am now. But to change it would be taking it out of the context in which it was created. I'm not really all that compelled to redo older works. What I normally do is say to myself, 'For that time, this was really pretty good,'" he said, laughing at his immodesty.

"There are so many dancers who yearn to be great. They may have the passion and the talent, but they never quite get there. As the director of one of the world's major ballet companies, how do you address this problem?"

"There are very few among us who have something that is extraordinarily special. This is true not only in dance but in all fields. It basically excludes 99.9 percent of the population. What do I say to corps de ballet dancers who are not going to be soloists? I try to make them sense their own worth. First of all, you cannot run a ballet company composed only of principal dancers. A ballet company needs all kinds of people. Some are chosen and destined to achieve more than others. Some people are handsome and some are not. That's just the way it is. There are times when I have to say to a dancer, 'I don't see you as a soloist. I don't think you have what it takes. You're free to go somewhere else. Maybe someone else will see you with different eyes.' But I always try to make them see that they are valued here and appreciated."

"I would imagine it's devastating for dancers who've devoted most of their life to dance and can't get beyond the corps de ballet."

"If they choose to leave dance. I tell them this: 'Don't get bitter. Quit now. You're young. Go to school and use this experience and the discipline of dance to help you achieve whatever you want.' There are so many dancers these days taking college courses. Let's face it: The dancer's career is relatively short."

"I imagine that the pressure to be commercially successful is enormous for you as artistic director of a world-class company. What's that like?"

"I do feel pressure to fill those seats. I'm always aware of the budget, the deficit, this expense and that expense. My goal is to see this company reach greater heights and broader audiences. But I also wear the hat of choreographer. I never start out choreographing a work thinking I have to sell tickets. I do it because I'm inspired."

San Francisco, 1999

Tough Bird

onna white

I could tell that Onna was nobody's fool when she phoned to bawl me out for spelling her name wrong in my letter of introduction.

"It's Onnnnnna, not Ooooooona," she yelled into the phone.

"I'm sorry, so sorry. May I come by this week to photograph and interview you?"

"Yes. Come on Wednesday after two o'clock. I'm busy watching my soaps in the early afternoon. And I never miss my soaps."

I jotted down her address and promised to be punctual.

When the day arrived, she buzzed me into her West Hollywood apartment and greeted me at the elevator. She was thin, almost frail, and walked with a slight limp that suggested she might have had a hip replacement—which is common among former ballerinas. She wore turquoise stretch pants and a sweatshirt emblazoned with a picture of a jazz dancer. I unloaded my gear in the middle of her living room and scanned the apartment for signs of her distinguished career. With little prodding, she pointed out old photographs and signed posters from such films as *Mame* with Lucille Ball, and Broadway shows like *Hello, Dolly* with Angela Lansbury. One of her prized possessions was a group photo of Oscar recipients.

"Receiving the Oscar for *Oliver* has meant the world to me," she said.

"I'm looking forward to hearing all about your amazing career."

"Well, then, let me begin at the beginning. I was born in 1922 in Nova Scotia, Canada. My family moved to western Canada when I was quite young.

"When I look back at my career,
I realize I had a lot of nerve.
I had stride. I had guts.

If you prove yourself, honey, it doesn't matter
if you're a man or a woman."

We lived in Powell River, which is about eighty miles from Vancouver. It is a paper mill town. My father was a barber and my mother a schoolteacher. I had two brothers. I was a very sickly child and would faint whenever I got excited. The doctor told my mother that I should have lots of exercise. So I started doing gymnastics in school and when I was twelve began taking ballet from a woman named Frieda Marie Richter Shaw. She was wonderful. I continued studying with her until I was seventeen. She knew someone in San Francisco and helped arrange for me to take classes at the San Francisco Ballet School. After a short time I was invited to dance in the company's chorus. I was very good at doing air *tours* and multiple pirouettes. It didn't take long before I graduated to soloist and then principal ballerina. I danced the white swan and black swan inter-changeably for what seemed like years. I was starting to get a little bored with the toe shoes when a girlfriend of mine suggested I move to New York and try out for some of the Broadway shows. So I did. My first audition was for *Finian's Rainbow*. The choreographer was a fellow named Michael Kidd. The part required a ballet combination, so I performed it and got the job!"

"Did you know then that you would eventually become a choreographer?"

"No, not really. I was just having a good time working with Michael. He took me with him to London to work on *Guys and Dolls*. I had no idea about choreography, but through assisting him I learned what choreographers do and how they are supposed to behave—when they should be patient and when they should be strict. I'll never forget when we were working on the "Take Back Your Mink" number and he asked me to do some little dance sequence and I said to him, 'That's easy for you to say. You're not wearing high heels.' So he says, 'What size shoe do you wear?' 'Size seven and a half,' I answered. He took my heels, put them on, and performed the combination flawlessly. Well, I shut my mouth and never doubted him again. I danced in the show and assisted him for a few years. In fact, I had both of my kids while working on that show. I eventually left and was replaced by Chita Rivera. From there I did a couple of seasons at City Center in New York, reviving shows like *Finian's Rainbow* and *Carmen Jones*."

"Having been a ballerina, stage dancer, and choreographer's assistant, did you feel you had all the necessary skills to be a successful choreographer?"

"Yes. I felt I had learned all I really needed to know for my style of dancing. I had studied piano when I was young and was knowledgeable about music. It would have been helpful had I known tap dancing, but even Michael didn't tap. What you do is just hire an assistant who can tap."

"Specifically what would you say defined your work or your process?"

"I was always devoted to the book—the story and the characters. I'm a stickler when it comes to making sure that choreographed elements belong in the show or movie. For example, I would never end a dance abruptly so that it looks like the number is in there for its own sake. The dance has to enhance the story and segue into the next scene, as well as reflect what's going on with the characters."

"What about dance movement, or dance vocabulary?"

"That would depend on the characters in the story. The moves had to match the characters. Who was going to do the dancing was another consideration. In *Bye Bye Birdie*, for example, I adjusted the choreography for Dick Van Dyke, who had no formal dance training. He was so scared. 'Oh, come on, Richard,' I would say. 'You can do this.' He was so cute and a great natural mover. I also had to do that with Mark Lester, the eight-year-old boy who played Oliver in the film. He had never acted or danced. So the choreography I gave him was something he could do. Today he's thirty-eight years old and working as a chiropractor."

"Did you find it difficult being a woman in a male-dominated profession?"

"If you prove yourself, honey, it doesn't matter if you're a man or a woman."

"How do you prove yourself?"

"You show them what you can do. A case in point is the film *Oliver*. The author didn't think I could do it, first because I was a woman and second because I wasn't English. But Columbia Pictures stood behind me and told him, 'We're hiring her.' So he said, 'Okay, but have her prove herself by choreographing the "Who Will Buy" number.' I quickly came up with a concept and got right to it. It was a dance that included 265 people. It required the use of eight assistants to coordinate the timing between dance sequences and multiple scenery changes. We did it all on one particular street but made it look like a London neighborhood."

"My goodness! Were you nervous with so much riding on that number?"

"No. I knew I could do it. I had learned my craft well. My brain was working fluently, and I was never at a loss for ideas. I just took charge. I read the script and saw immediately in my mind's eye what I needed to do. I went ahead and did my best, and it turned out pretty darn good. I've been lucky. Write in your book that luck has a lot to do with success."

"How do you know when you're doing the right thing, that you've taken the best approach?"

"It's very difficult to know ahead of time. You have to try it, and if it doesn't work be prepared to change it. You can't be stubborn with creativity. Keep the channels free and open. I don't have an ego, honey. I'm proud of what I've done, and I've always been willing to accept other people's suggestions. Sometimes you get wonderful ideas from your dancers or actors. That was the case with Ron Moody, who played Fagan in *Oliver*. He had performed the role on the stage and had a lot of little tricks up his sleeve that he let me use in the film, particularly in the 'Pick a Pocket or Two' number."

"Were there ever any instances where you wanted to change the script or convince the production team that you had a better way of approaching a scene?"

"Oh, yes. In *The Music Man* I felt very strongly about changing the library scene, but I had to convince the author, Meredith Wilson, to use the music man as an instigator. In the meeting she didn't say a word. I knew I would have to show it to her first. That was another one of those times when I had to prove myself. No one knew what Robert Preston could do. He had never done a musical before. But he came through beautifully, and she agreed."

"Sounds to me like you were pretty tough and self-confident."

"Well, I'm old now, honey, but when I look back at my career, I realize I had a lot of nerve. I had stride. I had guts. But I wasn't tough. I was honest. I just did what I had to do and tried to do it well."

"How about we immortalize you in a portrait?"

"Oh, honey, I don't like being photographed," she said. "Can you do a nice job with me?"

"Yes, of course, and we'll work on it together," I said.

Onna asked me to help her pick out a dress. While she changed, I set up a black seamless backdrop in her living room.

She reappeared wearing the black dress we had selected and pearl earrings. I invited her to sit on a stool in front of the backdrop. Sensing her discomfort in front of the camera, I gave her permission to look away.

"How do I look?" she asked.

"Not bad for a tough old broad," I answered.

West Hollywood, 1999

Tap Dancer

gregory hines

"You walk like a dancer," he said to me as I approached him in the lobby of the Westside Academy in Santa Monica, California.

"Thank you. I take that as a compliment," I said, shaking his hand. "I know you normally rent this space to practice. I appreciate your sacrificing some of your dance time to let me photograph you."

"No problem," he said. "Let's get to it."

"Well, I can't take your picture yet, " I told him, leading him into a studio where I had set up a backdrop and lights.

"You can't? Why not?"

"Well, for one thing, we're strangers to each other. How can I create a portrait of you if I hardly know you?"

"You're kidding, right?"

"No, not at all. I'm not interested in recording what you look like. I'm interested in revealing something about your nature, about you as an artist. I'd like to ask you a few questions before I photograph you, just so we get a little more acquainted."

"You know, that makes sense," he said, setting his tap shoes on the floor next to the chair I had prepared for him.

"You've been a tap dancer since you were a child. What is it about tap that still drives you?"

"What has always driven me and continues to do so is the search for a new step. Maybe that's innate in all artists, to drive oneself farther and discover new possibilities within. I know when I find myself inside a new step, it makes me feel soooo good. I'm always trying to get to that good feeling. I've heard artists say they quit dancing because they became bored with the sameness of it all. Maybe they didn't have the inclination to come up with something new."

"Do you remember when you first began searching for new steps?"

"Yes, I do. You know my brother and I had an act when we were kids. Our routine consisted of an opening number, a soft shoe, and a big close with acrobatics. We were performing at the Apollo Theater when I was about ten or eleven years old. Teddy Hale was also on the program. He did three shows a night. Here was this strung-out junkie, but what a great dancer he was! First show, he'd come out, do his thing, and he was hot. The second show, he's in the same shirt that had dried on his body, and he's doing something in a completely different tempo with all kinds of new stuff. I said to myself, 'This guy doesn't have an act.' Third show, still in the same shirt, he's snapping and sliding around, again something different. At this point I'm thinking to myself, 'That's what I want to do. This is it! I don't want to repeat the same routine night after night.'

"From that point, I was always trying to come up with a new step. We still had to perform our set routine, but whenever I was offstage and around other dancers, I'd be looking for a new step. Sandman Sims was always good for that. He'd always give me new steps. Once I started performing on my own, I couldn't wait to go out onstage without an act."

"Isn't that a little risky?"

"It's risky but very exciting. I've almost been fired a few times. Producers get nervous when they think you're just going to come out there and wing it. But I've managed to get my way. I have to have a couple of sections where I improvise."

"Whenever I see you dance in films or on television, I always feel like you're trying to really challenge yourself technically, outdo yourself. Do I have that right?"

"I come from the tradition of vaudeville, which is all about love me, like me,

applaud for me. Henry Le Tang, one of my teachers, used to say, 'If they start to applaud after you do it four times, do it nine times.' But I noticed at a certain point in my career that when my focus was mostly on the audience, it wasn't always so enjoyable for me. I gradually became more interested in listening to what I was feeling. Some people call that being in the zone. Once I'm able to connect with a particular emotion like joy or anger or humor, I can dance specifically to it. It becomes more meaningful for me. What I'm trying to do, in the best possible sense, is get into the zone and hang out there for as long as possible. When I'm onstage, I'm searching for the zone. It's a precious place to be."

"Do you usually end up there?"

"There are times when I get there and I can play around and linger inside it. But more often I'm only there for a short while, like maybe a minute or two. I get easily distracted. I could be dancing and then out of the clear blue my thought goes to, 'Was I supposed to bring home whole milk or skim milk?' Or I look out into the audience and see a beautiful woman with a real low-cut dress. It distracts me and I've lost the connection."

"How do you find or invent new steps?"

"What I do is improvography. I don't believe in pure improvisation. When I was working on the film *The Cotton Club,* directed by Francis Ford Coppola, I told him that I wanted to improvise during some of my dance sequences. He said, 'Fine, improvise Dutch Schultz being murdered.' I was in the first take, just getting going, finding things, when he stopped me and said, 'All right, I want that step that you just did with the rapid sound.' In each take I found new steps that both he and I wanted repeated in the next take. I had moments of sheer improvisation that subsequently evolved into fixed choreography. Once you begin to repeat steps and phrases, it becomes choreography. What I do, essentially, is go in and out of technique. The very first step that they teach you in tap is the time step. You learn it and do it, and then you throw it away. But you're doing the time step every time you jump up and down and flap. It's like a singer going in and out of the melodic line. Once you know the melodic line, you can

It's like I need a shot of whiskey, and I don't even drink."

embellish it. Nobody did that better than Ella Fitzgerald. She could sing a whole song without ever singing the melodic line. But you knew it was there."

"How did you develop your own style?"

"I think it was through my own evolution and emulating my dance heroes. I wanted to be like Sammy Davis Jr. When I was fifteen and sixteen I wore my hair like he did. I tried to get the same eyeglass frames he had. I walked like him. For three or four years I was Sammy Davis Jr. I learned so much from him. When I'd see him, he'd say, 'Hey, man, show me a step. You're really good! You're talented!' And then he'd look at me and smile. There's no way I can tell you what that meant to me.

"I stole steps from many great tap dancers—Honi Coles, Henry Le Tang, Sandman Sims, and so many others. One time I was doing this show back in 1988. I fell into this very hot step. I'd never done it before. The audience was applauding and shouting, and I was really in the zone. People were saying, 'Man, you really hit that step,' and I was feeling so good. Then about four years later, I'm watching this old Gene Kelly movie, and there's the step! The first time I'd seen that movie I was in my late teens. It didn't come out in me until 1988. I would say by the time I reached my mid-thirties I had developed my own style. I realized it only after watching a video of myself dancing, but I recognized flashes of all my teachers and dance influences."

"You have a spirit about you that is very uplifting. It shows in your dancing. Where does that come from?"

"Well, I'm one of the very lucky people who came from a very supportive family. If I radiate anything, it's because I received love in abundance. And I've been married a couple of times to wonderful women. Consequently, I am a happy man. I was also incredibly fortunate to have been exposed to tap dancing and able to spend time with my heroes. I'm sure there are kids out there who idolize Michael Jordan or Steffi Graf but don't ever get the opportunity to spend time with them. Can you imagine Steffi Graf saying to a young aspiring tennis player, 'Hey, kid, you've got a really good serve!'"

"What was it like for you working with Mikhail Baryshnikov when you did the film *White Nights?*"

"Well, I learned how to drink vodka! No, seriously, I was quite inspired by Mike. I call him Mike. I came from a tradition that when you get on the stage, you smile. You have to be happy all the time. The classical dancer usually assumes some dramatic role while dancing. We hung out together a lot, and I watched him rehearse with dancers from American Ballet Theater. I learned what makes ballet unique. We see the body. We see how it moves. I asked myself, 'Why am I always covering up with a tuxedo or jacket?' Tap dancers have traditionally shrouded their bodies in order to draw attention to the feet. I wanted to get sensual with tap dancing, to turn people on with the dancing, but also with the body. I started to lift weights, build muscle, and wear tighter-fitting clothes. The change was liberating. I saw immediately that people were responding to it, and it increased my employability."

"How do you maintain your dancing when you're away from it sometimes for months at a time?"

"Well, I'm finding I'm at an age when my skills diminish more quickly. If I'm working on a movie and I don't dance for a month or more and I put on my shoes, it hurts. When I was younger, I didn't need to dance beforehand. I would just hit the stage. I took for granted that I could dance whenever I wanted to and dance as well as I ever did. I get more out of it now than ever before. I love tap dancing. I love my tap shoes. I get so inspired, so filled up. It's like I need a shot of whiskey, and I don't even drink. Tap dancing is the second most wonderful thing that I can do."

"What's the first?"

"Lovemaking!"

"You know what? I think I might know you well enough now to take your portrait."

Santa Monica, California, 1999

Man with the Midas Touch

michael kidd

The man who choreographed some of Hollywood's most successful movies

(*The Band Wagon, Guys and Dolls, Seven Brides for Seven Brothers*) graduated from high school thinking he was going to be an engineer.

"I liked science and was very good in math. But when I got to the actual engineering courses at City College of New York, I became completely disinterested. It was too impersonal. The typical engineering student walked around with a slide rule in his pocket and was only interested in solving equations."

It was about that same time that Kidd saw his first modern dance performance.

"The dancers' ability to express personal feelings, emotions, and dramatic relationships in terms of movement intrigued me. So I began looking around for classes. Back then there were many dance classes available in New York City. I began studying with Anatole Vilzak and Muriel Stuart. It turned out that I had an aptitude for dancing. I was very agile and limber. I quit engineering school to pursue a career in dance."

Kidd would go on to establish himself during American ballet's formative years, dancing in Lincoln Kirstein's Ballet Caravan (1937) then moving to Eugene Loring's Dance Players (1940) and Lucia Chase's repertory company Ballet Theater (1942). Throughout these years he would dance in the ballets of Eugene Loring, Jerome Robbins, Agnes de Mille, Leonide Massine, Michel Fokine, Anthony Tudor, and many other prolific choreographers. Kidd would win five Tony Awards for his work on Broadway and receive an honorary Oscar for choreography in film. Now, well over thirty years since choreographing his last film, *Hello, Dolly*, he welcomed me into his spacious Brentwood home to talk over old times.

"You were first attracted to dance because of the dramatic relationships expressed through movement. How did that discovery influence your choreography?"

"Most of the dances created over the years, like those in the film *Seven Brides for Seven Brothers*, tell a story. You get to know the characters and how they feel about one another, how they react and why they are doing what they're doing. Abstract movement doesn't really appeal to me. It doesn't hold my interest. I look for stories whereby scenes are acted out in dance terms rather than verbal terms. The challenge is to create particular movements that look as if they evolved from those particular characters. A literal rendition of human movement would be uninteresting, so movement behavior is transformed into dance movement. My dancing is based on naturalistic movement that is abstracted and enlarged. All my movement relates to some kind of real activity. It's not pantomime, although there are pantomimic elements. It's really an expression of the emotions of the people involved and done on their own terms. If they live on a ranch in the mountains, like in *Seven Brides for Seven Brothers*, they have to do movements that would fit what they're all about. For that film I chose an acrobatic approach. Mountain men are not going to get up and do ballet. That would be ludicrous. In *Guys and Dolls*, I had the dancers use a jazz idiom and move on tempo. The characters were petty gamblers, con artists, and pickpockets, and their movement had to reflect that. During the crap game you feel them competing with one another, grabbing the dice and trying to win through exaggerated gambling behavior and energetic jazz turns and jumps. I got my ideas from various types I'd seen in real life, while growing up and living in New York City. I also used my imagination and did research."

"Did you typically need to dance the moves yourself or did you tend to visualize them in your mind before teaching them to the dancers?"

"I would first figure out in my mind what was supposed to happen among the dancers and usually get up and do each part by myself until it felt right. If it didn't feel right, I discarded it."

"The women's parts too?"

"Oh, yes."

"Do you need to see yourself reflected in a mirror when you choreograph?"

"Not necessarily. The mirror is more important during early dance training. When I studied ballet we always used a mirror. But when working out a dance sequence I don't necessarily need to see what I look like. I see the dancers perform it."

"How do choreographers hone their skill?"

"I think it's one of those crafts that you can't really study. The ability to devise a dance evolves from personal experience of having been in and performed in dance companies. That familiarizes you with the process of devising a ballet. I could not have walked out of a ballet class and choreographed a ballet without having danced for years in Ballet Caravan, Dance Players, and Ballet Theater. You also learn a great deal from assisting other choreographers. I assisted Eugene Loring, and that proved invaluable. I used to conduct rehearsals for him when he was busy doing something else. One of his most famous ballets was *Billy the Kid*. Later, when I joined Ballet Theater, they asked me to help them revive it because I knew it quite well. I staged it for them and danced the role of Billy the Kid. It proved very successful, and since they were always looking for new talent, they invited me to create my own ballet. And so in 1945 I choreographed my first ballet, *On Stage*, and played the part of a Charlie Chaplinesque stagehand who helps a shy little girl get into a ballet company. The entire ballet takes place during the course of a rehearsal."

"What inspired this story?"

"I had to come up with something, so I went home and just wrote out this scenario. I knew they didn't want to spend much money on a young, untried choreographer, so I thought of a ballet that required no scenery or costumes. The dancers could wear their practice clothes. In the end, the company did invest in a set and specific costumes because they didn't want to just leave things up to chance. The ballet was very successful and eventually led to my choreographing my first Broadway show, *Finian's Rainbow* [1947]. It turned out to be a big hit."

"Sounds like you had the Midas touch. Everything you touched turned to gold. Did you then begin to dance less and promote yourself as a choreographer?"

"I didn't want to end up like many performers who, after they stop dancing, have to open up an antique shop. I knew I couldn't dance forever, and I wanted to stay in dance, so I continued to take choreographic jobs."

"If you got a call right now to direct or choreograph a Broadway show, would you do it?"

"It would depend on the show. If I were really intrigued by it, I'd pursue it.

I've done so many shows and movies and I've loved it, but I don't have a burning desire to work just to work."

"Do you have a burning desire to create?"

"Well, I keep busy creatively. Choreography was not my everything. I was always interested in carpentry and making furniture. I made that table," he said, pointing across the room. "I enjoy photography and making short videos of family and friends."

"It's a little hard for me to imagine that the person who choreographed the films *Guys and Dolls, Can Can, Seven Brides for Seven Brothers*, and *Hello, Dolly* is not compelled to continue creating dances."

"I'm not like Jerome Robbins. I don't have that kind of persistent, relentless drive and desire to keep going. He never stopped. His output was phenomenal, always of a very high quality, always superb, always imaginative. When you look at the number of shows and ballets he's done, it's incredible. I danced in the first ballet he ever choreographed. It was called *Fancy Free*. I was one of the three sailors. It was very clear back then that Jerome Robbins was not just a beginner probing. He was a complete expert with a fully developed mature mind, doing a ballet to the smallest detail. It was obvious he would become a very important figure in dance. He worked until the very end. He never married and had no family. He devoted himself entirely to his work, and it meant everything to him. I don't think it was just nervous energy on his part. I don't want to give that impression. I think he was an extremely creative person who wanted to keep creating. That's probably why he was so harsh and difficult. He absolutely wanted things done exactly the way he wanted them done, and he could be very cruel to people."

"How did you treat your dancers?"

"I wanted things to be done well, but I didn't gratuitously insult or demean people. I just wanted the work to be done properly; otherwise it has no distinction. Despite everything I said earlier about the importance of dance being based on human movement, dance technique was always extremely important to me. My dancers had to be technically proficient and execute their moves cleanly. I think anybody who believes in his work wants it presented at the highest level."

"When I think of your work, I always come up with the word 'energetic.' Even Robin Williams characterized your work that way in the film *The Birdcage*."

"Yes, I got a kick out of that. I am energetic. I like things to be energetic. It's one of my personality traits. I think people's work reflects their personality and their spirit, whether they're a writer, musician, or dancer. When I danced, I was very active, very energetic, and very precise. I carried those things into my choreographic work."

"What's your take on today's Broadway scene?"

"The nature of musical theater has changed so much it doesn't really interest me. Back in my day songs had a melody, and the lyrics were important. The book was imaginative. Today's musicals seem rather manufactured and not very deep when it comes to content. But there are some very talented choreographers out there now, like Susan Stroman, Graciela Danielle, and Rob Marshall. I think they will continue to do good work."

(Within the next five years the three choreographers that Michael named went on to enjoy tremendous success. Graciela Danielle's *Ragtime* and *Annie Get Your Gun* became big Broadway hits. Susan Stroman's *Contact* and *The Producers* won an unprecedented number of Tony Awards. Rob Marshall directed and choreographed the film version of Bob Fosse's *Chicago*, the first Hollywood musical in decades to win an Oscar for Best Picture.)

"Why don't we take your portrait now? I just need to run out to my car and get my lighting equipment."

"Rose, I'd prefer to be photographed in natural light in my garden."

Kidd led me out back through a sliding door, past a sparkling swimming pool and into a glorious landscaped yard with blooming daylilies, tall trees, and perfectly maintained shrubs and bushes.

I pulled out my Hasselblad and started looking for a good spot. Michael seemed fascinated by my camera and asked if he could see it.

"This is one hell of a camera," he said, looking through the viewfinder as I wandered around the yard reading my light meter. "What kind of film are you using? How far away do you want to be? How much of me will be in the frame? How is the light over here?"

Together we worked out every detail of the shot, including precisely where Michael would sit. I worried when he pulled himself up to perch on the back of a wooden bench—both of his hips had been replaced. I shot a quick Polaroid and showed it to him for approval.

"Yes, very nice."

"Okay—camera and action!"

Brentwood, California, 1998

47

Improviser

toni basil

I phoned Toni to ask her if she had any ideas for a portrait.

"Let's go for the look of a 1950s Latin dancer," she said, explaining that her latest passion was salsa dancing.

"You mean something à la Carmen Miranda?" I asked.

"Yes, exactly."

"Great, let's do it."

When I rang the bell of Toni's Los Angeles home, she asked, "Who is it?" and hearing it was me, opened the door. She was half dressed and excused herself to return to her makeup artist. Meanwhile, I pushed her sofa and chairs into the dining room, rolled up her carpet, and set up a backdrop and lights. Toni reappeared about an hour later in full makeup and costume, as if she were ready to perform at the Copacabana. Before she would let me take a single exposure she went through a mental checklist in which she scrutinized every facet of the shoot. She examined my lighting setup, dictating where she wanted the light to fall and specifying "no shadows." A large mirror had been placed nearby so she could check her hair, makeup, fingernails, the folds of her dress, position of her body, and angle of her leg. Five hours later and utterly exhausted, I had learned that Toni Basil is a devout perfectionist.

About a week after the shoot I returned with the proofs for her review. She approved them, then we sat down to talk about her life in show business.

"Toni, your choreography is so innovative and creative. Where do you draw your inspiration from?"

"My work is very eclectic. It's made up of many different influences."

"Tell me about them."

"I was born into a show business family. My father, Louis Basil, was an orchestra leader who played in Chicago at the Lowe's and Chicago Theaters. He later moved to the Sahara Hotel in Las Vegas, where he worked until the day he died. My mother and her sisters and brothers were acrobatic comedians. Come, let me show you their photos." She led me to her photo gallery on the kitchen wall. "Here they are in costume. I think these were taken in the 1940s. This is my mother, Jacqueline, and my aunts, Iva and Christine, and then there's Uncle Pat and Uncle Billy. In this photo the man with the baton is my father. Show business is in my blood."

"So you knew early on that you would eventually end up on the stage?"

"Well, I knew I didn't want to be an opening act. I had my eyes set on the big picture. From as far back as I can remember, I was putting on costumes from the old trunk in the basement and dancing for the neighbors. In ballet class I used to ask, 'WHEN DO I GET TO DANCE? WHEN DO I GET TO DANCE? WHEN DO I GET TO DANCE?' I felt like all we ever did was exercises at the barre. My mother would say, 'Toni, you have to learn your technique first.' But all I wanted to do was make stuff up. Every time I heard music I danced to it differently. I was always searching for a new dance. You see, in thirty years my family's act never changed. From the 1930s to the 1960s it had the same music, the same juggling, the same boxing routine. The only thing that changed was the costumes. Even the couple of times they appeared on the *Ed Sullivan Show*, it was their same routine."

"Ah, so it's no wonder you wanted to make stuff up."

"My aunt Iva once told me, 'Whatever you could think up or imagine can be done.' So I formed cheerleading squads in the private school I attended in Chicago and made up dance routines. By the time I went to Las Vegas High School, I was staging pep rallies and halftime entertainment. Cheerleading gave me the opportunity to choreograph."

"When did you come to Hollywood, and how did you break into the dance scene?"

"I was seventeen when I arrived in LA, just as the go-go scene of the 1960s was emerging. I began taking dance class with David Winters, trained by Jerome Robbins and one of the original *West Side Story* dancers. Almost immediately I began to assist him. You might remember him as Arab in the film. It was an interesting time in LA because the more mature Hollywood choreographers weren't into social dancing, particularly go-go music. David and I, who were technically trained and completely understood contemporary music, jumped right into this new dance market. I assisted him on the TV show *Shindig*, the Hollywood beach movies, and the Elvis Presley–Ann-Margret movies. When David moved to New York for a job, I started getting calls to do choreography and established myself here in LA."

"Street dancing became your next passion?"

"Yes. Locking and popping became in the seventies what go-go dancing was in the sixties. It was happening in the streets of south central LA. I'd go down to the ghetto, on Forty-third and Crenshaw, and dodge bullets just to be part of the circle dances—the battles [improvisational dance competitions]. I survived several dangerous episodes in the early seventies when the Crips came in with guns. I'll tell you, nobody tried to save my ass. I had to dive under a car. But some of these improvisational dancers were as good as Fernando Bujones performing Don Quixote. You see, I was never sucked into the belief that street dance was less important than classical dance. I knew it was as creative and as difficult to perform. It took years for street dance to be recognized and appreciated. Today there is not a dance school in America that doesn't teach street dancing. New York dance schools offer classes in ballet, jazz, tap, hip-hop, flamenco, and locking and breaking, which is spinning on the back."

"Tell me about your group the Lockers."

"I didn't invent locking. The technique was created by a guy named Don Campbell, a street dancer from LA. His locking came out of the fact that he couldn't do the footwork of the Funky Chicken, the dance that was popular at the time. He came up with a technique that focused on the upper body. It caught on quickly because it enabled dancers to tell stories with their hands and arms."

"What does locking look like?"

Toni got up and began to perform staccato moves, pointing her index finger in different directions, isolating different parts of her body with very little footwork. "Now watch the difference. This is popping." She made the movements smaller and simulated the hands and arms popping out of their joints. "Then there is the electric boogaloo, which came out of San Francisco. It has a more rolling motion." Now she was moving her hips and shoulders in circles as she continued to pop.

"Ah, I see," I said.

"Choreography is not just steps; it's a vision, it's staging, it's patterns, it's scenery, it's lighting."

"The Lockers was a group of street dancers, about seven of us, that I formed into an opening act. You know, like what my aunts and uncles used to do. The street dancer's concept of choreography was to improvise competitively in a circle without imitating each other. I figured out how to make steps that all of us could perform without losing the 'in the moment' quality. I did it by creating stories around the movement. I did my own version of *Swan Lake*, combining classical ballet with street dance. Hell, we opened for Frank Sinatra at Carnegie Hall, doing *West Side Story* using locking and popping." Toni began to sing the Jets' theme—"Da-dum, da-dum—da-dum, da-dum, de-dee tada-hey"—and demonstrating part of the choreography. "The Lockers danced together for about five years, performing to varied audiences across the country and appearing on top television shows, including *The Tonight Show* with Johnny Carson, *Saturday Night Live,* and *The Smothers Brothers Comedy Hour*."

"As a choreographer you have a wealth of styles and vocabulary to draw from."

"Yes, I can pull up dance and movement information from all my different influences—my vaudevillian family, my ballet training, cheerleading, African American street dance, salsa, and all the different styles I've studied. I also own about a thousand dance reference videos, so if I need to, I just go into my video library and remind myself of the genre and put myself in that mind-set. Then I start to improvise through the vocabulary."

"What's the process like when you're working with pop singers, like Mick Jagger or Bette Midler?"

"So many people think that choreographers are just asked to choreograph dancers doing technical moves to music. But, don't forget, Rose, choreography is not just steps; it's a vision, it's staging, it's patterns, it's scenery, it's lighting. The master choreographer is someone who makes the performer look completely spontaneous, as if the artist never had a choreographer. Mick Jagger can never look like he's being choreographed. But he's on the stage for two hours, he can't just keep repeating the same moves over and over again. What I do is put together a blocking for each song—that means I create a pattern of where he should go and what he should do. Each song has its own theme, so to speak. Mick is an excellent actor, so I can provide him with imagery to act out. 'For this song, be a pimp like the Harvey Keitel character in the film *Taxi Driver*.' Or I might give him a step that he likes or would look good performing. Sometimes the approach would be in the staging itself. 'On this song, go out on the end of the ramp and stay there and sing beyond the ramp.' What I do is provide him with different textures to vary his performance.

"Bette is so eclectic and theatrical that I can pull from vaudeville or go-go or rock 'n' roll. For her stage show I have to come up with two sets of choreography, one for her and one for her backup dancers, the Harlettes—and they have to complement each other. Bette tells me what she has in mind and what the songs need in terms of movement. For example, her song "Miss Otis Regrets" is very fast-paced, so I have to give the Harlettes ass-kicking choreography. When they do the number with the wheelchairs, I have to create a variety of patterns for them to travel around on the stage. Do you know that Bette once made me put in on closing night a number she threw out at the beginning of the tour? We rehearsed it in the bathroom."

"You've been creating dance all your life. What continues to drive you?"

"You know, I had an incident that happened to me when I was very very young. I was walking with my mother toward the Chicago Theater, where my father was working. We turned a corner and entered an alley that led to the stage door. There, just outside the door, stood a mob of people waving autograph books and pencils. As we approached, the crowd grew quiet and parted like the Red Sea so we could pass. I thought to myself, 'If this is show business, then I want to be part of it.'"

Los Angeles, 1999

Risk Taker

david parsons

The ascent to David Parsons's third-floor walkup left me winded. Finally in front of his door,

I took a second to compose myself and then knocked. He appeared, holding a cell phone to his ear, and motioned me in.

"We can't possibly perform in two different Italian cities on the same day," he told the person on the other end.

I set my gear down on the floor of the tiny, sun-starved apartment and scanned it for clues to David Parsons' daily life. A couple of playbills, a recently used coffee mug, an assortment of papers surrounding an open Solzhenitsyn novel all occupied a small table. On his bookshelf I noticed a worn copy of *Curious George,* a children's book about a mischievous monkey, alongside a couple of books by photographer Lois Greenfield, whose images of Parsons, taken more than a decade ago, brought both dancer and photographer instant recognition.

"Hi," he said. "Sorry about that. Some mixup in Italy. Please have a seat."

I moved some newspapers from a chair and sat down. He sat on a bed that doubled as a sofa.

"How long have you lived here?" I asked.

"Since I moved from Kansas City, twenty-two years ago. I was a teenager when I rented this apartment. After high school I knew I wanted to be a dancer, so I hopped on the first train to New York City. I didn't even pick up my high school diploma. I got a job at the service station around the corner.

I pumped gas and washed windshields from eleven at night to seven in the morning so I could study dance during the day. I'd come back here, sleep two hours, and then go to class. I did that for eight months before I joined Paul Taylor's company."

"Why are you still living here? You have one of the most successful dance companies in the country."

"People can't believe I still live here," he said with a laugh. "In this apartment I find peace of mind. Rent control gives me freedom to work on my art and avoid monetary pressures. This apartment always reminds me of my beginnings. I never want to forget those early emotions, the drive and the dreams. You know, your environment says a lot about how you deal with your life. I suppose I'll move out of here one day when I feel financially secure."

"Does a successful dance career always come with personal sacrifice?"

"It does, but I'm not complaining. I began touring at the age of eighteen and haven't stopped since. My company has toured five continents and has given over 700 performances. I live a nomadic life. It's difficult to maintain long-term personal relationships when you're never in one place for very long. I've never had a pet, or even a houseplant. Dancing and the demands of running a company are all-consuming. I've been cultivating my artistic side so long I've forgotten to nurture my personal side. I realize it's not healthy."

"Do you have any regrets about the choices you've made?"

"My only regret is that I never went to college. Sometimes I feel inadequate when I'm with people who throw around major vocabulary, but I am beginning to realize that I have skills and experiences that most people do not have. My education took place on the road, on the stage, and in the studio. I speak Italian and Spanish, and can go anywhere on the planet comfortably with just a little suitcase. During the nine years I danced with Paul Taylor, I learned about music, history, and the knowledge of running a company."

"How did he affect you personally?"

"Paul Taylor taught me how to live and think as an artist. His unconventional approach to life, his ability to craft brilliant dances, and his love of nature greatly influenced my life. I learned that a simple existence can bring you great wealth intellectually and spiritually. One does not need monetary wealth. He showed me that you do not have to go the way society tells you. You can find your own truth. The real question is, Can you stay in dance long enough to really survive? Dance careers usually last seven or eight years. I have managed to stay on the scene while so many have come and gone. When I was twenty-two, Clive Barnes said in the *New York Post*, 'David Parsons is the problem with modern dance.' Recently he wrote, 'Very Important Parsons.' I think people are finally beginning to believe that I'm not just a flash in the pan."

"What must dancers possess in order to develop into artists?"

"Obviously they need a certain degree of competence, discipline, and drive, but quite honestly, they need the basic necessities of life. They need to earn money to live on, receive medical and dental insurance, and have a place to cultivate their craft. They need to feel emotionally and financially secure and have a sense of belonging. If you don't have to worry how you're going to eat and where you're going to sleep, you can feel more spiritual and improve technically. Your life is more conducive to creativity."

"What is the most difficult challenge for the dance artist?"

"Accepting certain realities about this particular art form. The dancer is unique among artists because, unlike the painter or musician, he always faces the eventual loss of his facility to perform his art. There comes a time when the body betrays you, and you must develop new ways to express yourself. I'm dancing less now and am faced with new challenges as a choreographer. I use other people's bodies to do what I used to do myself. Transmitting my vision to others can be tough without demonstrating all the movement for them. This is especially difficult for me because I'm finding my ideas become more conceptual and complex. Something else happens, too. When you stop dancing, you start picking yourself apart choreographically. You become more critical of your work and begin to focus on your weak areas. At the same time, I've had to assume a new identity as nurturer to those performing my choreography. I've had to cultivate a new kind of discipline to cope with all these changes."

"You're known as one who takes creative risks. Why not play it safe?"

"Experimentation and taking risks is the basis of contemporary dance. The need to push boundaries is built into the art form. I started my company as a platform to take creative risks, to play with lighting, music, and sound. You can't discover new things about your soul unless you take risks. The performing artist delicately goes out on a limb. The challenge to go out there becomes a challenge to the self. It's how you show your mettle as a person. When I'm too comfortable, I get nervous because I know I'm standing still as an artist."

"Where does the impulse to create dance come from?"

"The essence of dance is found in the body. When you rely solely on the physical body, you become aware of its restrictions. Through those restrictions and the use of dance vocabulary you discover its potential to convey ideas and emotions. I'm drawn to the human body and consciously resist the temptation to hide behind props, sets, and costumes. Onstage, the body is infinite in its beauty, emotion, and depth. It is this challenge that has kept me in dance all these years."

"How do you cope with choreographic failures?"

"Failure comes with the territory. You have to be able to handle the failures, even though they take the wind out of you. It can be unbearably painful when you fail. Afterward you just want to throw in the towel, give it all up, walk away."

"But you don't, do you?"

"No, I don't. I go back in and try not to repeat my mistakes."

"What sort of mistakes?"

"Well, for example, I've learned that one needs to understand the scope of a project and see that it is manageable. Does the vision you have in your head transfer realistically to the stage? Are the conditions and circumstances at your disposal realistic to the vision? Will you be able to maintain control over your choreographic ideas while collaborating with other artists? Will you be able to maintain your integrity and the integrity of the work? These are just some of the things I've become acutely aware of."

After about an hour of conversation I suggested we move outdoors for his portrait. We headed west toward Central Park, a few blocks from his apartment. En route he pointed out the gas station where he used to work.

We continued through the park until we came to a stand of tall, barren trees. Without warning, David slipped off his boots and scrambled up a tree, fifteen feet in the air.

"What are you doing?" I called up to him.

"Throw up my boots," he yelled.

"Are you sure about this? I don't want to be responsible for you breaking a leg or something."

"Oh, I'll be fine," he said. "Just throw me one boot at a time."

I heaved his boot up into the air, nowhere near his grasp.

"Closer, much closer," he called down to me.

After several tries, he caught the boots and put them on one at a time with the finesse of a tightrope walker.

"How does this look?" he asked, posing confidently.

"Just great!" I shouted back, shooting like mad. "By the way, is this what you mean when you talk about taking creative risks?"

New York City, 1999

55

Dance Organism

pilobolus

I caught up with the quartet that directs Pilobolus at the Joyce Studios in SoHo in the fall of 1999.

I had arrived early, only to find that the dance rooms were occupied and the interior of the building was too dark for taking photos. I quickly revised my visual concept and escorted the four outside to a random doorway in front of the studio. I then enlisted their aid in helping me come up with some interesting body sculpture—"like you do with your dancers." They looked at each other and then back at me, clueless.

"Why don't you give it some thought while I set up," I suggested. I metered the open shade, loaded my Hasselblad, and stepped backward into the street in order to get some focal length. Cars and taxis whizzed by.

"Okay, I'm willing to risk my life for this picture," I said. "Any thoughts?"

Jonathan Wolken experimented with an off-balance lean into the doorway but abruptly abandoned the pose in reaction to a sharp pain in his back. Robby Barnett, who had been resting against the building, lowered himself to a sitting position on the sidewalk and smiled playfully. Michael Tracy placed his hands on his hips and rested against the doorjamb, waiting patiently for my instructions. Alison Chase looked tired and said she was desperate for a cup of coffee. My half-hour window of opportunity was narrowing by the minute, and I knew that what I had before me did not reflect the uniqueness of this group.

"In the interest of time, I'll play choreographer," I announced. I started with Michael. "Look straight at me, as if you're trying to read my mind. Robby, why don't you look through this peephole in the door, your back to the camera. Jonathan, sit on the ground and look out into the distance as if you're day-dreaming, and Alison, why don't you face out as if you're waiting for someone to approach, like a guy delivering coffee." My concept was intended to show four distinct personalities who, in choreographic collaboration, form a well-balanced unity. I would not learn until two years later, in the course of my interview with them, that each of the directors is perpetually striving to infuse his or her individuality into the creative process and choreographed works.

In May 2001 I met with Michael and Robby in their Washington, Connecticut, office. They assured me that their voices echoed the views of the group.

"The idea for Pilobolus grew out of a dance class we took at Dartmouth College in the early seventies," said Michael. "Originally there were six of us, including Moses Pendleton and Martha Clarke. Alison taught the class and encouraged us to create and invent dances. Our early efforts explored movement with graphic and kinetic imagery that went beyond that of humans moving on a stage. We found ourselves referring to cellular life, insects, animals, and microbiological life-forms. The word 'pilobolus' refers to a phototropic zygomycete—a sun-loving fungus that grows in barnyards and pastures. We were interested in looking for references beyond ourselves, not only in the content of a dance but also in a physical vocabulary. We thought those kinds of investigations might be as interesting onstage as, let's say, the story of Giselle."

"Since you had little dance training, how were you able to physicalize your ideas?"

"Only Alison and Martha had studied dance," explained Michael. "The rest of us had no dance experience, had never seen a modern dance performance. Our initial understanding of what we were doing came from what we thought was dance, our sports training, and knowledge of other arts. We therefore responded freshly to movement without feeling the need to match a model of what dance was. We began as choreographers and had to become dancers in order to perform our choreography. The impulse was to create structures and forms that meant something to us. We didn't waste a lot of time trying to learn dance technique. Technique is learning well that which you already know how to do. We didn't think about technique in a formal sense until we stopped performing and had to teach our work to others. Suddenly we had to analyze the physics of doing multi-body structures. Dancers who wanted to do our work knew about standing on point and the alignment of their own body but had no understanding or training on how to do a three-person balance or move off the stage as a large object composed of three people."

"You had to go back and study your own technique in order to teach it to a next generation of dancers?"

"Yes, ten years after we started, we had to analyze every moment of choreography," Michael said. "While teaching it to new dancers, we discovered technical essentials we never realized. For example, I didn't realize I needed to do a subtle shift of weight in order to move the center of gravity back three inches. We had to understand these nuances before we could teach others so they could move onstage."

"Do you consider yourselves creative radicals?"

"Our focus is not to create dance within the context of what is done by others. What we do is a reaction to our own lives and our personal interaction," said Robby. "If anything, we are distinctly nonrebellious in that we are fairly self-involved. Ours is more an innocent approach to movement in that it allows us to respond freshly to things—or try to. One might call it cultivated ignorance or belief in naiveté."

"So the work is not intended to inform or influence others?"

"We try to put together something that is rich enough that there may be ambiguities about what it means, so that each person in the audience will be interested in it," said Robby. "We have very specific ideas about what we put into the choreography, but we don't have faith that these ideas will read to an audience. We are not inherently didactic. We very rarely develop a political stance and then create movement to elicit that. We don't know the answers to life's questions."

"How do you conceptualize work? Where do the ideas come from?"

"Everyone in the group has what I call restless intelligence," said Robby. "We are fairly discursive people with lots of interests. We read a great deal and listen to music diversely. All that stuff goes back into the pot, rattles around in there, and is available for us to draw upon. Art is created out of things you're reminded of. It's associative. Movement without reference has little interest to me. The more references you have, the more likely you are to experience an emotional response."

"Do you choreograph on a schedule? How does that work when there are four of you?"

"We create major company works two to three times a year, which can take many months," Michael said. "We take the blue-collar approach to cho-

"All our interpretations have equal validity."

reography. While inspiration is a wonderful thing, you can't really wait for it. We have a sense that if you put in your hours like a steelworker, and work long enough, work gets done. There may be some wasted time, but if you're in front of the typewriter or easel or behind a viewfinder long enough, a product will reveal itself."

"How do you start a piece?"

"We generally have thousands of ideas running through our heads that have accumulated throughout the year," said Michael. "Little by little, the ideas begin to structure themselves. Our interest lies in imagery. What are the rich associations or references that an image might spark in our minds, the dancers' minds, and consequently in the audience's minds? We begin collecting these references from each other and the dancers. In spite of the frustrations and inefficiencies of working in a group, when several minds are working rapidly at the same time, the speed of mutation is incredible. One person has a thread that will take you only so far, and then suddenly someone else will see this in a whole new way, and it will go shooting off. The quickness with which an idea can bud and flower and branch is really an amazing thing."

"What is the dynamic like for four people to choreograph? How do you come to an agreement?"

"Our work is interdependent and multifaceted over a long period of time. It has become increasingly an investigation of the individual within a group. I can't get involved in my own weird trip, because someone might say, 'Hey, that's lame.' We have to convince each other of each moment of choreography. It has to be approved before we can go on. There are lots of checks and balances. Our strength is that we can agree about a sequence of movement, but if you ask us what those movements mean, you'll get four different answers. All our interpretations have equal validity. This is the foundation of what we do."

"Robby, you can give me an example of what you go through as an individual inside the collaborative process?"

"We've worked together so long as collaborators that it's ingrained in my spirit to put out an idea, expect it to be second-guessed, moved off in another direction, added to, disagreed with. And all the while I'm trying to pull it back in the direction I want. Later, my general impression after looking at the finished work is relief that I'm surrounded by intelligent people contributing good ideas."

"Does it get combative at times?"

"Oh, it's not pretty," Michael said. "At times we really battle it out. Sometimes there are subtle machinations going on for political control or proprietary claims or various ideas. Fortunately, the dark competition behind the scenes does not get into the finished work. Maybe that's why we come back into the ring the next day and face off all over again. The essence of collaboration is that you feel your voice is heard and that the resulting work reflects one's own individual concerns. I think it's amazing to have four people look at the same work and say, 'That's mine.' We've managed to achieve this for the past thirty years."

"And after thirty years, how has the work grown and changed?"

"The first piece that we created was called *Pilobolus*, and a case can be made that it housed all the threads that continue to run through our company," Robby replied. "Within the work you find an interest in graphic design, eccentricity, a strong theatrical impulse, a sense of humor, a dramatic image sense, interest in visual impression, plus the kinetic versus psychological design. Even though as individuals our interests have vacillated, I haven't been able to identify at least in either Pilobolus's work or in my own approach to the work a singular line that's different now from the beginning. I'm struck more by how similar the work is after thirty years than by how different it is."

"And yet the work continues to evolve, does it not?"

"Yes, it does," said Michael. "Even though many of the same issues keep coming back to us, like community versus individual or theatrical versus kinetic, we've developed families and relationships, experienced psychological and emotional life changes, and discovered new interests. All of this informs the choreography. After thirty years, you'd think you've done it all. But we are always discovering new things. The exploration of life's mysteries is what keeps us interested, keeps us continuously going in."

New York, 1999, photo
Connecticut, 2001, interview

59

Rebellious One

anna sokolow

Anna Sokolow sat motionless on the sofa when I arrived at her Christopher Street apartment in New York.

She sensed my presence and turned her head slowly in my direction. She stared at me expressionlessly, silent. At the age of ninety, Anna was frail and in poor health. She required round-the-clock care.

"Hello, Anna," I said. "My name is Rose. I've come to talk to you about your life in dance and take your photograph."

"You'll really need to speak up," said Jason, her devoted caregiver.

"Anna," he yelled in a booming voice, "this is Rose. She's come to speak to you about your life in dance."

Anna nodded her head politely, her blue-gray eyes beginning to show some life. She looked pale, her skin almost translucent. I sat down next to her, pulled out my notes, and planted my tape recorder on the coffee table.

"What does it feel like to be among the pioneers of an art form?" I asked.

She looked puzzled by my question. Jason rephrased it and yelled it directly into Anna's right ear. With great effort she began to form words, but her speech was slurred, incomprehensible. I looked at Jason and whispered, "What is she saying?"

"Anna," Jason yelled, "you were one of the great pioneers of modern dance. How do you feel about that? Speak clearly so we can understand you."

"I never think about that," she said. "Dance was just something that I did."

"How did you discover dance?"

61

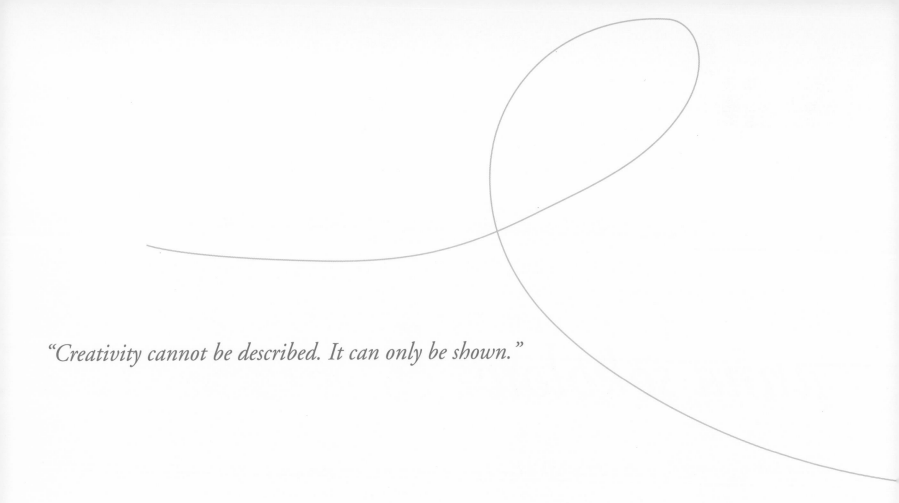

"Creativity cannot be described. It can only be shown."

"I just did it. I had it in me to move and to create."

"What were you trying to say in your dances?"

"Dance was always an expression of my feelings," she said. "I always spoke the truth in my movement. I knew when I saw a flower I could create movement to express how I felt about it. Music enhanced my ability to express myself, to bring up my emotions."

"What inspired you to choreograph such great works like *Rooms* and *Lyric Suite*?"

Once again Jason repeated my question loudly into Anna's ear.

"Choreography comes from ideas. All my dances were inspired by ideas, shapes, or visual images."

"How does one learn to create?"

"Learn, observe, communicate—express yourself," she said. "We learn through creativity, but creativity cannot be described. It can only be shown."

"Did dance technique ever get in the way of your expressing your deepest feelings? Did you ever get so caught up in executing a technical move that you forgot why you were doing it in the first place?"

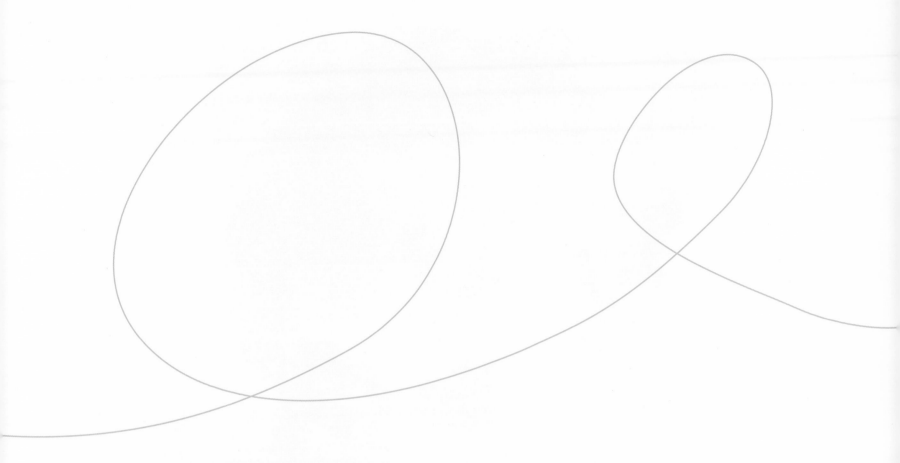

Anna began to giggle at the question, as if she understood it all too well.

"I'm sure that I did, I'm sure that I did," she replied.

When I asked if Martha Graham had affected her work, Anna burst into laughter.

"How shall I say it? Martha Graham didn't affect me. I affected her," she said. "The person whose work I respected most was Jerry Robbins. We were very, very close friends. I loved everything he did, and he loved everything I did."

"Is there something you still want to do as a choreographer that you haven't?"

"I have many ideas. There are always more ideas."

I could tell that the laborious interview process had tired Anna, so I suggested that we begin the photo shoot. Jason and I helped Anna stand and guided her toward the sunny window.

Suddenly, without warning, she raised her arms, forming an elegant pose, one hand folded over the other at the wrist. Praying that she would hold it long enough, I grabbed a camera from my bag, focused, and quickly pressed the shutter release. She lowered her arms, and the moment was gone.

I did not realize until later that she had positioned herself in front of a framed photograph on the wall, a photo that had been taken some seventy years earlier, in the same pose.

As I was leaving, she asked to see my photographs of dancers. I kissed her on the cheek and promised to come back the next day with my portfolio. Jason walked me to the door and said, "Anna still choreographs, you know. She choreographs in her mind. At night I watch her eyes moving behind her lids. She sees movement. She hears music. Dance is her life."

The following morning, Jason phoned to tell me that Anna had injured herself in a fall. She was not well enough to see me. I promised to visit her on my next New York trip, but I never saw her again. She died six months later.

New York City, 1999

63

Bad Boy of Dance

mark morris

Morris has cultivated the image of a dance diva with the manners of a truck driver.

When I arrived at his hotel room in West Los Angeles, he looked like he had just rolled out of bed. He was still in his nightclothes, unshaven, hair disheveled. My arrival apparently coincided with a temper tantrum caused by his inability to find an ashtray. I said a quick hello and tried to be as unobtrusive as possible, quietly setting up my lighting equipment.

Morris calmed down once he'd had a smoke. When the lights were in place, I asked if he wanted to change his clothes or comb his hair for the portrait.

"No, I'm fine like this," he said.

"This is how you'd like to be photographed? Don't you want to shave or anything?" I asked.

"No, I don't," he replied, annoyed.

"Well, first I'd like to ask you some questions if that's okay."

I walked toward the small table where I had placed my tape recorder. He followed me and took a seat.

"Audiences and critics appear to love you. What are you doing right?"

"People want to see my work because it's good."

"And that's it?"

"Yes."

"Do you have a central theme running through your work?"

"I choreograph because of music, and there is no other reason for it to exist."

"Well, how does a dance emerge?"

"I decide something will be a dance, and then I make it up."

"So it's really not all that complicated?"

"I work very hard to make things simple."

"Do you collaborate with your dancers?"

"Only in that they perform my work."

"What are your goals, aspirations?"

"I do exactly what I want and try not to lie too much."

Frustrated by his minimalist answers and indifference bordering on rudeness, I looked pleadingly at his manager, but she refused to get involved.

"Why don't I take some photographs now?" I said, returning to where I had left my camera and lights. Morris got up and plopped himself onto the sofa.

"How about over here by the window?" I suggested.

"No, we'll do it here."

He refused to get off the sofa or alter his position in any way. If I wanted to take his picture, it would have to be as it was or not at all. 'Two can play this game,' I thought. My Hasselblad would become an instrument of revenge. I double-exposed him, giving him four eyes, an ear protruding out of his fore-head, his nose extending out of an eye. In one exposure I filled the frame with his head and in the second showed him sitting on the sofa inside himself—a sort of illustrated inflated ego. I loaded some color film with the intention of

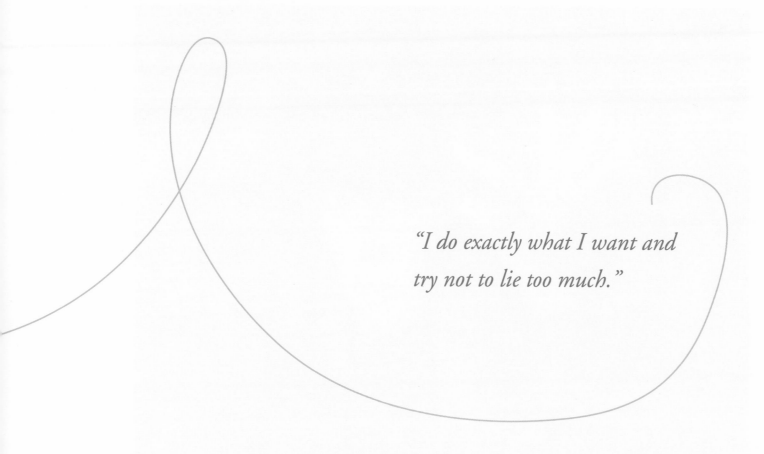

"I do exactly what I want and try not to lie too much."

altering it in the processing so that his coloring would look bizarre and surreal. All the while he ignored me, chatting with his manager and only occasionally looking in my direction. I was simply doing exactly what I wanted and trying not to lie too much.

That evening I attended his concert at Royce Hall at the University of California at Los Angeles. During the Q and A period, he was charming, funny, and personable. When asked how he creates dances, he gave the questioner a ten-minute response full of colorful examples of his process and specifics about how he chooses music. I wondered if Mark Morris was Dr. Jekyll in the morning and Mr. Hyde at night.

Los Angeles, 1998

Jazz Dancer

ann reinking

It was a busy time for Ann Reinking. Her show Fosse *had just opened on Broadway to rave reviews.*

It would later win a Tony for Best Musical. With only half an hour to spare, Ann arrived at my uptown sublet accompanied by her agent and a makeup artist, who marched into my bathroom and in minutes transformed it into what looked like the cosmetics counter at Macy's. While Ann was getting ready I was pacing, counting down the remaining minutes.

When she emerged, ten minutes remained. She looked beautiful in her black turtleneck, slacks, and a *Fosse*-style derby. I invited her to step out in front of the black backdrop that I'd set up in the living room. I picked up my camera, looked through the viewfinder, and focused on her enormous blue eyes.

"Wait!" called the makeup artist. "I missed a spot." In an instant she was back, buzzing around Ann's cheek. Eight minutes remained.

"Is there anything special you want me to do, Rose?" Ann asked in her famous raspy voice.

"I'd like you to just be yourself, show me who you really are."

A pro before the camera, Ann took a deep breath and opened her eyes wide, as if to say, "Go ahead, Rose, take a good look." Her gaze was as captivating as a Fifth Avenue department store window at Christmas. I continued shooting until Ann's agent tapped her wristwatch, signaling that time had run out.

Our phone interview took place nine months later.

"It doesn't matter how many pirouettes you own and how pretty you are. Usually the ones who get the role are the ones who do their homework, put their heart and soul into it, and want to serve."

"Ann, you've been closely associated with Bob Fosse's work. Have you ever felt the need to create in your own choreographic style?"

"Somewhere along the way, I have learned a craft and a certain degree of skill. I am expressive and pretty good at creating dance numbers, but whether I have my own style, I can't say. I feel that Bob Fosse was one of the greatest choreographers of the musical theater. He pushed theater forward to its present-day genre. Fosse's shows were innovative because they were character-driven. His cast members were required to act, sing, and dance. He had a great way of looking at things with sensuality, wit, and realism. His dance style reflected his point of view and manifested itself in shoulder shrugs, pelvic thrusts, and quirkiness. His talent is one of the greatest gifts ever given to me. I'm proud to present the style of Bob Fosse and privileged to be able to do it. I'm also enormously grateful for my association with Gwen Verdon, Michael Bennett, Michael Kidd, and Agnes de Mille. They all sank their own individual styles into me. That is perhaps why I don't have a style of my own."

"What do you think you bring to the Fosse style as a woman?"

"I've been told by others that my approach is softer, less cynical, less angry."

"Was some of his choreography cynical and angry?"

"Some of it was. At thirteen he was tap-dancing in sleazy striptease clubs just to survive. He developed an affinity for the dark side, the underbelly of society, and he could be self-destructive. When he was revealing the darker side of himself or society, one could feel a tremendous moral component. Even the stuff that was hard-edged had life-affirming qualities. *Chicago*, for example, deals with betrayal and corruption and vulnerability. I always found his work a little tender and brokenhearted."

"Do you think the choreographer's work is always a reflection of his or her own life?"

"I think everyone's work reflects their character. As a dancer I was privileged to interpret someone else's expression, but it was also mixed with my own feelings. Art is not science. There are no laws, no absolute patterns, and no formulas. The only sure things about creativity and individual expression are that they are purely human."

"Why do you think jazz dancing is so compelling to watch?"

"Because it is sensual, provocative, and a little dangerous. It is rooted in the twentieth century and tells stories in a twentieth-century way. Ballet, for example, comes to us from the eighteenth century, with its emphasis on the celestial, the otherworldly. Jazz is of the earth, of the streets, of this world. It is an

American art form, with its own syllabus and stylistic approach. When a jazz choreographer asks you to perform his steps, he's really asking you to express his point of view, his history, and his mood. Jazz employs an element of risk. There's a huge physical risk in ballet, too, but in ballet you hide the risk through its formal approach and refined nature. Jazz dancers are asked to fully reveal themselves and show their emotions and vulnerability. They are expected to show the risk taking and divulge the danger. That's what makes it so hypnotic and compelling to watch."

"Is the jazz choreographer bound by a specific dance vocabulary and stylistic formula?"

"Jazz is a very eclectic art form. It is a spontaneous mutation that employs information from many dance styles and schools of thought. It is therefore a very original, almost skittish art form. There are no rules with jazz. There are no rules in musical theater, for that matter. What matters is what you're trying to say and that you represent the time period accurately."

"What makes a good jazz dancer?"

"I always beg my students to take ballet, because if you can master ballet you can master anything. Ballet inherently gives you elegance, strength, and coordination. It gives you a beautiful carriage. You need that in abundance to perform jazz because it requires all of you."

"What advice do you give aspiring dancers?"

"I give my students practical information based on my own experiences. I try to prepare them for the tough times. I explain to them that careers go up and down and that they have to learn how to navigate the ups and the downs. But there is no guarantee that young dancers won't go out there and learn the hard way. It's tough when you have to waste a lot of time digging yourself out of mistakes. We all make them. I tell students, 'The minute you recognize you've made a mistake, fix it.'"

"What are some of the mistakes professional dancers tend to make?"

"The most common mistakes include acting like a prima donna (whether you have a right to or not), being disrespectful, showing up late, having bad working habits, and being really nice to people who you think will promote your career and rude to those who you think won't. People can tell when you're trying to deceive them with your tricks. They know where you're coming from. There are a lot of talented people out there, and if it comes down to getting the role, it doesn't matter how many pirouettes you own and how pretty you are; if you're difficult, the other person is going to get the job.

They'll go with the dancers who may not be as technically superior but whose hearts are in it, who do their homework and want to serve. I tell my students, 'If you take the money, you have a responsibility to be as good as you can be. It's not your right to criticize, pass judgment, or diminish the importance of a role or a particular choreography.' If I let a number die because I was tired or I didn't like it, that's as bad as a doctor saying, 'I think I'll let this patient go because she's not that pretty or I didn't get a good night's sleep.' You can't let a number die. It's that important! People who are writing, composing, and choreographing are putting their lives on the line so that their work might have a life. That needs to be respected."

"You've been enormously successful as a dancer, choreographer, and director. What continues to drive and challenge you?"

"I take very seriously my responsibility to educate young dancers. In my Broadway Theater Project in Tampa, Florida, I try to nurture and support aspiring artists because they guarantee the continuation of musical theater, a truly indigenous American art form. With the help of great entertainers like Julie Andrews, Stanley Donen, Savion Glover, Tommy Tune, Gregory Hines, Ben Vereen, and others, I teach students what's expected of them and how they should handle themselves—things rarely taught in technique class."

"You seem to fully understand the uphill climb of the aspiring dancer, but what is it like for dancers forced to take their last curtain call because of age or injury?"

"It's horrible. The feeling of loss and desperation is unbearable. You wouldn't dance unless you were absolutely and completely in love with it. It requires immense sacrifice, and it can be a hard life. So when you are forced to stop, you are losing something that gives you great joy and love and spirit. Fortunately, dancers today are becoming more educated. They know it's going to happen, and they start to prepare for it in advance. The upside is that most of them are still young and capable of having another life after they stop dancing."

"What's next for you?"

"I'm not sure. I've never been someone to design my future. I just wait for it to happen."

"Isn't that a little risky?"

"Well, yes, but I'm a jazz dancer!"

New York City, 1999

Director

vincent paterson

I was to meet him in the back studio of the Alley Cat Dance Studio on the Sunset Strip.

Vince told me he had a wonderful idea for a portrait and would supply all the necessary props. He showed up wearing a black suit. A pretty woman in a short skirt accompanied him.

"Here's what I had in mind," he said, pushing the baby grand against the back wall. He then pulled over a chair and instructed the woman to climb up and sit on the piano with her legs crossed. He leaned up against the keyboard and smiled.

"What do you think, Rose?"

"I think it's fantastic. Don't move!"

After our photo session Vince and I drove to a local diner for a sandwich and a long talk.

"What brought you to LA and how did you get started?"

"This is the movie capital of the world. In college I majored in directing and dramatic literature. I knew I wanted to become a director and thought I could break into the business by becoming a professional dancer. I arrived in Hollywood with $2,000 in my pocket and the name of a guy who I was told could put me up. Turned out he was this gay guy living with a manicurist/hooker. They let me sleep on their floor in a sleeping bag. I did that for nine months. When I was down to $35, I landed my first professional dancing job, on the *Dick Van Dyke Show*."

"Was that your big break?"

"No. Things really turned around for me when I got picked by Michael Peters to dance in Michael Jackson's music video *Beat It*. Having been an actor, I thought I'd have a better shot at getting picked if I came in character. So I dressed like a gang member with a toothpick in my mouth. Everyone else wore dance clothes. During the audition I was one of the few who could stay within a millisecond behind Peters as he spit out his fast-paced choreography with its intricate rhythms. My body just went there. I would eventually become Peters's assistant and also dance in Jackson's next big video—*Thriller*.

"Did assisting him inspire you to become a choreographer?"

"Michael was a brilliant choreographer but not a very nurturing artist. It was always his way or the highway. I loved the collaboration with him, but he never encouraged me to move on without him. Actually, he resented my finding my own choreographic voice. This eventually caused a huge rift between us. But I loved him as a mentor and a friend and learned an important lesson from him that I use to this day, and that is to trust your instincts."

"What happened next?"

"Michael Jackson phoned me and asked me to conceptualize, direct, and choreograph his next video—*Smooth Criminal*. I saw this as an opportunity to begin working behind the camera. I approached the project as a director might and dealt with the dancers as though they were actors. I asked each one of them to name their characters, come in with a one-page history of who they were and where they were from. I told them to remain in character whenever they were on the set."

"Did they look at you as if you were a little nuts?"

"Yes, they were shocked. I had never worked with a choreographer who had made such a request. But I felt that it was important for the dancers to understand the subtext of the movement, the reason it existed and what it meant. I thought it would make them better dancers."

"Then came your association with Madonna."

"Yes. I met Madonna while working on a Pepsi commercial and would eventually choreograph her video *Express Yourself* and her Blond Ambition Tour. That was a very challenging job because I had to come up with a dance for each of her twenty-two songs and put them together very quickly. I found myself using something that I learned from working with Michael Jackson. He once told me, 'Don't try to impose your ideas on the music. Let the music talk to you and tell you what it wants to be.' Once I allowed the music to guide me, the dances just poured out of me. In time I developed a process of visualizing movement that I still use today."

"What is that process?"

"I wear headphones to bed and listen to the music as I'm falling asleep. It's like I'm choreographing in my subconscious mind. In the morning the idea for the dance appears before my eyes. When I first started choreographing, I didn't trust those initial visualizations. I'd come into the studio with that vision and then start layering movement on the dancers the way a painter applies paint to a canvas. I'd keep adding more and more and more, as if I were desperate to have something to show at the end of the day. Eventually I'd end up stripping off those movement layers and come back to my original idea. I spent many years wasting time until I learned to trust myself and my first impulse. Too many artists fall into this pattern because they think they're not good enough."

"Next, you had another big break—feature films!"

"Yes, I got a call from director Mike Nichols, inviting me to choreograph the dance segments for *The Birdcage*. I cast the dancers, hired the musical director, and chose the music. With Nichols's vision in mind, I created the nightclub scenes, as well as the history-of-dance demonstration by Robin Williams. Watching Mike Nichols work made me realize how wonderful it could be to direct feature films, so I decided not to choreograph any longer unless I could also direct."

"Didn't you choreograph *Evita*?"

"Yes, but I agonized over whether or not to take the job. Every time I make a decision fate challenges me."

"Really? Why does it have to be all or nothing?"

"Well, let me tell you about Hollywood. Most producers see the job of the choreographer as very mysterious. They don't really understand what he does. I think they're a little baffled by it. If it says in the script, 'and they danced,' then the choreographer becomes the writer of those scenes. He interprets what that sentence means and creates it visually for the screen."

"So what's the problem?"

"The problem is that producers think that a choreographer is someone who *only* knows how to put dance steps together. Because they are not in the room when the choreographer is working, they don't see that he understands character development, progression of story line, et cetera. Michael Kidd, Gene Kelly, and Herbert Ross started out as dancers/choreographers. The problem is that once you've been labeled a choreographer, it's very hard for others to see you in any other way. The writer or the cameraman has a better shot at being asked to direct than does a choreographer."

"So you choreographed *Evita*, despite your vow not to choreograph unless you also direct."

"Yes."

"How was the experience?"

"Challenging but wonderful. I had studied acting, so I could speak the language of the actor. I had studied dance, so I could speak the language of the dancer. Working on *Evita* enabled me to utilize both, my knowledge of acting and of dancing. I auditioned five to six hundred Argentine tango dancers and chose one hundred to dance in the film. I had to convey to them in dance language that their performance for the film required a contemporary look with universal appeal. This was tough to communicate, because the dancers wanted to present a more traditional view of tango. I also met with great resistance when I asked them to dance to the music of Andrew Lloyd Webber instead of traditional tango music. Because I knew how to relate to them as dancers, I was successful.

"Antonio Banderas is not a dancer, but his character dances in the film. My job was to help him deal with the dance sequences. He would ask the type of questions an actor would ask. 'Why would I do this move? Why would I do this now? Why would I be here?' I'd answer him, 'You would do that because this is what she is thinking,' or 'You're part of this fantasy.' That's all he needed. He wanted the subtext for the movement, and because I understood this, I could give it to him."

"Did working on *Evita* reinforce the feeling that you had the necessary skills and the knowledge to direct films?"

"Yes, absolutely. After *Evita* I reaffirmed my decision not to accept a choreography job unless I was also directing the project."

"Vince, are you going to keep making that threat your entire career?"

"Yes, I'm going to insist until it happens," he said, laughing. "It's funny—in my life I have to give myself these ultimatums. I find myself every couple of years at a very low point. I get terribly suicidal until life admits me through the next door."

"Was *Dancer in the Dark* that next door?"

"Yes, it was. Working on the film with the great Danish director Lars von Trier was a life-altering experience. At the beginning of production I fantasized creating huge musical Broadway-style numbers. I soon realized rather dramatically after an intense meeting with the director that my approach was wrong. The dances had to look as if they were coming out of the mind of the main character, a woman enamored with the old Hollywood musicals but who had no dance training. The choreography would need to look pedestrian—organic and natural, not polished and exact, which is more my style. My ego took a beating when I decided to let the artist within me create for character and do what was best for the film."

"Isn't this how you should have been working all along?"

"Yes, I should have, but I've come out of Hollywood, which is all about ego. Suddenly I was working in a foreign country with people who didn't think that way. We became a big creative family inside one of the most creative environments I've ever encountered. I think this allowed me to trust my instincts and leave my ego behind. Ultimately, I directed the dance sequences in the film with my own crew and framed all the dance scenes. I also acted and danced in the movie, which I hadn't done in years. It became a total and complete experience for me. I saw that what I had been saying I could do, I could do. I stopped struggling with the ego and started to think and work as an artist."

Hollywood, photo 1998, interviews 1998, 2003

Bold and Brave

debbie allen

I arrived at Debbie Allen's Santa Monica home on schedule.

Her housekeeper let me in and told me to make myself comfortable. I set up my lights in the living room and wandered around the house, hoping to find Debbie. Next to the sofa stood a table displaying several of her Emmys and other awards. *Sweet Charity* and *West Side Story* posters dating back to Debbie's Broadway career decorated the kitchen. Stepping out into the backyard, I noticed a small structure that looked like it had been added on to the house. Upon closer examination I saw that it was a dance studio. I removed my shoes, stepped onto the hardwood floor, and took a few minutes to stretch and do a few pliés and *relevés* in front of the mirror. Still no sign of Debbie. Walking back into the house, I was confronted by Debbie's husband, Norm Nixon, former Laker basketball star.

"Who are you?" he demanded.

"Ahh, I'm here for Debbie. We have an appointment. Do you expect her anytime soon?"

"What's your name? How did you get in here?"

"Oh, your housekeeper let me in. I was expected. My name is Rose. I'm working on a ..."

Before I could finish, he said, "Fine" and walked away.

Half an hour later Debbie walked in, weighed down with shopping bags. She apologized for keeping me waiting and offered me a cold drink. Then we sat down in the living room.

"Debbie, you've been a successful dancer, actor, and choreographer. Now you're moving into directing and producing. How does the dancer inside of you maintain itself?"

Debbie turned serious. "That's my original self. Every artist goes back and forth and does a lot of different things, but they always come back to their original self. The dancer inside of me is still very much alive. I dance almost every day and look for projects that include dance in some way. I have a studio out in back."

"I would imagine that your private studio is a sanctuary of sorts."

"I go in there just to make sure that I fit in my own skin. For me it's more than therapy, it's how I live. There is nothing like going in there, putting on a song that I've just fallen in love with, and moving to it. I am happiest when I'm dancing. I just go and do it. I don't need permission from anyone. It's when I feel most myself. I get really annoyed with people who think that just because you're over thirty or fifty or eighty, you can't dance. Katherine Dunham danced very late in her career, as did Margot Fonteyn, who took class seven days a week religiously, almost every day of her life. And let's not forget Martha Graham, who as she aged became even more powerful in her expression."

"I understand you had to fight very hard for your dance career."

"Yes, as an African American I was faced with many obstacles. I grew up in Texas in the 1950s, where segregation was a big problem, especially if you wanted to dance. I wasn't allowed to take dance class or even attend dance performances. Everyone kept telling me, 'No, you can't dance here,' but they were really saying, 'We don't take black people.' When I auditioned for the North Carolina School of the Arts, I was rejected and told that I should try modern dance because my body was not suited to ballet—that, of course, was pure racism. But my passion for dance was very strong, and I was encouraged by my parents to follow my dream. I learned that persistence pays off."

"You eventually learned many different dance styles."

"Yes. I studied ballet and experienced the techniques of Katherine Dunham and Alvin Ailey. I performed the works of many great choreographers, including Jerome Robbins, Bob Fosse, and Donald McKayle. I lived in Mexico for a year and worked with the Ballet Nacionale. All of those experiences broadened my dance knowledge and enlarged my vocabulary."

"I've always recognized a sort of tenacity in your work, a kind of gutsiness in your physical attack. Are you conscious of that tendency?"

"Well, I think that's built in when you train as a dancer. Dance can make you very bold. The dancer always says 'yes,' thinking, 'Oh my God, how do I do this?' Then she goes out and figures out how to do it. When I did my first Broadway show, they asked me if I could sing. I said yes, but, honey, what could I sing? Not a note. I immediately signed up for opera lessons. I studied hard, and before long I found those chest tones. By the time I played Anita in West Side Story, I was belting out those tones and holding the notes forever. The cast was arguing about where I was holding the breath. 'She doesn't need a beat, let her hold that note,' they would say.

"Even now I'm not afraid to try new things. Last year I did a one-woman show in which I played Harriet Tubman. Child, I was scared to death! I spoke every word and played every character in the two-hour production. My mind was on such overload I didn't think I'd survive. But it was a very powerful experience that proved to me that I'm capable of many new challenges."

"Why do you think some people knowingly put themselves on the edge like that?"

"They're crazy, really crazy," she said, laughing. "No, I think it's really human nature to be at risk. Not too long ago, when we were hunters and gatherers, we were on the edge every day. We were either going to eat or get eaten, so we made spears and bows and arrows. The feeling of danger forced us to be inventive and creative. Being on the edge also makes you hypersensitive. It's like men in battle who become so primed and alert they can hear things like insects in the grass—sounds they would normally not be able to hear. If we don't continue to push those envelopes intellectually and artistically, I don't know how we will develop as a people."

"Have you been able to chart your career?"

"Honey, please. If I've been charting the course, I've been in the eye of the storm the entire time. I've been tossed this way and that. You never know what's coming. That's just how it is. I've started to create my own projects, and, even then, the outcome is unpredictable. But if you don't take on challenges, you'll never know what you're capable of. Do you think it was easy to get the film Amistad produced? Everyone said no, and the door kept slamming in my face. But I persisted and, with the help of Steven Spielberg, brought it to the screen."

"So dance has taught you never to give up."

"Yes, it has, and it gives you confidence to achieve what you need for yourself. I've always tried to teach my children and my students that the dedication, discipline, and, let's not forget, the physical pain get you ready for the challenges of life."

"How do you step out of the chorus?

Knock somebody down, honey, and take their part."

"You sound a little like Lydia Grant, the dance teacher character you played in the original *Fame.*"

"Well, I do love to work with young people, especially when you can push them and mold them. And there is another thing—we need to keep passing on those batons or our dance heritage will be lost. I try to pass on dance knowledge through my choreography. When I work with dancers, I treat them as if I'm giving class. This summer I was doing a musical ballet at Kennedy Center, and before every rehearsal I'd focus on another dance technique just so the dancers would have a richer experience. One day I'd do a Graham class, the next day I'd do Dunham, another day I'd do swing. I even invited Norma Miller, God bless her heart, to come work with the dancers. Norma was the star of the Savoy Ballroom when she was fifteen. She was eighty years old when I tracked her down living in Las Vegas. I wanted her to help me with authentic swing moves when I was choreographing the film *Stompin' at the Savoy.* She came in with those little tennis shoes and taught us all how to swing. That's what I mean about passing the baton."

"How would you advise a young dancer to break into the business?"

"First of all, it's about getting the training and having the talent and the inclination to do it. It takes years to master techniques. I say 'techniques' because you have to learn many different ways of moving. Your dance vocabulary has to be very broad in today's world. You can't succeed if you only know one way of moving. Study with great teachers in a great school. And then, after all that, it's just whether or not you have the spirit. That's not something you can buy or borrow. It's magic. It's fire. It has to come from you."

"Let's say you have the training, the passion, and the spirit. How do you step out of the chorus?"

"Knock somebody down, honey, and take their part. Tie up your competition and lock them in the dressing room, or steal their shoes if you have to," she said, bursting into laughter. "Seriously, that's a tough question. There are so many reasons why talented dancers never make it out of the chorus. In the dance world you are dealing with highly motivated but temperamental people. If the choreographer doesn't like the color of your shoes or thinks you're too short, you won't get picked. It's that subjective. There are many things beyond one's control, and they can hold you back. Keep a positive spirit about yourself. Faith can be a big comfort in those situations. Some people can get positive energy from religion. Use whatever is at your disposal to stay focused and positive."

"When you were working on the original television series *Fame,* about a high school for the performing arts, how did you go about creating a new set of choreographed dances every week?"

"My Lord . . . I think the reason that I was able to do that volume was because I had such a wide dance vocabulary. I could bring all that knowledge to the show and adapt the choreography to fit the show's premise and weekly episodes."

"What do you know about choreography that the rest of us don't know?"

"I'll never tell," she said, leaning back in the chair and laughing. "I'm taking that with me to the grave! Hey, I have no idea. It just comes to me. All I need is a big empty space and it's like this light shines in on me. All I know is that to create is to do something that is original to your perspective—your feelings. I'm drawn to certain things, and they can be radically different from each other. Like most people, I have different sides to my personality."

I thanked Debbie for her insights and suggested we move on to the portrait.

"You look pretty comfortable in that chair, with the Emmy perched behind you on the mantel. I think I'll just shoot you here."

"Go ahead, honey, make me look gorgeous."

Santa Monica, California, 1999

Dynamic Duo

dee dee wood and marc breaux

Dee Dee and Marc were still flying high from the previous evening, when they had been honored with the American Choreography Awards Career Achievement Award in Los Angeles. I was covering the event and invited them to visit my studio before leaving town.

"Looking at the montage of your films last night made me realize what an incredible body of work the two of you created. How did you both get started?"

Dee Dee began. "I started studying dance in high school. When I was seventeen I landed a scholarship to Jacob's Pillow Dance Festival. There I was exposed to many different styles of dance, including Haitian dance, which completely captivated me. After that I made up my mind that I wanted to become a professional dancer. I moved to New York City to study Afro-Cuban dance at the Katherine Dunham School and also took classes at the School of American Ballet. My big break came in 1951 when I got a part in Michael Kidd's Broadway show *Guys and Dolls*. But I didn't get the part right away. I wasn't picked at the audition, so I waited outside the stage door for two hours until Michael Kidd came out. I ran over to him and asked why I didn't make the cut. He told me that I needed to be able to dance in high heels. He said, 'Listen, we are having another audition in three weeks. Go home and practice dancing in high heels and try it again.' I didn't even own a pair of high heels. So I borrowed a pair and practiced and practiced till I could do just about anything in heels. This time I was picked and would go on to dance in several Broadway shows. I eventually became one of Michael Kidd's assistants."

"How about you, Marc?"

"I started dancing in 1948. I was twenty-three. I happened to accompany a girlfriend of mine to the Humphrey-Weidman Studio in New York City. I watched Charles Weidman teach class, and then Doris Humphrey approached me and asked if I liked what I saw. I said yes, so she invited me to take class. It felt wonderful to me, like water off a duck's back. They offered me a scholarship on the spot. Charles allowed me to live in the basement of their school, and I washed windows and floors to earn my keep. I enrolled in singing and acting classes, and within a couple of months I was performing in concerts and was made a member of the Humphrey-Weidman Dance Company."

"How did the two of you meet? And when did you first start choreographing as a team?"

"We met in 1955 while dancing on Stan Kenton's TV show," Dee Dee replied. "We married six weeks later. We've been separated for over twenty years but remain best friends. Marc joined me to assist Michael Kidd on an industrial show for General Motors and then on the Broadway show *Li'l Abner*. When a job came up on a TV show for *The Bell Telephone Hour*, Michael suggested we take it. Word got out that we were talented, and before we knew it we were regarded as choreographers."

"Michael Kidd really helped you get started, then. In what way did he influence your choreography?"

"We learned a tremendous amount from Michael," said Marc. "When you have a teacher like that, you learn to work with everything you see. He liked to experiment with props and sets. He could look at someone screwing in a light-bulb and transform it into an innovative ballet. His influence is present in much of our work. For example, in *Mary Poppins* we used the broom as an important dance prop in the chimney sweep dance. We researched what a chimney sweep does and what equipment he uses and then incorporated that into the dance. When we did *Chitty Chitty Bang Bang*, we used bamboo sticks for the 'Me Old Bamboo' number. In *The Sound of Music*, the set designer and I chose locations that would enhance the choreography. For the 'Doe a Deer' number, we constructed the dance so that the actors could jump down steps as if they were piano notes."

"Michael's work always had a lot of vitality and humor to it also," said Dee Dee. "He believed in having fun, and so did we. In *The Sound of Music* we did all sorts of funny things with the actors, like having them get into a pillow fight or exit a scene by kicking each other in the behind in assembly-line fashion. That was not in the script. We put that in."

"Marc, I imagine that Charles Weidman must have also had a tremendous impact on you as a choreographer."

"Oh, yes. Charles Weidman taught me to understand that the human body is capable of moving in many different ways. He believed in creating real movement. He inspired me to choreograph work that people could easily relate to. He was also very theatrical and comical and was a wonderful mime. I'm sure I inherited some of that from him. I also learned a very important lesson from another great choreographer named Glen Tetley. Glen eventually went on to direct the Stuttgart Ballet. I had the opportunity of dancing with him in a show. He had just broken his ankle, so he moved in slow motion while I tumbled and did all these quick, acrobatic moves. His minimalist dance was extraordinary. It dawned on me that you don't have to knock people out to get attention. If you want to see a beautiful sky, you can see higher if you lower your arm as you're pointing up."

"What's it like to choreograph as a team? Do you delegate sections of a dance? How does that work?"

"Well," said Dee Dee, "with something like *The Sound of Music* we would take on the roles of the characters. I would be Julie Andrews, and Marc would be Christopher Plummer. Then we would bring in some stand-ins to perform what we had worked out so we could see what it looked like. Typically we worked on a big sound stage with a mirror."

"So you'd work it out on your own bodies and then teach it to the actors?"

"That's exactly how we did it," Marc said. "But once I was unable to execute the moves, I stopped choreographing. I will not instruct someone to do what I can't myself execute. I have to feel the movement in order to produce work. Once I even put on toe shoes to create a ballet sequence just so I would know what it's supposed to feel like. Choreography was never second nature to me like it was for Doris Humphrey, who I remember could choreograph sitting in a chair."

"Marc, there is a vocabulary of movement that you can use to describe what you want the dancers to do!" Dee Dee insisted. "Dancers understand the dance vocabulary. Plus, you can always use an assistant as long as they understand your style. A good assistant is like an extension of yourself."

"Nevertheless, that's not the way I want to work," he said adamantly.

"The two of you created some of the most memorable dance sequences ever recorded on film. How much of your choreography was done with the camera in mind?"

"We created the work as if it were a stage show, but we had every shot visualized," explained Marc. "We knew there would be close-ups, shots from the waist and feet. We had it pre-planned by using a storyboard. The studio artist would come down to rehearsal, and he or she would draw the scene, the placement of the dancers and the actual camera shots. For example, that very famous scene in *The Sound of Music* when Julie Andrews is on the hill was completely staged. We had to match a long shot to a close-up. I told the cameraman, who was in a helicopter, to cut to the close-up as soon as Julie turns toward the camera."

"Yes, Marc was in the bushes with a bullhorn and had to cue Julie when to turn. He had to scream, 'TURN, TURN, TURN' at the top of his lungs for Julie to hear him over the noise of the helicopter."

"Did you ever have problems with directors who wanted to edit your choreography? I've learned that it is not uncommon for editors or directors to cut some great scenes out of a movie."

"Tell her the *Mary Poppins* story, Dee Dee," said Marc.

"I think the most important work we ever created was the chimney sweep dance in *Mary Poppins*," said Dee Dee. "It was a very complex dance, with action going on inside the house, on the roof, and in the street. We had at one time as many as thirty dancers on set. The dance was approximately twelve minutes long. Robert Louis Stevenson, the director, wanted us to cut it down to two minutes. When I heard this, my mouth dropped open. Fortunately Walt Disney loved our work and used to come to our rehearsals every day after lunch. So Marc went to him and told him what the director wanted to do. Walt Disney said, 'If you think it should stay in, then it should stay in.' Disney instructed the director to 'keep it exactly as it is.' We were pretty tenacious about it, but we felt it was worth fighting for."

"When you're choreographing for a film, is it difficult to find your true artistic voice?"

"Regardless of the limitations of story line or lyrics," said Dee Dee, "you are still creating work that is uniquely your own. No one else in the world is going to do it exactly like you. You are creating original work every time. For example, when we are working with the pianist, we might decide after a certain lyric to add three or four sets of eight. That lyric might kick us into adding a musical moment that wasn't originally intended. We do it because it feels right and it comes from a very deep, creative place."

"Exactly," agreed Marc. "We find we have to extend that section because it's too beautiful, too wonderful. It's a moment you can't miss."

"And because it feels so damn good," interjected Dee Dee. "I can hardly wait to get with the pianist and get my hands on the material. There is no high like a dancer's high. There is nothing in the world that can touch it. There are no drugs that can equal the euphoria you feel when you're in the throes of a dance moment."

"Do you think you have to be a great technician to be a great choreographer?"

"Well, I had very little technical training," said Marc. "All I had was a couple of months with Charles Weidman and then a summer with Hanya Holm. I drew on my other strengths, like character work, my sense of humor, and background in gymnastics. Dee Dee and I complemented each other because she is technically meticulous, very musical, and loves to have fun."

"We just took life and translated it into energy, character, and emotion," said Dee Dee. "For us it's never been about how high is the leg or how swift is the jump. Dance is not about pushing the body to the limit. It's about what is the body saying, expressing, and emoting."

Marc and Dee Dee followed me into my studio and sat down on a low bench I had prepared for them. The second I pointed a camera at them they turned silly. Marc made funny faces at me and insisted on doing "bunny ears" behind Dee Dee when she wasn't looking. She retaliated by resting her elbow on his head and dislodging his glasses. The antics continued through four rolls of film.

Los Angeles, 1998

Anthropologist

katherine dunham

In June 2002 Jacob's Pillow Dance Festival honored Katherine Dunham with a special evening.

I was invited to document the event, but I hadn't anticipated the crowd of local photographers and reporters who had gathered outside the gift shop waiting for this ninety-three-year-old icon of dance to arrive. When she and her escort drove up in a golf cart, the photographers turned paparazzi, furiously clicking their shutters as if she might suddenly vanish. I stood back and waited. When the shooting frenzy stopped, I walked up to the legendary choreographer and introduced myself.

"Hello, Miss Dunham. I'm honored to meet you. May I take your portrait?"

"Yes," she said with a nod. I used my finger to direct her attention toward my lens, adjusted my camera, and proceeded to take her in. After shooting half a roll with her facing me, I suggested she look away, hoping the late-afternoon light would fill her eyes. It did. She looked radiant.

That evening, speeches and performances were given in her honor. But it wasn't until the following day, during an address to students and guests of Jacob's Pillow, that I would experience the intense magnetism of Katherine Dunham. Again she arrived by golf cart and once inside Ben and Estelle Sommers' Studio was transferred to a chair. She took her place at the long table, flanked by some of her former dancers and friends—Julie Belafonte, Madeline Preston, Walter Nicks, Reginald Yates, Joe Nash, Donald McKayle, Cleo Parker Robinson, among others. I placed a tape recorder on the table, attached a tele-

photo lens to my camera, and positioned myself at the back of the room, now full of students and fans. Miss Dunham looked out at her audience for a moment and then, without any notes, began to speak.

"I'd like you to think about a technique you can call your own. Something you can use to express what you mean. In order to do that, you have to know what you mean. Ask yourself, 'Who am I?' And after you know who you are, ask yourself, 'What am I here for?' And then ask yourself, 'Am I accomplishing what I was put here to do? And if not, why not? How can I do things that will bring me closer to my meaning in life?' Each of us is a different soul, a different person, a different human being.

"When I refer to the soul, I'm talking about spirit. The Dunham technique is made up of elements of body, mind, and spirit. We have to know this body we're in. We might think of it as a shell. You fill that shell in a way no one else can. There is no one like you in the whole world. No one has the same meaning of being, the same values, or the same intention.

"You have a big job ahead of you. You never know your full potential. You never know as much as you can know. We are born to want to know more. Sometimes it frightens us. We pull away and say, 'I can't go on. This is too much for me.' But you really do want to know more. Everything that passes before you contributes to your potential to know more. You end up expanding yourself into the mindness and beingness of other things and other people. We are an endless well of curiosity. We want to know more and feel more. This is what life is like.

"Unfortunately, there are some who get tired. They get tired too easily and say, 'I don't care.' They do care, but they're lazy. They have very little to do with us. Let them go their way, and they will, which is the way of nothingness. I feel that every second of every day I become wiser. That's because I want to be. I don't want to go backward. I have to develop toward what I aspire to be. I have felt on many occasions that I have not arrived at my destination, but I don't let that discourage me, or pull me down or hold me back. I believe we all want to get to another level.

"Discrimination will show you the difference between 'isness' and 'nothingness.' You need to know the isness—the being of is. And when must you know it? Now. I want to know the nowness of now. I need to know the nowness of now," she repeated, pounding the table. "I need to know that there is a tomorrow, but my awareness is now! Lately I have begun using these words to make my point clearer."

She went on to decry the state of our civilization, the urbanization of our villages, and the loss of personal identity and power. She encouraged assertiveness, activism, the pursuit of knowledge. After more than an hour, her stream-of-consciousness recitation came to a close, and she called for questions. Not a single hand went up.

"Ask yourself,

    'Who am I?'

    And after you know who you are, ask yourself, 'What am I here for?'

    And then ask yourself, 'Am I accomplishing what I was put here to do?

                           And if not, why not?'"

"Don't be concerned about the silence," she said after about a minute. "Silence is very good. We need to be able to be quiet, too. Silence helps us to know ourselves better and meld our mind, body, and spirit. Silence helps us find peace and tranquility."

A couple of arms poked out of the crowd.

"Who were your mentors?" someone asked.

"I immediately think of the people like anthropologists Melville Herskovits and Robert Redfield, who helped me go to the West Indies to do my research. But when I look at myself as I am, I think about psychoanalyst Eric Fromm. Many of you are probably not familiar with him. He was a very important thinker. He came into my life when I was a junior at the University of Chicago. He taught me so many things. I am what I am today because of Eric Fromm. Once people bring you knowledge, nothing in the world can ever take that from you."

I asked the next question.

"Ms. Dunham, why as an anthropologist did you choose the concert stage over continued field research?"

After a long pause and looking somewhat uncomfortable, she said, "I don't know why I did the things that I did." The audience responded with laughter. I knew I had hit a nerve. "I am still unfulfilled," she continued. "I am rich and full, but I know there is so much more to learn. I'm not answering your question," she said suddenly, "because I can't. I've spent my whole life wanting to know more, and I've spent my life wanting to create. We must be very careful when we say, 'I am a creator.' There should be a reason for your creation. When you form something out of nothing or something out of very little—and form it into something that other people need, want, love, and respect—then you are creating. I think there is no greater joy."

"How do you want to see your legacy preserved?" a young man asked.

"I hope the good things that I've done will remain and have meaning. I have established a training center and museum in St. Louis, where we try to awaken in people knowledge of this holistic approach of body, mind, and spirit. This work and living the academic and artistic life help me maintain my legacy and give me peace and tranquility in my life."

Lee, Massachusetts, Jacob's Pillow Dance Festival, 2002

Dance Architect

gus solomons jr.

Gus Solomons Jr. and former Alvin Ailey dancer Dudley Williams were working on a movement sequence
when I arrived at Gus's downtown studio on Broadway near Nineteenth. I pulled a 35 mm camera from my bag and shadowed the two dance legends as they moved across the hardwood floor. Fully absorbed in the details of the choreography, they seemed oblivious to the camera. I shot a roll before Gus decided to take a break for our scheduled portrait session. Dudley took advantage of the interruption to grab a bite.

Attracted by the natural light and the view of the city, I suggested that Gus position himself at the window. As he did so, I realized that the light coming in through the glass only partially illuminated him. I noticed a standing lamp next to Dudley, who sat on an old trunk munching McDonald's fries.

"Dudley, can I borrow you and that lamp for a second?"

"Sure," he said, bringing it over to us.

"Just point it up at him," I instructed. Then I knelt down and aimed my lens at Gus in such a way as to accentuate his six-foot one-inch frame. He crossed his arms and gazed out at the city. I had my portrait.

"Thank you, Dudley," I said. "Now you can add lighting assistant to your already distinguished list of accomplishments." He threw me a smile and went back to his fries.

Gus then led me through a door into his adjoining one-room apartment—a seamless configuration consisting of living room, office, kitchen, and bedroom.

We sat down in the designated living room. Gus stretched out his long legs and rubbed his thighs vigorously to soothe aching muscles. I began my interview by asking him about his journey and desired destination as an artist.

"I've never had a destination," he said, raising his eyebrows. "Once I started dancing I knew I would never stop. I never think about retirement, even today. I'm more concerned with how I can dance effectively with the equipment I have at my disposal."

"What do you speak about in your dances?"

"I'm not concerned with saying things in my choreography. With dance you're doing things, not saying things. I tried to say something in the first solo I ever choreographed. It was called *Expression of a Man*. I was bare-chested and wore black tights. I used percussive music and pounded my body, leaped around and got myself exhausted in the first three minutes. I performed it for Murray Louis, who said to me, 'Gus, what was all that suffering about? What do you know about suffering?' I never forgot his criticism and stopped wasting my time trying to convince an audience that I was saying something of importance. I just create work that makes me feel good, and if others read something into it, then that's great."

"Do you consider yourself an artist?"

"Yes, I do. But to me 'artist' is not one of those sacred words like 'genius.' Anybody can claim to be an artist, but whether their art resonates to the public is another matter."

"What makes art resonate with the public?"

"Familiarity, something that an audience can relate to. My early work was very much like that of Merce Cunningham's in that many viewed it as inaccessible. People had a hard time identifying with its abstract nature. When you set movement to noise or random sounds, people don't know how to relate to it. It was important to me that audiences relate to my work, so I interspersed music in between sections of movement that did not alter the intent of the piece. The dances became acceptable to audiences because they had something familiar to connect with.

"People also relate more easily to a dance when the dancers show a great deal of emotion. A neutral body that shows no obvious emotion makes viewers uncomfortable because they are unable to empathize with the performers. When people pay money to see dance, they want to be moved in some way. The work of the Alvin Ailey American Dance Theater is highly emotional and immensely successful for that reason."

"Should the artist indulge the audience?"

"The artist can do one of two things. He can either stay in his downtown loft, driven by his vision, and perform to a select few who get his thing or he can moderate what he does, like I did, and bring the audience closer if it doesn't offend his vision."

"Is there a difference between art and entertainment?"

"Art is like the main course, the protein; entertainment is the dessert. The art nourishes you because it makes you think about things outside the moment. Entertainment satisfies the moment; it lets you escape from your reality. Art helps you deal with your reality."

"Dancers often complain about their bodies, their instrument. They can't go out and buy a new one the way a musician can."

"Yes, part of the angst is trying to make peace with the parts of your body that you don't like and the limitations they impose on you. That tension creates a kind of drama in the dancer's psyche. Dance legend has it that when Martha Graham was at the Denishawn School in the early 1920s, she was told every day that she wasn't pretty enough to be a dancer. They told her to teach yoga and forget about performing. But she said, 'Goddamn it, I'm going to make myself the princess if I have to build a whole new kingdom.' And she did. She created a new vocabulary of movement. It is believed by some that she derived the contraction, the cornerstone of her technique, from her knowledge of *mula bundha*, the yoga principle that leads to levitation. It's a lifting of the perineum, which activates the transverse abdominal muscles." Gus hollowed his torso in a Graham contraction.

"Martha opened the possibility of moving in a whole new way," I said. "Are today's choreographers trying to come up with new movement techniques to cope with their own physical deficiencies or limitations?"

"Perhaps. As long as we keep doing it, we'll continue to find new possibilities for the body. Merce Cunningham shows us this every day. His use of the computer has allowed him to make up physical combinations that aren't kinetically determined in the body. In the process of executing these possibilities, dancers are forced to do things they'd never 'naturally' come up with. Don't for-

get, we are also finding new uses of energy because of state-of-the-art physical training and explorations. When I started dancing in the 1950s, it was a really big deal to execute a double pirouette. Today, the physics of spinning around on one foot make doing six simple. Sixteen-year-olds do it with no problem."

"Gus, as a choreographer and artistic director, how close were you to your dancers?"

"When I had my company, I kept the dancers at a distance. All I asked of my dancers was that they do the steps that I had created for them."

"Sounds to me like you were somewhat of a control freak."

"Oh, please. I invented the term. Just look in the dictionary, you'll see my name," he said, laughing. "As I got happier and less neurotic, I started including the dancers' personalities in the work. I'd give them tasks: 'Okay, let's see what you would do with this idea.' The work eventually became more collaborative, and they ceased being my puppets. Interestingly enough, when I stopped being so controlling, I stopped needing that purchased relationship. I no longer needed a company or even to make dances."

"Before that you did?"

"Oh, yes. It confirmed for me that I was alive. I was in a deep depression from 1970 to 1985. I used my art to medicate my depression. It kept me from going over the edge. It kept me useful."

"What was the cause of your depression?"

"It was a chemical imbalance. I didn't know that at the time. I eventually got medication and therapy and basically outgrew it, like an allergy. Now I'm working with Carmen de Lavallade and Dudley. Our company is called Paradigm. It's completely collaborative. I furnish the movement skeleton, but what they bring to it—because of who they are—is extraordinary. It would have threatened me no end to work with dancers of that level years ago. Now this is all I'm interested in."

New York City, 2002

91

Little Giant

patricia birch

Pat greeted me at the elevator of her uptown apartment with a warm hug and led me to her home office.

"Rose, how about a nice glass of Chardonnay?"

"Yes, that would be lovely."

When Pat left the room to pour the wine, I studied her trophy wall, covered with awards and framed posters of shows and movies she had either appeared in or choreographed—*West Side Story, Zoot Suit, A Little Night Music, Candide, Pacific Overtures, They're Playing Our Song, Grease, Parade*, and many more.

"What an amazing body of work, Pat," I said as she handed me the drink.

"Yes, I've done a few things," she replied modestly.

She sat down in a swivel chair, kicked off her clogs, and dangled her thin legs over the side. I clipped a microphone to her blouse and started recording.

"Tell me about your introduction to dance."

"I always loved to dance, so when I was twelve years old my parents sent me to a summer camp that featured dance classes. I immediately developed an insane crush on the dance teacher. His name was Merce Cunningham. I prayed that he would fall madly in love with me and carry me off into the sunset. I would then become the most beautiful dancer in the world and live happily ever after with the most beautiful man that ever lived. Of course that didn't happen, but when camp ended Merce arranged for me to study with Martha Graham and at the School of American Ballet."

"Wasn't it unusual to study the Graham technique and classical ballet at the same time?"

"Oh, yes. Back then it was practically unheard of to study two very different, opposing dance techniques. Today no one thinks twice about it. But Merce felt that was what I needed. Martha was not at all happy about it."

"What comes to mind when you recall Martha Graham?"

"She was very dramatic and liked to face her students and say, 'One of you is *doooomed* to dance.' There we stood, a bunch of young girls, all hot and sweaty, thinking 'Oh, let it be me, me, me. Please let it be me!' Martha saw everything in terms of doom and danger. I was *doom eager,* but try as I might, I didn't know how to be tragic and anguished. I had an upbeat personality and longed to be a ballerina. I was too short for ballet, so I remained with Martha, eventually becoming a soloist in her company."

"What did Martha teach you?"

"I really learned how to move from Martha, even though I didn't understand some of the crazed imagery that possessed her. I didn't particularly care for all that Greek stuff—yuck. But I do acknowledge that much of what I know has its foundation in her training. Nobody knew how to cut a stage better than Martha—diagonal, straight across, front to back. Nobody made spacing count for emotional content better than Martha or was more theatrical than Martha. No one lit a stage better or understood set design better. One of the most important lessons I learned from her is that the stage is a sacred place. You put a toe out there, and you're making a huge commitment."

"Did Merce Cunningham influence your dancing?"

"Not really. I was too young when I took classes from him, and his work was far too abstract for me. Merce, who had left Martha's company to do his own thing, was very afraid I might get stuck there. He used to say that people often get stuck in dance companies and end up going nowhere. He didn't want that to happen to me."

Pat stood up, dislodging the microphone, and picked up a framed photo on a nearby bookshelf.

"This was taken in 2001," she said, handing it to me. The photo showed Pat and Merce sitting next to each other on lounge chairs, laughing and having a good time. "We've been lifelong friends."

"You didn't get stuck in Martha's company?" I asked, reclipping the microphone to her blouse.

"Oh, no. As it turned out, I married young and ended up with a bunch of kids. I had my first child at the age of twenty-one. How could I go on tour with a houseful of kids? I had to help support the family, so I started to think about doing something else. I wrote a letter to Agnes de Mille and asked to be involved in some of the Broadway revivals she was putting together for City Center."

"Did Agnes take you on?"

"Yes. While I didn't work directly with her very much, I learned from the shows she created. Agnes was a master storyteller with incredible comedic timing. She had an amazing eye for detail and understood that dance could be used to advance the plot, reveal the character's personality, and help integrate the libretto, the score, and the stage direction. Much of what I know about musical theater I learned from her work. She encouraged me to find out what it was that I really wanted to do. She used to say, 'You have to know what you are in this world. Martha Graham is a genius. I am a carpenter, an excellent carpenter. What are you?' After that I began putting steps together and saw that I had a talent for musical theater and that I was pretty funny."

"You also worked with Jerome Robbins and played the role of Anybody's in *West Side Story.* How did you get the role?"

"It was terrifying! I went to the audition and read for the part. When Robbins asked me if I could dance, I said, 'A little.' I didn't mention that I was still a soloist with the Martha Graham Dance Company. So he left me with his assistant to learn the part. Overnight he must have done a little research, because when I came in the next day he said, 'I don't know what you're trying to pull here, but I'm on to you. Give me a triple knee turn!' Oh, Jesus, he was so angry he gave me the most grueling audition of my life. But in the end I got the part, and it was one of the most amazing experiences of my life."

"How did that experience affect you?"

"Well, it was incredible to be in *West Side Story.* I learned a great deal about choreography just from performing his work—to stick to the point and make every move count, to work with economy, and to avoid being decorative. What Robbins demanded was mind-blowing. He would give you a result without any guidance, and you'd have to figure out how to get there. He could be wonderful, and he could be evil."

"Are you conscious of the influences that exist inside of you?"

"Yes, I know they're there, and they color how and what I do, but I don't think about that very much. When I do a show or film, I'm focused on the movement and body language that goes with a particular character in a par-

"The stage is a sacred place.
Understand why you're there
and celebrate it."

ticular time period. What they do and how they move are dramatically driven by the story, the era, and who they are as characters. I'm working on a film right now—*The Stepford Wives* with Nicole Kidman and Glenn Close. Glenn and I played around with what the body language of a Connecticut lady would be. I gave her a few suggestions—chest up, open carriage—and along with the dialogue and the development of her character she easily found the appropriate body behavior."

"I suppose you need to be part movement therapist and part dance historian."

"Yes, that's right. I had to do the same thing with the characters in *Grease*. The story is about high school students in the fifties. The physicality and dance moves of the characters had to match the body jive of the times. John Travolta, who is not a trained dancer, made it so easy because he has the gift of motion—and his moves are as smooth as butter. He understood his character from the start and simply became Danny."

"How do you go about researching a character and a specific time period?"

"I watch films and tapes and often refer to my library here."

Her shelves were laden with books on dance, theater, and art. She stood up again, sending the microphone to the floor, and handed me *The Encyclopedia of Social Dancing* by Albert and Josephine Butler. I flipped through the heavy book, taking note of essays and commentary as well as instructions on everything from swing to square dancing.

"You have been busy," I said, placing the book on the coffee table. "Are you content with how things turned out for you?"

"Well, I'll tell you, it's very different when you're a mother. You can't always do what you want to do. There is always this pull to be with your children. I had to make certain choices in my career that dancers without children don't have to make. I remember trying to take dance class, but my adorable four-year-old daughter, noisily bouncing around like a bunny rabbit, made it impossible for me. My butt was getting bigger, and I'm thinking, 'How can I go on tour? Is the career over?' If not for my family, I might have had my own dance company and had a much bigger film career. But in spite of what could have been, my family has meant the absolute world to me. Plus they've kept me attached to the real world; otherwise I might have gone spinning madly out of control."

"Do you have any favorite works?"

"I don't think in terms of favorites. But I have spent the last umpteen years trying to escape *Grease*. When you have a megahit like that, it tends to haunt you a bit. There are smaller things that I've done that have much more meaning to me. Creating a commercial success does not necessarily mean that it satisfies and fulfills you on a personal level. I've learned to separate the experience from the outcome."

"I sense the dancer in you is still very strong. You haven't stopped moving throughout this entire interview."

"Oh, you noticed that. God knows how I try to sit still," she said with a laugh. "We dancers feel all kinds of physical pulls that others don't feel. We are pulled by gravity and space. We always know where we are, and that makes us want to move. We've been given the gift of motion. We have to honor it, and we do that by dancing and choreographing and squirming around."

New York City, photo 1999, interview 2003

95

Dance Environmentalist

rob marshall

"Picture this, Rob," I said. "You're in a backstage dressing room—mirrors and makeup lights;

a counter filled with jars of cold cream, lipsticks, and powder puffs; fishnet stockings, lingerie, and brassieres hanging everywhere. Downshift into a grainy black-and-white photograph. Fill the frame with sexy long-legged, half-dressed Kit Kat Club girls putting on their false eyelashes. And there you are in the middle of it all."

"Wow! I love that."

"Think we could get backstage before a performance of *Cabaret*?"

"I think I could pull a few strings."

It would take another year before Rob and I actually met at Studio 54, where the Tony Award–winning revival of *Cabaret* was in its fourth season. Rob, the show's director and choreographer, arranged with theater management to let me photograph the dancers in their dressing room. After signing a liability form presented by a theater representative and being given clearance, I pushed aside a flimsy curtain separating the dressing room from the backstage hallway and entered. The women were half dressed, standing and sitting in front of mirrored lights, putting on makeup and false eyelashes. Lingerie and stockings hung off a clothesline that ran across the room. To my surprise, the scene perfectly matched the image I had described to Rob a year earlier. I introduced myself to the dancers, who had been expecting me. They welcomed me graciously, even though it was only sixty minutes before showtime. When Rob walked in

a few minutes later, the women jumped up and screamed for joy. In an instant they were hugging and kissing him, and he disappeared into a huddle of arms and legs. Having no time to lose, I hurried everyone along and began composing my shot. I asked Rob to lean against the dressing table and had three women in underwear and fishnet stockings surround him. Without another word from me, the dancers slipped into character. We had our picture.

Before we sat down in the back of the theater for the interview, Rob made sure that a ticket for the next evening's performance would be waiting for me at the box office.

"You've rechoreographed works of Broadway's greatest choreographers, like Jerome Robbins, Michael Bennett, and this one, of course, by Bob Fosse. How do you deal with the ghosts of genius?"

"Well, it's tricky, because you don't want to compete with such great choreographers. What you want to do is reconceptualize the show's story so that you can create your own vision. *Cabaret* takes place in Berlin in the 1930s, a dark and violent period in history, and deals with the ugly side of life. The story unfolds in a dimly lit third-rate nightclub with broken lightbulbs, dancers in

ripped stockings, with needle tracks and bruises on their arms. The girls and guys of the Kit Kat Club are drugged out and burnt out. By the time you get to the second act, you feel pretty uncomfortable—like the doors have been locked and you can't get out. I wanted to create an environment in which the viewers feel they're inside the experience, not just voyeurs. That's why the floor is filled with round tables and small lamps, as if we're in a nightclub." He pointed to where the audience sits. "I hired artists Otto Dix and George Gross to create an ambience that would feel authentic for that era. They transformed this theater using murals, wallpaper, period lampshades, and all kinds of things."

"How did you capture that era in your choreography?"

"Our look was based on historical re-creations of the time and creative elements, including dance moves, that helped us find our production vocabulary. During the rehearsal process, I'd have the dancers hit a pose, and then I'd deconstruct it so it looked jagged and disjointed. The poses and movement phrases, like the sets and costumes, were made to look distressed. I'd do things like have the dancers start their steps on the wrong foot to make them look awkward and ugly. I avoided clean lines and perfect technique. These 'dancers' would not have

"Create an environment. Bring your characters to life and invite the audience in."

had real training or serious dance technique. You wouldn't find a prima ballerina in a seedy nightclub. In shows like this and *Damn Yankees,* for example, I look for dancers who can also act and become their characters. They need to be believable. The steps are the last things I think about. I'm always preoccupied with what illuminates the characters and furthers the plot. In a musical, dancing can help define the character, show the inner core and true colors. The dancing needs to enhance and move the story line along. If the dancers in the cast identify with their characters, then the dance moves move themselves."

"When you work collaboratively on a project, does your artistic expression become diluted?"

"I want to be fulfilled, but I also want the people I work with to be fulfilled. In this line of business you really have to lose the ego and compromise. I'm flexible and don't mind hearing other voices, because someone may say something that's really smart. I don't have all the answers; I have some ideas. It's wise to take advantage of the wealth of knowledge and talent around me."

"Is it important for you to leave your mark on your various projects?"

"I'm not interested in being like a *Where's Waldo* picture. I don't want to be spotted in the work. I try to disappear, because it's never about me. It's always about the characters and the story. What I do best is bring characters and stories to life. One of my strengths is to tap in to people and give them ideas that will set them free. If I'm creating for Nathan Lane or Julie Andrews or Kathy Bates, the only thing I concern myself with is making the work look like it's coming from them."

"How does being a director/choreographer help you achieve this?"

"As a director you see the entire production as a whole and are better prepared to find the honesty in the work. I want the work to be seamless. If the dance stops and the story begins, then you haven't done your work."

Two years later Rob would emerge as a successful Hollywood director with his film version of *Chicago,* which won the Oscar for Best Picture.

New York City, 2001

Communicator

sophie maslow

"Hello," she said in a heavy Russian accent. "I am Tatiana. I take care of Sophie. Come in."

The tall, robust woman led me into the living room. We passed a bedroom, and I caught a glimpse of Sophie sitting in a wheelchair applying lipstick. A few minutes later Tatiana rolled her out to meet me. I offered my hand and thanked her for welcoming me into her home.

"Please have a seat, my dear. Tatiana can fix us something to drink."

"That would be nice," I said, pulling one of the dining room chairs from the table and placing it near her.

"Sophie, what attracted you to dance?"

"My first exposure to dance came when I was three years old. My mother took me to see Isadora Duncan dance on the stage. I was very little, but it left a big imprint on me. She danced with a red shawl and spoke to the audience with a bouquet of flowers in her arms. I never forgot it. I began taking dance lessons at the age of seven. When I was fourteen, I read Isadora's autobiography, *My Life*, and was very influenced by her ideas on movement, love, and marriage. I identified with her. When I graduated from high school in the early 1930s, I began a three-year course at the Neighborhood Playhouse on the Lower East Side of Manhattan. This was a unique performing arts school run by Alice and Irene Lewisohn, two wealthy Jewish sisters. There were just twelve of us in the course, including Anna Sokolow. Anna had been taking classes there since she was fifteen. Dance was taught in combination with other theater art forms. The faculty included Martha Graham, who taught us movement and developed her new dance ideas on us. Louis Horst taught choreography, emphasizing formal structure and the importance of understanding music in choreography. We had an instructor trained in the Stanislavksi Theater who taught diction and the craft of theater. We were even taken as a group to the Metropolitan Museum of Art to observe Greek and Egyptian art."

"Was it during that time that you started to choreograph your own dances?"

"Yes, I started right away. In those days if you wanted to dance in front of an audience, you had to compose your own dances. Martha taught us only technique. Even when we danced in her company, we didn't perform solos. Several of us, Anna included, worked with Louis Horst to create our own dances. He then took us out to perform them in lecture demonstrations. That's how we began to learn the craft of choreography. His insights on how music relates to movement were vital to our understanding of dance construction. He was very innovative in his approach and worked only with modern and pre-classic music. I remember one day I asked him why he didn't use music of the Romantic composers like Beethoven and Brahms, and he said, 'There's nothing as old as yesterday's newspaper.'"

"So while you were in Martha's company, you never had opportunities to express your own dance ideas?"

Sophie laughed at the notion. "Certainly not in the beginning. But later on, when she became more successful, she allowed a few of us to occasionally have solos."

"When you danced in her company were you just background?"

"Oh, I wouldn't say we were just background. Sometimes it was very important what we were doing. But Martha was the soloist. We were there for her. There was never any doubt about that."

"Did you use Martha's movement vocabulary when you choreographed your own solos and group pieces?"

"Why, yes. I had no other technique to draw on. I had never trained with anyone else, and it was Martha's technique that made me a dancer. I never felt there was anything wrong with that. Besides, I found her technique very powerful and very expressive. I loved it and never wanted to dance in any other style."

"Did her technique limit you at all since it was specifically created to mirror her own expression?"

"No, not really, because I used a lot of folk elements and themes in my work. My parents were Russian Jews, and I had an affinity for folk culture. I would add Russian or Spanish elements to the choreography, depending on what the piece was about and what the music dictated. I never felt at a loss for movement. What concerned me more was that people understood what I was trying to say. Many choreographers want to leave their work up to personal interpretation. Whatever the audience reads into it is fine. That's not how I felt about it. I chose the subject matter for my dances very specifically because I wanted people to understand what was important to me and what I was expressing. If there was any doubt about what a dance meant, then it was my fault. I had failed the choreography."

"Was your motivation to alter perceptions or inform people about things?"

"I never tried to convert people politically or religiously or even teach them lessons. I simply wanted to express myself and be understood. This was my reason for becoming a choreographer. It was my way of being sociable. I couldn't sing. I couldn't paint. I wasn't a good writer. What I could do was make dances, and that was my way of communicating with other people. I hoped people agreed with my views, but they didn't have to."

"So you based success or failure on whether or not the audience understood what you were saying in the dance?"

"Yes, audience response meant everything to me. I used to have a list of my dances, probably over one hundred of them. The ones I was most proud of were the ones that moved audiences and made them laugh or cry. *The Village I Knew* was a dance I did based on the stories of Sholem Aleichem. He was a Yiddish writer who romanticized Jewish life in Eastern Europe at the end of the nineteenth century. I was very surprised at how the work impressed non-Jewish audiences, especially since it was being performed during the time when Nazis were killing Jews all over Europe. I wanted to help in some way, even though I personally felt that nothing I could do in dance could ever measure up to the horrors of the Holocaust."

"Do you think that art in general has the capacity to reflect real life?"

"No, I don't think it's really possible, except maybe through the medium of film. It's easier to re-create or simulate real-life situations through cinematography and acting. But with dance and music you are abstracting real events, and that removes you from the reality. I do believe, however, that art can be enormously comforting emotionally and promote psychological healing. That's why I chose the Sholem Aleichem stories. Even though they were sad, they also had a great deal of humor, and I thought that uplifting."

"What are the choreographer's tools for creating dances?"

"That's a funny question to ask," she said, looking perplexed. "That's like asking a composer what are the tools for writing music?"

She paused for a couple of minutes to contemplate her response.

"Well, I could talk about the need for dance vocabulary, but I think what is more important is that you have a deep appreciation for the art form and a specific point of view. It's essential that you know what it is that you want to say. Beyond that, I think it's extremely important to be interested in people and what's going on in the world."

"Why what's going on in the world?"

"I can only speak from my own perspective, but I am affected every day by what goes on in the world. Whether it has to do with people who live on my block or in some other country, I am deeply affected by the human condition. I hear about AIDS in Africa, or the violence that's going on in the Middle East. Even when I would choreograph a time-period piece I always made sure it had relevance to our present-day world. Choreography is my way of responding to that which affects us all."

"As you reflect on your life now, would you say you've lived a good life?"

"I'm ninety years old and have lived a long time. I've been a choreographer since I graduated from high school. Dance was my way of communicating with others, and it gave me a profession that I loved. I've had a happy life and good marriage, but I had some tragedies too. I lost my first child, and that was a tough blow. Creatively speaking, there were things I would have liked to do. If I was held back artistically, it had only to do with the lack of funds. Not having money limits what you can do as an artist. I had to get along on a modest budget, and that affected my ability to dress my dances properly. I often had to forgo scenery, costumes, and even the music that I wanted to use. Sometimes circumstances dictated what my work would look like. For example, I choreographed thirteen Hanukkah specials at Madison Square Garden accompanied by the New York Philharmonic Orchestra. It's a big sports arena, and we had no stage or curtains, but I always felt it was very important to expose 20,000 people to dance, even if I couldn't present the work the way I might have liked to."

I could tell that Sophie was getting a little tired, so I suggested we move on to her portrait.

"Before you do, I'd like to show you some of my dance photos," she said. She called for Tatiana, who came in drying her hands on a dishtowel.

"Tatiana, please take my photos out of the drawer." Tatiana pulled out several creased and aged prints taken by Barbara Morgan in the 1930s and 1940s. Some of them I had seen in books.

"That was me in Martha's company," Sophie said proudly.

"These are very precious," I said. "Do you have more?"

"No, this is all I have."

I wondered how such an illustrious life in dance could result in so few photographic mementos.

"Come, Sophie," said Tatiana. "Why don't you use your walker and show Rose how well you're doing?"

Sophie stood up with great effort and painstakingly made her way across the room to the sofa. Tatiana helped her sit down while I metered the light. Sophie struck a pose, and as I rattled off two rolls of film, I made a mental note to send her a print for her photo collection.

New York City, 2001

103

Ambassador of Spanish Dance

josé greco

José Greco greeted me on the front porch of his home in Lancaster, Pennsylvania.

At eighty-one, he had not lost the sex appeal that had served him so well over a career that spanned more than sixty years. The mere sight of him had captivated audiences on stage and screen.

"I saw you perform on *The Ed Sullivan Show*," I said. "I was around eleven years old. I never forgot it."

"Oh, is that right?" he said, laughing heartily. "Please come in, my dear."

He called out to his wife, "Ana, here is Ms. Eichenbaum."

A woman in her late forties joined José at the door and invited me in. The living room decor hinted only modestly of Greco's brilliant career. A pair of bronzed dance boots rested near the fireplace, and a portrait of Greco in his prime hung on one of the walls.

"Everything I've read about you says that you were the greatest Spanish dancer of modern times."

"Well, ahhhh, I cannot really comment on that," he said. "I was never really interested in reading what critics said about my work as a dancer or choreographer. When I danced with the late Argentinita, one of the great Spanish dancers of the 1930s and 1940s, John Martin, the most eminent dance critic of the *New York Times*, wrote that I had no future."

"You proved him wrong."

"He thought I was not serious enough or whatever. It did not make me feel too happy to read his words. From then on, I never read reviews. What critics said about me would be good, if it was good for business. It was always with the audiences that I had rapport. In time, I became very famous. My name meant something at the box office. But even so, I never considered myself a super dancer. I could have improved technically. I always felt I needed to learn more about combining the elements of theater with dance. But I always danced the best I knew how. I left people with an image."

"Why do you think audiences embraced you so? Was it a sudden interest in Spanish dance?"

"I tried to make my shows very theatrical, with wonderful staging and drama, but it went way beyond that. People were drawn to the image I projected. For the female, it was an admiration for a strong, virile male. The women wanted to have me. The men wanted to be me. They identified with the strong masculine figure I assumed on the stage."

"How did you know what would appeal to audiences? How did you create your presentational style?"

"I drew from my early experiences as a performer in cabarets and from my exposure to the theater. When I was in my twenties I had a job running show tickets for a scalper on Broadway. I used to slip into the theater with the crowd and take every opportunity to see a show. I quickly developed a love of theater. I particularly adored *Porgy and Bess, View from the Bridge*, and *Dial M for Murder*. I didn't realize it then, but I was absorbing everything I saw. Later, I applied all these elements of theater to my own shows. I was fascinated with lighting, costumes, and staging, and the contrast between one production and another. The dramatic shows, in particular, gave me the idea to add suspense to my performances. I'd purposefully create tension on the stage and then I'd present the hero—that, of course, was me," he said with a laugh.

"How did you manage to stay popular for so long?"

"Everybody seemed to want us in their show or on their stage. We performed around the world every year for almost thirty years, from 1951 to 1978. We maintained our success in part by diversifying our presentations to fit each circumstance and venue. For example, we put flashy numbers in nightclubs and reserved duets, trios, and dramatic pieces for the concert stage. When impresarios booked us in huge football stadiums, our performances reflected a dynamic Spanish revue. I welcomed the various media because it exposed us to a mass of people. We appeared on *Ed Sullivan* and *The Tonight Show* with

Johnny Carson an estimated twenty times. If I had to cut a dance from five minutes to two rather than be preempted on television, I'd do it. I always felt it was better to be seen than to make a scene over the length of a dance."

"What was it about performing that turned you on?"

"I loved the applause, the attention. Ever since my debut performance when I was cast as a Spanish gypsy in *Traviata* at the age of sixteen, I adored the attention. We had performed in the great Hippodrome Theater in New York City. It no longer exists. But when the applause roared through that enormous auditorium that first night, I just loved it. I decided there on the spot that this is what I wanted to do the rest of my life."

"And later when you performed on the great stages of the world, what did that feel like?"

"Once I'd see the lights and feel the stage under my feet, everything became my possession. This was my kingdom! Everything I saw and witnessed was mine. I owned it all."

Greco jumped out of his seat and assumed a classic flamenco pose, one arm overhead, the other folded at the wrist and resting on his waist. He began clicking the hardwood floor in a rhythmic pattern with his street shoes. He looked past me as to a large imaginary audience. "Oh, yes, oh, yes," he said, switching arms and dancing about the living room. "I'd move this way and that way. I would go down, and up, in the air and throw myself here and turn around. Ahh . . . I never forget the thrill of moving, the satisfaction. I loved it so."

Ana and I applauded loudly as José bowed, a huge smile animating his face.

"Did you ever have trouble getting into character or into the dance?"

"No. Never! I don't think I ever had that disagreeable feeling that I was not dancing at my best or felt out of touch with my character. Once I felt the heat in my body, I could do anything. I felt such passion for the dance. I even danced when I was sick with fever because I felt the dance would heal me."

"Did you feel you had a responsibility to show the audience a good time?"

"I always wanted to give audiences a great show. I felt strongly that audiences should get their money's worth. But I also felt I needed to be true to the art form. People always expect surprises and tricks, but in Spanish dance you've got to remain true to the character. You are interpreting emotions. I never felt that I was there to show them that there is more to Spanish dance than there is. I never saw myself as an innovator or vanguard of the dance."

"Did you ever improvise dances or experiment with choreography?"

"With Spanish dance, improvisation can occur only if the guitarist knows

> *"Once I'd see the lights and feel the stage under my feet, everything became my possession. This was my kingdom. . . . I owned it all."*

what you want to do. He must anticipate your steps; otherwise it's easy to go off beat. When I tried new things, I felt as though I was cheating the audience. I had plenty of turkeys during my choreographic life. At the height of my career I thought my fame was so great I could get away with anything. I could give them Chinese dance and they wouldn't care. But that wasn't true. After a while I stopped monkeying around with new concepts and stuck to what I knew. You don't victimize an audience. If you want to experiment, go to the university."

"So you had some failures when you tried to be innovative?"

"Yes, I did. It's risky to try new things. I suffered much more than my audiences did when things didn't go. I was accustomed to big ovations, so when the curtain came down and there was nothing, I was devastated and demoralized. I would begin to second-guess myself. Did I take enough time to stage the numbers, light the pieces, and costume the dancers? Maybe I emphasized this, instead of that. Perhaps I used the wrong person for a particular number. After thirty consecutive years, you wonder what you can bring that's new. When I experimented and things went badly, I'd tell myself, 'I'll do better next year.' I had to, or no survival."

"You are of Italian heritage and were raised in Brooklyn. What was it about Spanish dance that so captivated you?"

"I was an Italian with a Spanish heart. I loved the dance, the rhythm, and the pride of what a Spanish male is supposed to be—strong, masculine, and suave."

"How did you create a look and feel that non-Spanish audiences could relate to?"

"When I choreographed dances, I drew my inspiration directly from the stylistic variations of the Basque, Andalusian, and northeastern regions of Spain. I tried to be as authentic as possible. I was always careful to provide appropriate theatrical staging, lighting, and costuming. *The Dance of the Horsemen* grew out of a personal experience I had in southern Spain while filming a movie. We were on a bus heading back to the hotel after a day of shooting when I looked out the window and saw four powerful horsemen galloping off into the sunset. It was the most beautiful sight I had ever seen. It was this moment that gave me the idea to choreograph a dance that would convey the poetry and passion that is Spain. It became my signature piece and would stop the show."

Once again José jumped up out of his chair and began a slapping a beat pattern on his thigh. "We tried to re-create the sound of galloping horses through rapid footwork that sounded like this," he explained. He then stopped and posed elegantly as if in full costume. "I wore a Spanish sombrero, a short fitted jacket with very tight trousers, and boots up to here," he said, placing his hand just below the knee. "The costumes were impeccable. I still have all my costumes. Would you like to see them?"

"You mean you have them here in your home? Costumes from your world tours? Yes, my goodness, I would *love* to see them."

José and Ana led me through their kitchen and down a staircase into the basement, illuminated by a single bare lightbulb. Racks of trousers, ruffled shirts, vest, capes, and multicolored dresses, covered by plastic and garment bags, gave proof to a thirty-year career on the great stages of the world. Boots and shoes of various styles and colors were stored in boxes and on shelves. Hats and sombreros, along with props such as whips, fans, castanets, and other paraphernalia, were also carefully filed away. Though in hibernation, the costumes and props looked at if they might someday awaken to the call of the dance. Greco needed only to twist his torso and crack his whip.

"Would it be possible for you to wear one of your old costumes for our photo?" I asked.

"I'm afraid they no longer fit me, my dear," he said with a laugh, patting his belly.

"How about one of your hats, then?"

"Yes, that would be fine." He grabbed one of his big black hats off the shelf and placed it carefully on his head.

"How do I look?" he asked.

"Like an Italian with a Spanish heart," I replied.

Lancaster, Pennsylvania, 1999

107

Tall Talent

tommy tune

Tommy Tune's electronic image exploded on the towering marquee of the Las Vegas MGM Grand Hotel.

I knew I'd come to the right place. And if there was any doubt, his portrait appeared everywhere, from the parking lot to the elevator walls. And not just his image. When I later phoned for room service, the recorded voice was none other than that of Tommy Tune, inviting guests to his show. I wondered if Las Vegas had become Tune Town.

The following afternoon a hotel guard escorted me to the star's backstage dressing room.

"Make yourself comfortable," he said. "Tommy will be here shortly."

I pushed open the door and beheld a white room. The walls, carpet, furniture—everything was white. I removed my street shoes and began setting up the lights. I pondered why the star of *EFX* had purged the room of all color. Just then Tommy walked in, wearing a black turtleneck sweater and black slacks. I was stunned by the sharp contrast of this extraordinarily handsome six foot six man in black against the stark white background.

"Hello. I understand you have some questions for me," he said in a pleasant voice as he dropped his long body onto his even longer oversized bed.

"I'm actually curious about this white room of yours."

"I have a good reason for that," he said with a laugh. "Have you seen *EFX*?"

"No, not yet."

"If I stop to think about how am I doing this, the dance stops."

"Why don't you be my guest tonight, and after you see the show, you'll understand."

"Fair enough."

I parked myself on the bed facing Tommy and plunged into the interview.

"You've won nine Tony Awards and the respect of audiences and critics alike. To what do you attribute your enormous success?"

"That's easy. Love is the key to success. You can call it different things, and get technical about it, but that's what it comes down to. Love is the most powerful source from which all creativity grows. People often believe that it's angst or torment that inspires creative work, but for me it's love. I try to infuse my work with this magical ingredient, and when I do, everything is taken care of. Success comes when the intention to serve what you love and feel passionate about is realized. You may not become financially successful or publicly celebrated, but that is not always the true measure of success. For example, the short-order cook who makes a perfect scrambled egg because of the care he's invested is a success. I feel like I'm doing what I was put here to do. When you find something that you love to do and people love to see you do it, that's the happiest that a man can be. What makes me feel successful is using the gifts that have been bestowed upon me and giving them back in the form of entertainment."

"How does one recognize true success?"

"Success comes from having a fulfilling experience and being inside the moment of that experience. Success does not come in retrospect or as a recollection or even as an evaluation from others. It's not something that you can physically hold on to or repeat at will. Only when you acknowledge the special moments can you truly feel the effects of your most wonderful achievements."

"When you're developing a show like *EFX*, how much of the work is created with the audience in mind?"

"We are in Las Vegas, where the sexual vibe is stronger than any place I've ever performed. I don't know if it has to do with the gambling or the appetite for stimulation, so everything I do in this show is a sort of seduction, visually and kinesthetically. I kept that in mind when I staged this show. When I choreograph I always ask myself, 'Am I happy looking at this?' Then I ask, 'Will the audience be?' What it's like on the stage and what it's like from across the footlights are very different. Occasionally I'll be on the stage, feeling it and getting it right, and then I go out into the house and it's not right at all. The proscenium arch creates a distinct field of vision. I'm forever amazed at what I'm seeing from the seats as opposed to what I'm feeling on the stage. The emotions are very different. Up on stage you're expressing, and out there you're experiencing."

"You wrote in your memoir that when you create an opening number for a show, you need to define the rules from which the audience can sense the world they are about to inhabit. What are those rules?"

"Well, they are different for each show. For example, in this show the orchestra will be playing in the pit, and curtains will be going up and coming down. Then just as that starts to get boring, the curtain opens from the middle and then closes together. If you begin with curtains, you can't lower a cement wall and expect the audience to stay in the same evening with you; you've introduced architecture into a curtain world. It's necessary to remain consistent so the audience doesn't need to constantly change perceptual gears."

"When you're thinking in terms of pleasing an audience, how do you bounce back and forth without losing sight of your original idea?"

"When I'm creating or directing, I try to view everything with baby eyes. The audience doesn't know what's in my head, so I have to approach the work with the purest of intentions and break it down thoroughly. All I'm trying to do is communicate and communicate well. I'm not doing it for myself. I'm not masturbating. I am there to lift their spirits. This is show business. I entertain, and I hope I do it artfully. I'm not just there to fill out eight bars of music. If you underpin whatever you're doing with a hidden metaphor or rich motive, it will travel further to the deeper part of the soul. The audiences may not get it on a surface level, but their soul will get it. If I as a performer can get there myself, then they can get there too."

"I would imagine the ultimate goal is to feel transported by the work."

"You can feel it when you land there, and it takes you into one of those successful moments. But as much as I try, I don't always get there. It takes a long time to click in and feel the performance shift gears. That's why I love long runs. Some people get bored doing the same show night after night, but

I thrive on it. Each time out, you have a chance to go higher because your foundation is stronger. Every time you perform that piece, you create another layer of support for yourself. The floor gets thicker and thicker until it becomes a launching pad."

"When you get a tepid response from the audience do you ever get annoyed or upset?"

"Oh, no. The audience doesn't owe me anything. They paid their money and their fanny is in the seat. Now what do I do to make it worth their while for having spent the money, gotten dressed, and come to the theater? It's up to me to compensate them."

"If an audience is not happy with a show, do you ever get angry with yourself?"

"Oh, I think I'm past beating myself up. I went through that many years ago. That happens when you don't like yourself."

"So far we've talked about the relationship between performer and audience. What are your thoughts about the dance critic?"

"Dance critics often come to a show with expectations of what they want to see. If you fulfill their expectations, they write you a great review. But if you do something they're not expecting, look out. I've pretty much stopped reading reviews. At this point in my life I just want to do my best. When I go to bed after these two shows a night in Vegas, I'm exhausted, but I feel good because I know I haven't cheated the audience. That's success."

"Do most dance reviewers really understand dance?"

"Typically a dance critic will write, 'And the dancer took her arm and moved it over there and did this or that.' Dance is better seen, not described. Fred Astaire once asked, 'What is dance? We don't know. It can't be defined. You know when you're doing it, you know when you're seeing it, but what makes it different from running or jumping or flying?' I don't know what it is either. I only know that when I'm doing it, I enter another state of being. If I stop to think about how am I doing this, the dance stops."

"What would you say are the hardest lessons you've ever had to learn?"

"Never underestimate the benefits of down time. If you don't force creativity, your subconscious has an opportunity to kick in and take care of whatever creative blocks might be plaguing you. One day during rehearsal for *The Will Rogers Follies*, I reached a block. Everybody was yelling, 'What do we do now, what do we do now?' I didn't know. So I excused myself and retreated to the theater's backstage bathroom. It was absolutely filthy. Near the sink sat a can of Ajax and a sponge. I got down on my hands and knees and scrubbed the floor clean, and then I cleaned the sink. I washed and dried my hands, came back out, and somewhere between the floor and the sink, I had solved the choreographic problem. While I was engrossed in the cleaning, my subconscious kicked in and took care of business. I have since come to realize that you can't force a creative thought. Down time will help you get there."

"The most serious crisis you faced, according to your memoir, was when you broke your foot. You contemplated suicide."

"I was in trouble after I broke my foot. The doctors said a full recovery was unlikely. What is a dancer who can't dance? I had never before in my life come to a full stop. But interestingly enough, after I wrote those words, that feeling receded. I think sometimes when you face up to some deep fear that haunts you and you shine a light on it, it seems to evaporate. I haven't had suicidal thoughts since I wrote that. I was going through a very severe time, and I needed to dance in some way, so I danced with my pen."

That evening I attended Tommy's show in the MGM Grand Ballroom. When the soft-shoeing star moved downstage in his white tuxedo and tails, the capacity crowd cheered. Tommy looked like there was no other place on earth he'd rather be. The show progressed into a high-tech computer-generated special-effects extravaganza, complete with fire-breathing dragons, swashbuckling daredevils flying through the air, and a 3-D light show. I understood immediately Tommy's flight to white. It allowed him to clear his visual palate before and after each *EFX* performance. He would do this eye-dazzling spectacle more than 900 times before his contract in Las Vegas ended.

Las Vegas, 1999

Jazz Master

luigi

When I received the phone call to cover Jazz Dance LA Foundation's tribute to Luigi (Eugene Facciuto),

I immediately took the assignment. Covering the event would allow me to get to know the jazz great and also watch him in action. He was scheduled to teach several master classes here in Los Angeles at the studio of his former student, Hama. I phoned Luigi, and he agreed to be photographed in my studio. The minute the seventy-three-year-old dancer and his devoted protégé, Francis Roach, walked in, I felt as if I were seeing two old friends. I offered them some hot tea, and then we sat down to get acquainted.

"Luigi, your career has really been an amazing one. Not many can say they came back from paralysis to dance alongside Gene Kelly."

"Yes, I've been a very lucky man, very lucky."

"I can't even imagine what you've been through. What did you think when you found out you were paralyzed?"

"The first thought that crossed my mind was, 'Will I ever dance again?' I wasn't even thinking about the fact that I might never walk again. The way I saw it, dancing meant being alive. Dancing was the most important thing in my life. What was life without it? Nothing. I had danced ever since I was a kid. Without it, I had no profession, no reason for living."

"How did your accident occur?"

"The year was 1946. I was twenty-one and had come to LA after fightin-

"Learn to feel your technique, and your technique will become your feelings."

in World War II. I was hoping to make it as a dancer in musicals. I was on my way to buy ballet shoes in Hollywood, when the driver whose car I was riding in lost control. It was a rainy day, and the road was very slick. I was thrown from the car and my head was crushed against a curb. I was in a coma for several days. When I awoke in the hospital, I couldn't move. The doctor came in and said, 'You'll never walk again. The left side of your face and the right side of your body are paralyzed.' I also had a fractured skull and a broken jaw. My eyes were so badly jarred in my head that they sustained permanent damage. You see, Rose, how I'm cross-eyed."

"Yes," I nodded.

"In the surgery to repair my eyes, they tied the muscles too soon. It left me with permanent double vision. Incidentally, that's why I can't do pirouettes. I'm unable to spot—but we'll talk about that later."

"What happened next?"

"Lying there in the hospital bed, I heard a voice say, 'Never stop moving, kid. If you stop moving you're dead. Don't ever stop moving.'"

"How did you manage your recovery? Did the doctors prescribe physical therapy?"

"The hospital gave me conventional physical therapy, but I could see that movement had to come from the inside. I took it day by day and gradually found a little feeling in my muscles. It felt like a twinge, and then I was able to get control of it. I started to feel the body's ability to heal itself. A year after the accident I began taking ballet classes at the Falcon Studios in Hollywood. I studied the Cecchetti and Fokine methods of ballet with wonderful teachers like Bronislava Nijinska, Eugene Loring, Michel Panaieff, and Edward Caton. I took classes in tap from Louis Da Pron and modern dance with Michio Ito. Eventually Miss Edith Jane, who ran the school, took me on as her protégé. Studying with these great artists inspired me to resume my professional career. All the while, I continued to push through the paralysis."

"How did ballet technique serve your recovery?"

"It helped me find my balance and placement. Once I learned to press down lightly on the ballet barre and feel my feet solidly to the floor, I discovered my own center of balance, and that gave me control. Up until then, I would just fall down. Because ballet works both sides of the body equally, I was able to stop giving in to my paralyzed side and build up strength evenly. I began to recognize where the muscles begin and end and identify the appropriate muscles needed to execute specific actions. It also became clear to me that if the body is in the right placement—lifted torso, hips in alignment, et cetera—I could move effectively. This is the cornerstone to my technique. I always tell my students, 'There's only way to dance—*the right way.*'"

"I've heard the phrase 'Your space is your barre' in reference to your technique. What does that mean exactly?"

"This is one of the basic foundations of my technique. I explained to you how I used the ballet barre in my recovery. Well, basically it's finding that same inner feeling when you are away from the barre. You imagine it's there when it's not, and you do it with the use of imagery. This helps you maintain balance, control, and natural alignment."

"How is this applied to motion in space?"

"It's really about integrating the body and the mind and letting the body flow and feel connected. I don't believe in isolating body parts or movements. I talk about putting yourself in a circle and reaching beyond the circle, which becomes a continuous flow. During my recovery I discovered the *epaulement*, which is a ballet term that refers to the use of the shoulders and the upper body. It gives the body balance and direction in order to move through space. My leg will only go where my body tells it to go."

"How did you break into Hollywood musicals?"

"Two years after my accident I was dancing in a recital at the Falcon Studios, when a talent scout from Metro-Goldwyn-Mayer spotted me. He took me over to meet Gene Kelly, who then hired me to dance in the film *On the Town*."

"Were you were still partially paralyzed?"

"Yes, but I could do most things. I appeared in *Annie Get Your Gun, Singin' in the Rain, An American in Paris, The Band Wagon*, and many other musicals. During those years I danced the choreography of Michael Kidd, Robert Alton, Hermes Pan, Eugene Loring, and others. I also appeared alongside some of Hollywood's most famous entertainers: Judy Garland, Cyd Charisse, Leslie Caron, Vera Ellen, Donald O'Connor—and the list goes on."

"It's sort of miraculous, isn't it? You had a very successful Hollywood career despite your physical handicap."

"I had big dreams before the accident. I was very cocky, saying to myself, 'Fred Astaire and Gene Kelly, move over. Here I come.' But fate stepped in. I feel that God chose me to fulfill another mission."

"How did you come to develop your own dance technique and begin teaching it?"

"During rehearsals on movie sets I found that there was a lot of time spent waiting around. I'd go off to the side and do my warm-up routine so my muscles wouldn't get stiff. Pretty soon other dancers wanted to join me. They encouraged me to teach, so I rented a space at the Rainbow Studios in Hollywood and held classes. It was also around that time that I started choreographing my own nightclub act and performing in movies and on early TV shows. In 1956 I got a part in *Happy Hunting*, a Broadway show starring Ethel Merman and Fernando Lamas. So I moved to New York and continued to perform in shows and assist choreographers like Onna White and Alex Romero. I knew that I loved teaching, and so when June Taylor asked me to teach in her dance school, I accepted. I've been teaching now for fifty years."

"Luigi, it's obvious that you love ballet, and ballet has been good to you. How did you end up a jazz dancer and teacher?"

"I didn't intend to be a jazz dancer. It just came out that way. The reality was that as much as I loved ballet, I was limited by my paralysis to perform it. Jazz has its structural foundation in ballet technique, so it was very easy for me to execute its moves. Also, don't forget that the dancing I performed in the Hollywood musicals was very jazz-oriented mixed with tap. But let me tell you a little story. One day when I was in New York, I went in to audition for Lucia Chase, who was the director of American Ballet Theater. I came in and knew I could jump like hell, do splits in the air, and had beautiful lines. She asked me to do turns in the air. But I couldn't do them because of my eyes. I heard Lucia Chase say, 'I thought they said he could dance.' That's why I knew I'd never be a performing ballet dancer."

"Do you have a motto that you live by?"

"Yes, I have several: Learn to feel your technique, and your technique will become your feelings. Put your hand to your heart and listen to the sound of your soul. *And*, my personal favorite—*Never stop moving!*"

After the interview, I invited Luigi to step into my studio. I had him stand up close to the backdrop and threw a spotlight behind him.

"I normally like to look away from the camera because of my eyes, you know."

"I think people who view this portrait will be looking way beyond external appearances. They'll be seeing Luigi the artist."

"Yes, you're probably right. Okay, dear, go for it," he said and leaned back into a pose.

Los Angeles, 1998

On the Path

judith jamison

Judith's assistant of many years escorted me to a small room on the third floor of the Ailey School, near Lincoln Center.

I quickly unloaded my rented gear and converted the space into a makeshift photo studio. When Judith arrived, some forty-five minutes later, lights were in place and cameras loaded.

Wearing a black shirt and slacks, a string of African beads and a crown of braids on her head, the artistic director of the Alvin Ailey American Dance Theater projected a commanding, almost regal presence.

"Rose, so sorry I'm late. The traffic was awful," she said, waving her arms chaotically. "You should have heard me yelling out the window at those cabbies. They haven't heard the last of me. I hope I didn't keep you waiting."

"No, no, I'm fine."

"Where would you like me to sit?" she said, walking toward the designated photo area.

I directed her to a chair facing the lights and sat down opposite her. The soft white light of my photo umbrella accentuated her flawless skin and high cheekbones. I fought back the urge to pick up my camera right then and instead began the interview.

"Judith, do you think you can pinpoint a time in your career when you felt you really came into your own as a dancer, when you really knew what you were doing?"

"Nothing has ever occurred to me in any logical chronology or clear way.

I began dancing at the age of six and never contemplated where it would lead. I've always been where I was supposed to be, when I was supposed to be there. I've been guided all my life and very blessed. I'm simply on the path and have to be prepared for whatever comes my way."

"Did you consciously strive to become a great dancer?"

"From the time I was a child my goal was to be the best. It didn't matter what the activity was. If I ran a race in the schoolyard, I had to win. When I was in the choir, I had to sing the loudest. In Modern European History, one of my favorite subjects, I had to get an A. When I finally got on the stage, I had to dance the best. I had to be the best at everything. That's who I was."

"Where did that push to be the best come from?"

"It came from being surrounded by what I thought was the best. My mother had an absolutely rigid back. She was erect and spoke the Queen's English, as did my father, even though they both had only a high school education. They believed that a good education, including exposure to the arts, was essential. Growing up in Philadelphia, I was always in and out of museums and surrounded by breathtaking art and sculpture. Going to church every Sunday filled me with beauty, pageantry, and faith. I had a very rich childhood."

"How did you know to follow the dance path?"

"I didn't. I was just having fun. I am overtly passionate about the things that I love. I'm very obsessive-compulsive by nature. I do it with people, I do it with food, and I do it for long periods of time. Dancing has always been like breathing for me. I simply had to do it."

"Do you identify yourself as an artist?"

"No, I have a thing about that. I'm still aspiring to be an artist in its truest sense. Today everybody is an artist. The term is used too lightly. You're not an artist just because you perform steps or you have been at it a long time. I don't fully comprehend what it means to be an artist—not yet. To me, the highest compliment I could receive is to be called a dancer. I've spent my whole life being a dancer, and I'll always be a dancer. A dancer is God-like to me. If you want to tack on the word 'artist,' that's an evaluation of something else that I don't yet comprehend."

"What makes an artist an artist?"

"I don't know, because if I did, I'd turn a lot of people into artists! There are so few true artists around. In fact, there are very few true dancers around. There are a lot of people pretending. You aspire to be an artist, and you either get there or you don't.

"To me, an artist is someone who brings out what's deepest within you. They pull everything, everything, *everything* out of you, and you gladly give it to them. If it were possible, you'd turn yourself inside out because of what they are giving you. An artist makes you feel a part of the universe and takes you out of yourself and plants you in a space of total freedom. Only a true artist has the power to do that. You thank them with applause, but really that's hardly sufficient."

"You've been called Alvin Ailey's muse. Did you identify as his muse?"

"I never thought of myself exclusively as Alvin's muse. He created solos for all of us in the company—Dudley Williams, Donna Wood, Mari Kajiwara, Sarah Yarborough, and many others. There was really nothing muselike about it. But by 1971, by the time we got to *Cry*, the piece he choreographed as a tribute to his mother, everyone started to attach this thing to it that I was his muse. When Alvin phoned me at four in the morning to read me Clive's review in the *New York Times*, I thought he was out of his mind. 'What are you doing?' he asked me. 'I'm sleeping, Alvin,' I said. 'I've got a matinee tomorrow.' I had no idea what lay ahead for either of us. When I did my curtain call that night, I didn't notice anything out of the ordinary. People yelled and applauded the way they normally did. When the curtain came down, Alvin came backstage and said, 'Now what am I going to do?' I didn't realize what he meant until much later, when all the publicity hit. He had just made a classic work, and I was about to be thrust into the limelight. He was already on the next page, saying, 'What am I going to do next?' People immediately began calling the box office, asking, 'When is Judi going to do it again?' It was a very vulnerable place for him to be."

"Did your relationship with Alvin change once you achieved international stardom?"

"No, our relationship remained the same. We loved each other dearly and did everything people in relationships do. We laughed, we fought, and we shared our innermost feelings. The trust between us was very deep. He entrusted me to translate what he was trying to convey to the world. That's a choreographic shoe that's hard to wear."

"I think you just described what a muse does."

"Yes, I suppose I did."

"Were there any particular roles that you performed that altered you in some way, changed you by their very nature?"

"Well, I would have to say *Cry* changed me greatly because of all the attention it brought me."

> *"When you stand*
>
> *on the shoulders of others . . .*
>
> *you can envision more,*
>
> *dream bigger, and*
>
> *plié deeper,*
>
> *to jump higher."*

"I was really referring to the character itself and what it meant to be inside her skin. As I understand it, *Cry* was created in dedication to all black women everywhere."

"Yes, Rose, I understood your question. You see, if you've never had celebrity status and it's suddenly thrust on you, it changes you internally. You're never the same again. What it did for me was plant my feet on the ground. It reinforced for me the things that are really important in life. I remembered how I got started and all the people who pulled me along. Being a celebrity crystallized that. The public started to look at me as an icon and ask me for autographs. I wasn't really too crazy about that. It's difficult for people to understand that who you are onstage is not really you."

"After experiencing such a successful performance career, was it difficult for you to stop dancing? How did that affect you?"

"It affected me in a wonderful way. I was ready to stop dancing. My body hurt! I burned my candle at both ends and in the middle. That I'm still walking and breathing and still in one piece is a miracle. If you are trying to be the best dancer that you can be, you have a lot of candle burning to do. Concert dancing is hard, really hard. I performed *Cry* twenty-six consecutive times, and it nearly killed me. It was an extremely physical and demanding piece. I tried dancing on Broadway, and that takes your body and mind in a whole other direction, and my body still hurt. I came to a point where I said what I had to say on the stage, and I was finished with that statement."

"You wrote in your autobiography that you were proud to stand on the shoulders of Alvin Ailey. What did you mean exactly?"

"We all need shoulders to stand on," she said. "Alvin stood on the shoulders of Lester Horton and Katherine Dunham. When you stand on the shoulders of others, you can see out to the horizon, because you are uplifted and supported from below. You can envision more, dream bigger, and plié deeper to jump higher."

"Do you think Alvin's dream to create an African American dance tradition has been realized?"

"Alvin's dream was to create an African American tradition of dance in America *and* a modern dance tradition in America. They go hand-in-hand. He did not want to be remembered as an African American choreographer but as a choreographer, and a brilliant one. He thought it was very important that the beauty, intelligence, and drama that people of color have be expressed on the stage and represented as a universal experience. He did not want the African American experience to be seen as parochial or for blacks only. He hoped that all people of color and people in general would understand the validity of the human spirit. The culmination of his trying to do all this is us today, our two performing companies, our school, and continued vision for the future."

"And for you personally what does it mean?"

"When Alvin asked me to take over the direction of the company, naturally I said I would. I didn't know what it meant at the time, but I've always been where I'm supposed to be. And this is where I'm supposed to be, continuing Alvin's American dream and watching a new generation of dancers turn into extraordinary artists."

New York City, 2002

119

Emissary of the Dance

dwight rhoden

I slipped quietly into the rehearsal room at the Ahmanson Theater in Los Angeles.

Dwight Rhoden and co-artistic director Desmond Richardson were doing a run-through of *From Me to You in about Half the Time*. I maneuvered through overstuffed dance bags and parked myself against a mirrored wall. Desmond broke formation and welcomed me with a handshake. Dwight winked a hello without losing sight of the dancers.

"This work," he told them, "deals with personal relationships. There's a certain emotion when there's no turning back. When it's over, it's over. There should be sentiment building to that final moment. When you get into that section, realize this is the last time you will ever relate to this person in this way. Make it have meaning. Now, let's try it again."

At the close of rehearsal Rhoden excused himself and invited me to his dressing room for the interview.

"You articulate very directly what you expect of your dancers."

"I try to come from an honest place. If I feel that something is getting contrived, I'll stop and give them a break or say, 'It's over for today.' I consider myself more of a director, one who is gently pushing the process along and exploring it as I go. Unfortunately, I don't always have the luxury to halt rehearsals just because I may not be feeling productive. Complexions is a project-based company, and therefore we have performance deadlines and monetary obligations. This forces me to be efficient and very clear about what I need from the dancers."

"I get the impression that you can tap into your choreographic voice rather easily. Have you always been able to access your creative side?"

"Yes. I think it stems from a great need to express myself. I felt this way even as a boy. People used to say, 'What a serious child.' I was very intense—didn't play much—and it wasn't because I was unhappy. I was just more keyed in to other things. I grew up in a very creative environment. My mother changed the decor in our house probably three or four times a year, and we were always relocating. I always had crayons and paints. Over the years my mother invested in every musical instrument you can think of, hoping I'd find my thing. She used to say, 'Can you get some focus?' None of them held my interest. But when I found movement, I found out who I really was. Six months after I started dancing, I started choreographing. I was more comfortable expressing myself within a dance than through normal avenues of everyday life. My grandmother was a pianist and very creative. I'm sure all that creativity seeped into me somehow."

"How much of your self do you invest in your choreography?"

"I'm always amazed at how much of myself I expose. I'll often look at the work after the fact and think, 'Oh, my God, I'm practically naked.' I don't set out to be so revealing, but my work instinctively reflects what I'm going through at particular times in my life. I wear my emotions on my sleeve. I created *Higher Ground* to the tunes of Earth Wind and Fire during a very joyful period. I was feeling very creative, and the company was starting to grow and enjoy a good deal of success. I wanted to do something that was a lot of fun and would make people want to get out of their seats and dance."

"What happens choreographically when you're in a more serious mood?"

"A full evening of my choreography can be a lot to take because it takes you through a plethora of emotions. Some of my dances can be very intense, like *Solo*, a piece I created in 1998. The company was only four years old and struggling to be noticed. For me it was about feeling anonymous and not present. Desmond performed it, but I was somewhat embarrassed because it revealed too much. I didn't really want everyone to know that I was down."

"The movement I saw in the rehearsal room today was very powerful—extreme body undulations, warp-speed turns, and jumps, risky jumps, falls, and slides. Are you trying to create a new dance vocabulary?"

"I'm not really conscious of that, although it may be happening without my trying. It's been pointed out to me that Complexions dancers tend to move in a specific way. It's dense, purposely multilayered and thick. My vocabulary is composed of everything that I've ever experienced—modern dance, ballet, jazz, lyrical, funk, and musical theater. We believe in studying pure forms—classical ballet, Graham, Horton, Limón, and Cunningham. Desmond and I work really hard at the how of movement, not the what. There are not that many steps that are new. So for us it's in the timing, the phrasing, the theatricality, and the poetry of the moment."

"Your dancers are considered among the most talented in the world."

"Dancers are my first priority. I feel a responsibility to my dancers to keep them challenged and inspired technically and artistically. I want dancers to feel ownership of the work. I'll take what I know about them and how they move and create from there. I tell them, 'This is a pas de deux. You're leaving your lover. This is the framework. Here are a series of steps, and you have to be off the stage by the end of the music. What you do inside of that space is your own.' Sometimes I say, 'Improvise on that,' and I'll remove myself. I give the dancers a lot of freedom. But not all dancers are comfortable with freedom. Some want to be guided all the way. I respect that, too."

"How do you push the dancers to technical heights without their going over the top and becoming exhibitionistic?"

"It's great to show technical virtuosity, but it has to serve a purpose. I tell my dancers, 'If you're going to add that seventh pirouette, it should be about building up to something. If you're holding a pose for more than two counts, it should be about reaching for something—pushing a thought or expanding an idea. You have choices here, remember why you're doing this.'"

"How much does Desmond enhance what you do?"

"A great deal. Desmond is very much like a poet. He takes my words, which are the steps, and gives them inflection and resonance. Sometimes he may change my words, but he never changes my meaning. Desmond reinterprets movement through brilliant phrasing, and that comes from a deep understanding of the way movement works. He sees his body as a tool for communication and continuously strives to increase his range, move beyond himself, and become more expressive. After thirteen years, he knows what I want and is able to get there very quickly."

"Tell me what it was like to work with Alvin Ailey."

"Alvin was an amazing mentor. When I first got into the Alvin Ailey American Dance Theater, I choreographed a dance for the school. Alvin introduced it in a showcase and refused to let me hide in the back of the room. He made me come out and take bows. I could tell he was really, really proud of me. One time he introduced me to the French choreographer Maurice Béjart and said to him, 'Oh, Béjart, this is our future competition. Watch out for him.' He was always building me up, and his support made me feel great."

"Was there one particular gift he left you with?"

"Yes. If you danced Alvin's work, you came to understand that he liked to leave a lot of room in the choreography for interpretation. He gave the dancers these amazing images to work with and then set them free. This is something that has come into my work. I leave room in the choreography for the dancers to interpret."

"Do today's young dancers understand the concept of freedom within choreographic limitations?"

"No, not really. When I'm at the Ailey School coaching young dancers, I see that they don't get it. They're worried about the arabesque or the big jump. I do like a clean, clear instrument that is technically proficient, but at the same time I'm always pushing them to explore what they're doing and why. I ask them lots of questions. Dancers don't like to talk. I want them to be expressive human beings. If they're not full people, they're not going to be full artists."

"Do you try to convey a message to audiences through your choreography?"

"My message is global unity through dance. The mission of Complexions is to bring artists together to express their uniqueness in culture, race, and background through dance. Coming from a mixed marriage, a real rainbow coalition of a family, I understand what conflict and cooperation are all about. On a larger level, dance has the power to bring people together. If you look beyond the steps, you can see we are all cut from the same cloth. We just look a little different. That's about it."

Los Angeles and New York City, 2001, 2003

Caribbean Man

garth fagan

"My formative years were spent in Jamaica," Garth Fagan told me when we met for an interview

in his uptown New York hotel room. "The rhythms, colors, textures, and fabulous fragrances of the island still stay with me. I spend a fortune on tropical flowers year-round, even in the winter when the snow is deep. The florists in Rochester, New York, where my company is based, love when I order calla lilies and birds of paradise. I also keep a menagerie of birds just to remind me of home. The Caribbean in me is very strong."

The award-winning choreographer of *The Lion King* began his professional dance career in Jamaica and toured with the renowned Ivy Baxter and her national company. Before moving to the United States he was also influenced by Pearl Primus and Lavinia Williams. In America he "fell mercifully under the spell of the great modern dance pioneers: Martha Graham, José Limón, Alvin Ailey, Merce Cunningham, and their wonderful dancers Mary Hinkson, Dudley Williams, Clive Thompson, Mari Kajiwara. I witnessed dance in its finest form and soaked up everything like a sponge."

"I see that you are a repository of dance knowledge, from the Caribbean's great dance masters to America's most celebrated dance pioneers. Do you ever stop to think about whose technique you might be using or whose influence you're drawing from?"

"After all this time their styles are fairly integrated within me. I generally don't worry where something is coming from, I just thank God that it's coming.

125

"Resort to craft when you need to,

but come back later and make sure it's honest."

When I see it, I grab it and hold on to it real tight. Then I bend and twist it and explode it into the form that suits me."

"Where does *The Lion King* fit into your career as a choreographer?"

"The fame I am receiving for *The Lion King* has come late in my career. My focus has been to maintain Garth Fagan Dance, the company I created in 1970. The company has always come first and required a great deal of personal sacrifice. It sounds dramatic, but it's true. It's taken work, work, and more work and necessitated real stamina to cope with the disappointments, rejections, and times when the grants didn't come. As an artistic director, you have many responsibilities, not least of which is caring for your dancers. Dancers commit to you and make big sacrifices for you. Without them, your vision exists only in your head. So you promise them a career and a salary to pay for diapers, food, and doctor's bills. It becomes a very deep, mutually beneficial relationship."

"The drive to create must be very great."

"Yes. It is very, very great. We, the afflicted, quest for the better dance— the fabulous dance—the idiosyncratic dance—the one that goes against the grain. We are always trying to come up with something that hasn't been done before or seen before. I am always trying to break barriers—invent movement and be the original one. It's this chase that keeps me going, keeps me interested."

"What are your dances about?"

"I try to present positive images for African Americans to identify with. I do this only because there are so many negative stereotyped images paraded about us. If you watch TV, you think most black people are drug dealers and murderers. It's a very small percentage of black people who do that, yet that's all you see on the front page of the newspaper. I try to present more positive images. Not heroic or lofty ones—I might just focus on a family that is trying to put a kid through college and pay the mortgage. I think there is a certain kind of heroism in that. Not everyone has to be a Martin Luther King Jr. I also like to ask questions in my work and present alternative ways of thinking, as opposed to dictating my opinions."

"I often hear choreographers say that their work reaches more people when they talk about the truths that affect us all."

"I don't want to take on universal truths. The problem with doing that is that your truth and my truth can be different because our experiences and our perspectives are different. When I put a work on the stage, it has my name on it. That means it is my idea, my expression. I'm only willing to take full responsibility for my own personal truth."

"How do you ensure that your company's public image represents your true artistic vision?"

"I have a company of young, beautiful dancers full of exuberance and energy, as well as seasoned dancers who have been in the trenches for thirty years. There is a tendency to just use the young dancers and throw the others away. I think that is such a mistake. When I look at my stage, I see a community of people of different experiences and walks of life—working, blending together, and even sticking out, and that's okay. Projecting a public image that rings true to my personal vision is tough, because my oil and canvas are people—human beings. They bring into the studio their personal triumphs and tragedies. If they had a fight with their wife, husband, boyfriend, gigolo, lover, parakeet, dog—whatever—they bring it with them and dump it on my lap. They don't do it maliciously, but they bring their emotions to rehearsal and sometimes onto the stage. What can I do? They are not machines. They are human beings."

"Sounds like you really respect your dancers and are very attuned to them. What's it like when you do commissions and don't have the luxury of familiarity and friendship?"

"I try always to handpick the dancers who will perform my work. When I did a work for the New York City Ballet, I chose dancers who I'd seen perform and respected. Because they were not familiar with my style or approach, I tried to gain their trust but at the same time needed to keep them vulnerable so I could shape them. For *The Lion King*, I chose fourteen dancers out of over four hundred. I picked the crème de la crème. Working with puppets and elaborate costumes was a whole new concept for me. I had to take a real hands-on approach with this work because it required a different way of constructing movement and a great deal of creative energy. Many of the dancers had to be hunched over or squatting for long periods as they simulated natural animal movement. I had to keep in mind the dancers' muscles, joints, and alignment in relation to the costumes they were wearing."

"What normally inspires you to start a new work?"

"It varies. Sometimes it begins with an idea, like when I choreographed one of my favorite pieces, *Passion Distanced*. The piece deals with the idea of distancing yourself from painful events in your life. I lost my daughter and tried to put distance in front of that. I found it couldn't be done. One day you think you're over it, and you turn on the radio and hear on the news that someone has thrown a newborn baby in a garbage can. Your heart swells, and it sends you right back to your own passion, your own pain.

"Sometimes I create from movement—movement that bursts out of my own body. I show it to the dancers, and we turn it into something. Sometimes I'll observe a dancer and she looks so beautiful, or he looks so expressive, that I'm moved to create a work for them. Sometimes it's just a sublime piece of music that knocks me out, and I've got to use it. You see, it can be many things."

"What happens when the mood strikes, but the dance won't come? How do you maneuver out of a blocked state and get the process going?"

"Sometimes I start off with something wonderful and end up in a dead end. I might have to discard some or all of it. If I have time, if it's not a deadline on a premier, I leave it alone and come back to it later. If I'm pressed to complete it, then I resort to craft. It doesn't satisfy me, but it keeps the process moving. Later, when I come back to clean and polish it, I often end up saying to myself, 'Hmmm, this was really not so bad,' or 'Oh, this has got to go. What was I thinking?' Resort to craft when you need to, but come back later and make sure it's honest. At this stage in my career I know when truth is knocking."

"What is the most important lesson you've learned?"

"'Do it till you get it right!' I learned that from Martha Graham. I'll never forget when she asked me to go across the floor in a simple unadorned walk. She didn't demonstrate what she wanted. She used images to explain her request. Only after I went back and forth about twelve times did I realize that she wanted me to let go of all that 'look at me aren't I gorgeous' stuff. This taught me to strip down to the real thing, pay attention to the details, and do it until I got it right. When she saw that I finally got it, she clapped her hands and said, 'I think you're going to be going places.'"

"And you did! Let's take your portrait now," I said, noticing Garth checking his watch.

"What would you like me to do?"

"Give me a minute," I said, pretending to fix the lights, but really trying to think how to create an interesting portrait in his humdrum hotel room.

"Stand on the bed," I instructed.

"Okay," he said, as if that were a normal thing to do.

He put on his dark sunglasses for effect and stepped up on the mattress, wobbling from side to side in his platform sneakers.

"What do you think?" he asked, standing on one leg.

"I think you look pretty funny," I said, clicking a few frames. Since he seemed unphased by my first composition idea, I suggested that he recline on one of the upholstered chairs. Within moments our portrait revealed itself.

New York City, 1999

Singing Body

meredith monk

Meredith made it sound so simple. "Just take the N train, get off at Canal Street, and then turn on Broadway, walk up a few blocks, and my building is right there."

What was not so simple, however, was carrying two heavy camera bags on a hot, humid day from the subway station to Meredith's apartment. When I finally arrived, she buzzed me into the foyer and told me her apartment was on the fifth floor.

"There's an elevator, right?" I asked.

"No," she said. "You have to walk up."

I just stood there contemplating the ascent.

A few minutes later Meredith called down from the top floor. "Rose, where are you? Are you down there?"

"Meredith," I shouted, "you didn't tell me you lived at the top of Mount Everest. I could use a sherpa about now."

"Oh, I'm sorry. I see you have heavy bags. I wish I could help you, but I have a bad back."

"It's okay. I'll get there eventually. Just get ready to call the paramedics."

By the time I reached the fifth floor, I was woozy and my clothes were drenched. Meredith guided me through her front door and sat me down in a chair. After handing me a glass of water, she fanned me with a magazine. I felt embarrassed in the face of her kindness now. When the room stopped spinning, I told her I was feeling better, and we moved into her spacious studio, where the light was pouring in from a side window. It was an ideal space to photograph her.

Even though she had already done her morning exercises, she offered to show me how she warms up her voice. She pulled a standing microphone into the light and demonstrated how she "dances" the voice, using its quality, pitch, and range. I photographed her from various angles, amazed at her vocal capability. After shooting each roll of film I paused for an explanation.

"The voice," she said, "is as flexible as the body, and the body is as articulate as the voice. I call my process dancing voice/singing body." She explained her interest in working "between the cracks," finding powerful moments between the musical notes or movement phrases.

"What drives your work and keeps you interested?"

"My work is all about letting go of expectations and seeing things you might take for granted, or being open to deep memory and emotions we don't have words for. The work encourages the viewer to temporarily drop out the discursive part of the mind, which is always evaluating or trying to understand things in a linear way. My work is more like poetry of the senses. I've tried to open up the idea of movement as an expressive medium within a larger context that includes a theater of images, sounds, vocalizations, and gesture. I think I've opened up ideas about what else dance can be."

"I would imagine the dance audience is particularly responsive to your work."

"I love the dance audience because they understand nonverbal communication. They tend to be the most open-minded and openhearted. They understand the language of the body and, because my singing is also very kinetic, they understand the language of the voice. For me the body and the voice are one."

"When you begin to work on a performance piece, how do you know when you're following the right creative impulse?"

"It's like tending a garden. You throw seeds into the ground. Some plants will grow and others won't. All you can do is nurture it and then just get out of the way and wait. I don't decide in advance what something is going to be or how it will look. Part of the creative process is discovering what shape or form the thing will take. I spend a lot of time hanging out in the unknown. That's what keeps me interested."

"Are you particularly conscious of working within a given style, your style?"

"Your whole life is about developing your own style. But as soon as you start thinking, 'This has to be my style,' you start repeating yourself. My pieces are recognizable because there is a style, but I don't consciously try to create in my own style. When the work has a certain level of honesty and authenticity, it's always going to come from the deepest part of your nature, and that, I think, is what allows style to happen."

"Do you ever create work that surprises you, when you say. 'Hey, that's unusual for me'?"

"Each piece is a world in itself. When you decide to hang out in the unknown the way I do, you're basically throwing everything away and starting from zero. That's the hardest thing to do, because we all have a past, and ultimately it gets in the way. We are who we are, so whatever we do, we will put our own stamp on it. My goal as I go along is to start from the freshest place that I can and try to explore new areas and new dimensions."

"I've found that many prolific artists tend to be obsessive in their work. Do you think it's helpful to be obsessive?"

"I enjoy obsessive energy. Over the years the tone of my obsessive behavior has changed slightly, but it has retained the same kind of urgency. I like it when my whole energy is devoted to the world that I'm working in. Some pieces make themselves, as if they have a life force of their own. With others you have to fully rely on your craft, and of course that's a lot harder, but the obsession is still there regardless. You know, Rose, I love these questions, because I see they are questions you personally need answers to."

"Yes, I do. I think when you have burning questions it makes sense to seek out those who might have the answers."

"That's interesting, because most artists don't have the answers. Creativity is a mystery to all of us. Some artists work in manufacturing. Those are the ones that are product-oriented. I feel like I'm in R and D, research and development. I need a lot of time to create because I'm basically deep-sea diving every piece. Sometimes I get exasperated with myself because I wish I could produce more work and that it could come easier. But really what keeps me going are those unanswered questions and moments of discovery."

"How do you cope with the highs and lows of the artist's life?"

"You just cope. I've had years when I've had so much doubt. Sometimes I

"Practicing your craft daily

leads to amazing moments of inspiration."

ask myself why can't I be like those artists who do their work and never question themselves. But then I realize that doubt is part of the process. Every time I've had doubt and asked the right questions, like what is missing or why am I so unhappy, I've felt a surge of energy. I realized that what I needed was to go back to a more playful process and that I'd been taking it all too seriously. When you take on a creative challenge, you are really charting a new path. You're stumbling along on the path with no one to guide you. Sometimes you just hover like a helicopter until you find your way, and only then do you land. I'm lucky because I have people in my ensemble who tolerate this tedious process with me. They're like midwives who help me through labor and the birthing process."

"So it's important to have people with whom to collaborate?"

"Yes. When I'm doing a group piece, I love working and interacting with my ensemble, but first I need a lot of solitude and preparation time. I require at least a year or so before I go into rehearsal with a new work. When I'm working on a solo piece, it's a lot like being a painter, except a painter can step back and look at his work."

"I think you would agree that your first responsibility is to your art. Is your next responsibility to your audience?"

"You want to be authentic to yourself and work toward some sort of per-

fection, even though you realize perfection can never be fully realized. At the same time you want your work to communicate. But an audience is made up of individuals, so what I try to do is set up a situation that is very evocative, and within that, people can respond in their own way. I think it's a fairly nonmanipulative and openhearted approach. My work is different from, let's say, something you might see on Broadway. Broadway shows are directed toward mass appeal, with specific and predictable responses."

"What are some of the most important lessons that you've learned along the way?"

"Making art is not about the ego. It's about letting go of the ego and staying out of the way of your art, so that whatever is coming through can come through. You're really a catalyst for energy, and you should give the work what it needs and not be afraid to go where it takes you. I've learned also that one of the most important things you can do for yourself as an artist is tend to your artistic development. Practicing your craft daily leads to amazing moments of inspiration."

New York City, 2000

131

Choreographer Incognito

moses pendleton

It was raining heavily when I pulled up in front of Moses Pendleton's New England farmhouse.

The front door was open, so I walked in and called out, "Hello. Hello?"

Moses bounded down the stairs and welcomed me with a grand wave of his hand and the smile of a seasoned stage performer.

"Moses," I said, meeting him for the first time, "you know, you bear a striking resemblance to General Ulysses S. Grant. No, wait a minute! Vincent van Gogh."

"Yes, well, Grant is actually an ancestor of mine. I may have inherited some of his features. And I think I share some of the madness of van Gogh—so therein lies the resemblance."

"I see. Well, maybe we'll be able to capture that on film."

"I hope you can. You picked a pretty dark and wet day to take pictures."

"Yes, this New England weather is intense."

He led me into a living room full of unmatched furniture and the clutter of a person who spends much of his life on the road. One corner warehoused performance props and theatrical sets; another served as a repository of books, magazines, papers, and posters. If the room had one iconic theme it was sunflowers. Past their bloom, they drooped pathetically from vases and old jars atop tables and bookshelves.

Moses walked around the room lighting strategically placed candles to create a séancelike atmosphere. Then, without a word he left the room. Ten minutes later he returned, holding two steaming mugs of coffee scented with maple syrup.

"Wait a minute. I know this flavor. Danny Ezralow made coffee for me that tasted just like this."

"We are very close friends. Years ago we danced together. I introduced him to the idea of sweetening coffee with maple syrup. Come, why don't we sit here on the sofa?" he said, pulling a tape recorder from his pocket and placing it next to mine on the coffee table. "Just so I know what we talked about," he said, pressing the Record button.

"Does living here in Washington, Connecticut, free you from the distractions of city life, fuel you creatively?"

"Yes. I follow the natural cycles of New England and experience the seasons ritualistically. Living in this old house with my family, eating home-cooked meals, and enjoying heirlooms like this old Oriental rug that belonged to my grandfather are a great inspiration. I believe we are natural extensions of our environment and, as you can see, I happen to also thrive on chaos. In fact, I made a film once about the chaos of a messy room. I realize that there is a limit to mess before it really begins to shut you down. Fortunately, I have people who take care of scheduling and logistics when it comes to running Momix."

"How would you describe Momix to someone who has never seen the company perform?"

"Momix is visual theater that uses bodies, light, music, props, and ideas of stagecraft to make a show that is evocative and stimulating. The work is abstract and at the same time fanciful. We have humans doing things that are not human, with references to plants, animals, and minerals, even architecture. We've been accused of doing things that have no relationship to humanity, but when I see one of our dancers create a beautiful abstract form made of pure muscle, it can bring tears to my eyes. That's human."

"Are you on a choreographic quest?"

"I try to be a catalyst for choreography. I set up performance situations through improvisational play. I never go into the studio with a particular dance phrase in mind. I'm not interested in literal work or making shapes in the mirror. I'm more interested in a spontaneous reaction to various stimuli that often include music or props. My studio is wired with quadraphonic sound and set up with video cameras to record everything we do. If we can excite ourselves in the studio, perhaps a greater audience will find it interesting as well."

"When you set up these play improvisations, do you anticipate a particular outcome?"

"I never say where the work should go, but I like to entertain with humor, irony, and slightly irreverent behavior. There is a natural humor to much of my work, the humor of surprise encased in some utopian dreamlike vision."

"What do you look for in the dancers who perform your work?"

"I look for dancers who have full dance capabilities and possess what I call Joe-Action; that means they inherently possess some kind of spark. There is a quality in that person that catches your eye and makes you want to follow them. The other important requirement is that they appreciate the humor of their director. If they laugh at my jokes, then they're in."

"Ah, I see. What does your work reveal about you?"

"Probably that I don't want to reveal myself. Maybe that's why my work is so abstract. Choreography is a good mask for my internal operation."

"What keeps you in dance?"

"I think if I didn't stay connected with my body, I'd probably be a drug addict or have committed suicide years ago. Even now, I spend 80 percent of every day working my body, whether it's running, swimming, or bicycling. It keeps me grounded; otherwise I live too much in the mind, and for me that's dangerous."

"Can you recall the first time you realized the power of the body-mind connection?"

"Yes, when I won the Vermont Cross-Country State Race in 1967. I was skiing under adverse conditions and got off the starting line thirty seconds late. I was so enraged that it pushed me to another physical level. I experienced a second and then a third wind. I realized that the body can do much more than the mind thinks it can. It was this athletic courage that helped me win the race."

"So you applied this concept to dance?"

"Yes. I found that it could serve choreography very well. It's based on the principle of 'push.' Push harder, break that barrier, get to your second or third wind, and you enter a sort of spiritual automatic pilot. It occurs when your natural endorphins are released. Athletes call it 'getting in the zone.' They can do almost superhuman feats, drilling three-pointers one right after the other. Robin Williams does it with verbal improvisation. He becomes like a medium for many other voices. The idea is to pick up the spirit and the energy, channel it, and then increase your flame."

"How do you apply 'push' on a personal level?"

"I run five miles every day, faithfully. And while I'm running, I free-associate or 'rap,' if you will, into a tape recorder. I believe if you stimulate the mind through the body, then the mind can stimulate the body. Once that body goes into its second and third wind, it can push the brain further. So what I do through verbal discharge is like panning for gold. You've heard the expression 'My life flashed before my eyes'? I talk myself into a physical state to the point where I envision my life in the same way one does who's having a near-death experience. I do this as part of my daily routine. I come back with some pretty intense findings and then listen to them the next day for important sound bites. I keep literally thousands of recorded tapes. See that old trunk over there?" He pointed across the room. "It's filled with hundreds and hundreds of hours of early Pilobolus 1970s improvisations." (Pendleton was a cofounder of Pilobolus along with Jonathan Wolken, Michael Tracy, Robby Barnett, Alison Chase, and Martha Clarke.)

"In other words, you take your psychological and emotional pulse on a daily basis and record it for creative use. That's pretty unusual."

"Well, it is, but it enables me to go out on creative expeditions while still attached to an umbilical chord. Recording my nondeliberate stream-of-consciousness ramblings assures me that I can get back again; otherwise madness would set in, and I'd probably never return. Listening to the tape the next day to recharge myself is part of my workout."

"Do you feed these sound bites into the choreography of Momix?"

"Not necessarily. What I'm doing is archiving the drama in my head. General Ulysses S. Grant didn't have a life until he began to write it down and record its meaning. That's part of what I do, only on tape."

"Moses, why all these dead sunflowers?"

"The sunflower stabilizes me. They're fascinating in terms of their construction and vibrancy, and there are no two exactly alike. When I meditate on a sunflower it takes me to a state beyond myself. I'm passionate about them and suffer when they wilt or are consumed by deer. I have a two-acre sunflower garden and draw strength and inspiration from it. I've been accused of spending more time in the garden than in the studio. Making dances is not my only interest. Frankly, I'm just as inclined to grow sunflowers."

"What drives you so hard? Why so much 'push'?"

"I have a great fear that I won't be able to satisfy my urges to attain greater knowledge. There is still so much that I don't know. I'm very disturbed that I haven't seen the greater light."

"Do you know what you're looking for?"

"The fourth wind. I'm looking for the fourth wind. But I don't know how to find it. Not yet."

"It's getting late," I said. "Why don't we spend some time on your portrait?"

Moses left the room to change his clothes. I scouted the property for an appropriate photo environment. The rain had slowed to a drizzle. When he returned, we went outdoors to grab a few shots in his off-season sunflower garden, but the cold soon forced us back into the house. We ended up in his second-story stairwell. Above the landing, diffused light entering the beveled-glass windows created a luminous glow. A dried sunflower that had been propped up next to the banister hung like a showerhead over the stairs. Masks made of plaster decorated the opposite wall between long strands of peeling wallpaper. Moses stepped into the scene and threw his gaze away from the camera as if to deflect its probing eye. The photograph composed itself.

Washington, Connecticut, 1999

135

Dance Painter

lar lubovitch

I had been cautioned that Lar Lubovitch was intense and serious. So when I met him at the security guard station
of the American Ballet Theater building on Broadway, I was relieved to see that he had not shaved that morning and was dressed casually in a black polo shirt and jeans. He lifted my box of photo gear and hauled it up a flight of stairs to the next floor. I followed, weighed down by camera bags. We unloaded and sat down at a round table. I chose my questions carefully.

"Do you think you can articulate what it means to be a choreographer today in the postmodern dance era?"

Lubovitch objected to being categorized. "I don't feel that I am a choreographer within any given era. I just feel that I've been evolving according to my own aesthetic from the time I began making dances over thirty years ago. I've been moving at my own speed and within my own needs and interests."

"Do you feel any pressure to move the art form along or leave behind a prolific body of work?"

"I have no external pressure that I respond to or that has influenced me to make particular artistic choices. I do have a great deal of pressure within myself to stay interested and move beyond where I was when I started."

"How does one stay interested and focused?"

"For me, I think it has to do with constantly looking for visual experiences, which in my case includes an emotional, spiritual, or physiological component. I think what I do best is exercise my ability to visualize movement, to see

137

inside with an inner eye and then materialize outwardly what the eye is seeing. I consider myself more a movement painter than a choreographer. I come from an art background. I painted and sculpted from the time I was very young. My reference to shape and space has in many ways a greater relationship to my experiences as a visual artist than as someone who puts steps together."

"Why did you feel the need to shift from paint and clay to movement?"

"When I saw dance for the first time, I knew immediately that I wanted to be a choreographer. Dance completely captivated me. From then on, I felt compelled to paint with movement instead of paints and sculpt with bodies instead of clay. In order to do that, I had to become a dancer. I needed to learn the world of dance and its language. I was twenty years old when I began studying dance."

"So you abruptly chose a new creative path?"

"Yes. There are times in your life when your eyes are wide open. You see the right path, so you take it. But it is frightening to take an unintended path. You have to find your way in the dark. Everything challenges you to take another road. Your will and integrity are tested at every turn. There's no one to pat you on the back and say, 'I believe in what you're doing.' The artist is always met by a prevailing energy that prevents him from doing what he must to fulfill himself. One sees this throughout history with political upheavals. Every time a fascist dictatorship comes into power, the very first thing they do is subjugate the artist, because artists are purveyors of free will. Free will is always being tested."

"Have you been able to remain solidly on the dance path?"

"Well, that's an interesting question, because I just became aware of a film that shows my very first choreographed work. It was shot at the University of Iowa, where I was an art major. I performed a solo. When I viewed the film, I realized that I haven't been doing anything all that different from the time I started thirty years ago. What I did then without thinking, I've been doing in one way or another ever since. I feel very enriched by that and take it as some small piece of evidence that I've remained on the same path all this time."

"What do you reveal about yourself in your work? What do you hold back?"

"My work isn't focused on myself. It's not intended to say things on a personal level. I'm more interested in taking subject matter and exploring it. No doubt I'm revealing and holding back a variety of things, but not on a conscious level. I do know, however, that I try to keep feelings of resentment from entering into my work. Art never comes from hate. I don't believe it's a source, I believe it's an impediment. I also avoid irony. Irony in art is so highly admired, but it is just an excuse for sarcasm and cynicism. Too often people are afraid to commit to their emotions, dreams, and hopes. They use irony as a defense mechanism and build a wall between themselves and their true feelings. I find this quite prevalent in dance. It seems to me a fairly limited point of view."

"Ever have the equivalent of writer's block, as though you might dry up creatively?"

"It's happened to me many times. I didn't know where an idea would come from, or if I could make up another dance. I don't know how I've done it till now, so I don't know how I'll do it the next time. It's a mystery to me. I don't know how to 'choreograph,' if you want to use the popular word. Each time I make a dance, I have to reinvent how to do it. It's not really different every time, but I don't seem to remember the process. I don't know what I know. I know many things, but none I could put down on a list of how-tos."

"Do you care what people think about your work?"

"Be patient with the process . . .

Be patient with yourself.

Quiet all your fears and take the time it takes to create.

Own up to your true voice and trust that what you make is unique

and has a place in the world."

"Yes, I do care. I care a lot. When I make a dance, it comes from a very deep place, so I do hope that people will accept it and even love it. It hurts me very badly if people hate my work. I feel bruised and very vulnerable."

"Anytime you expose yourself creatively or otherwise, you set yourself up for criticism. That's just the risk you take, isn't it?"

"I feel it's a small risk to withstand people's criticism. You're not really risking all that much, because you are a privileged person if you've had a life in the arts. You've had the opportunity to create beauty, to create art. This is the most wonderful of opportunities. If you are going to create, you're going to create whether it's an obsession or the utilization of a gift. You're not really risking the real source, only some external manifestation that comes along for the ride. Nothing will stop you if you are of the spirit to create. There could be momentary setbacks because of the pain of some opinion, but the drive of the artist will regenerate itself because that's who he is."

"With your thirty-eight years in dance and thirty as a choreographer, what would you say is the most important lesson you've learned along the way?"

"I've learned to be patient—patient with the process and patient with myself. I struggle with this because frequently my impatience has gotten in the way of my being true to myself. I've wanted things to happen quickly and have gone too fast. I've learned not to take shortcuts and not to do things out of fear just to get them out of the way. The only way to create that unique thing is to be patient. Quiet all your fears, own up to your true voice, take the time that it takes to create, and have trust that what you make is unique and has a place in the world."

The time had come for the portrait. I had scouted the building the day before and set my sights on some old theatrical trunks stored in one of the back rooms. I thought they might make an interesting backdrop. Lar agreed. I set up a couple of strobes and had him find a comfortable pose leaning up against the trunks. But the minute I started shooting, I felt a wall go up between us. He had turned distant and restless. He looked like he just wanted to get out, despite the rapport we had established earlier. I remembered the stairwell with its Art Deco banister of twisted grillwork. I finished the roll and said, "Let's move into the stairwell." Lar seemed surprised that I wanted to relocate, but he offered no resistance.

I carried my lights, power pack, and cords into the stairwell and reconfigured the lighting setup while Lar looked on. I suggested that he stand on the landing. He looked uneasy. It seemed that he wanted to be photographed but not seen. I put my camera down on one of the steps and walked up very close to him and whispered, "Why are you avoiding me?"

"If you really want to know who I am," he said, "you have to see my work." I remembered what he'd told me about his choreography. "My work is curvaceous," he said, "because there are no straight lines in the universe. All of space is curved, and so are all of my dances."

I suddenly understood that a portrait of Lar Lubovitch without reference to his work was like movement without direction. I went back to my camera, lifted the viewfinder to my eye, and shot a Polaroid of him through the banister's circular shapes. I pulled the Polaroid out of the camera and waited for the image to develop. The sixty seconds of silence was a welcome respite. I peeled off the emulsion backing. There it was. I walked down several steps and handed him the Polaroid. He studied his likeness, showing no emotion.

Finally he looked me in the eye and said simply, "Yes!"

New York City, 1999

139

Movement Maven

"There is a big difference between
creating art and getting therapy."

murray louis

Murray motioned me into his Greenwich Village apartment and pointed at the sofa in his sitting room.

He had grown a handsome mustache since our photo session four years earlier.

"Let me just finish this conversation," he whispered. "I'm on the phone with my publisher."

He was no doubt talking about his upcoming book, *The Unique Gesture,* a philosophical manual and autobiographical account of his forty-five-year collaboration with Alwin Nikolais.

"Nik's piece should precede mine," Murray insisted. "His section flows, and mine breaks frequently as I describe technique and approach. No! You don't understand. This is how I want it!"

The conversation continued for several more minutes, allowing me to focus my attention on his fine collection of paintings, figurines, and porcelains.

"Yes, my dear. So sorry to keep you waiting. As you heard, I spend lots of time giving my publisher hell."

"Retirement agrees with you, then."

"I'm seventy-six now," he said, taking a seat next to me. "I quit dancing ten years ago, and it was enough. I danced on the stage for fifty years. I've done everything, traveled everywhere, met everyone in the world of any consequence. I made a lot of money, and I was very happy. I had no reason to bemoan leaving the profession. I had always planned to write after my retirement. For me now it's a summation of fifty years in dance and a way for me to link together the events in my life."

"You're not interested in directing a performance group to extend your shelf life?"

"No, I'm not, and that's not possible anyway. Only a few choreographers, like Nijinsky, Isadora Duncan, Martha Graham, and Fred Astaire, will be remembered beyond this century. A new generation comes up every twenty years, and they have to learn from scratch about the great dance choreographers. The people who teach them are going to teach only the names they know and the steps they themselves can do well. So the generation, after that limited learning, is going to be dancing to an even more codified version. Look at the Graham technique, for example. It's now in about its seventh generation but hardly reflective of the initial material, and that's only because of the way it's been taught."

"I've always been struck by your dances because of their unusual movement-within-movement quality. It runs through all your work, pure movement in time and space with effort and shape."

"You describe what I did beautifully and appear to have understood it. I create out of a palette I make for each point of view, and then I put together the principles: the time of it, the shape of it, the space of it, and the movement motif. The other important ingredient is finding people who can perform these principles, who understand movement the way I understand movement. One of Nik's greatest contributions to the art form was that he acknowledged that dance was an abstract art and that its message lay within what you did—not within an imposed message on top of it. If you lifted an arm with the idea of releasing from gravity or with tension, or suspension, the message was going on inside the movement. The message rested within the lifted arm. It was not being done as a passive, sweet gesture because that implied a message. Is that clear?"

"Yes."

"There was a word for it. It was called motion. Motion became the thing to be experienced and viewed. Inside the shape there was a vibrancy, a motion going on, or an attitude. The message came with the shape. Making that clarification enabled one to work cleanly with the abstract principles of the art form. Motion existed in space and time. You could reach into it, you could form it, and you could deal with it. Motion became inclusive in all the principles. You still with me?"

"Yes. But what happened if you performed all these motion-endowed principles to tell a story?"

"Then you were dealing with narrative. I wasn't interested in that because the ego of the performer and the lazy imagery of the viewer lead to very benign messages. The viewer begins to read into the work; it's him experiencing this, and she did this and they did that, all out of nothing but their own Rorschach. The stimulation of their own sensory processes produced nothing new in them. They fell back into it's a boy and a girl and he's turning her down. I found all those easy narratives and the performing of them a distraction to the viewer who might otherwise witness a wide range of experiences and insights."

"Often choreographers want to use their art for self-expression or to tell their own story. But that was not your interest?"

"I'm skeptical about people who put too much of themselves into their work because they drown that fragile work of art with their own problems. There is a big difference between creating art and getting therapy. I look for the motion, not the emotion. The emotion of the piece comes out of the motion of the piece."

"If your pieces were highly abstract, how did viewers understand your intention or motivation for creating the work? Did you provide notes in the program?"

"I took my thematic material from things I was familiar with. Listen, I'm a human being. My head thinks a certain way, and my heart feels various emotions, but I present abstract work. I never provided notes, only a title. I didn't care what people read into my dances. That's not my job as an artist. All I needed was an audience with an open mind."

"How do you define art?"

"A stimulus to the soul. To experience and re-experience that which will feed the soul and encourage interior growth."

"How did you discover this way of thinking?"

"It was Nik. He was my mentor. When we met, he was just beginning to formulate his theories of movement within movement. He was well versed in the craft of dance, lighting, music, and theater. He attended workshops at Bennington College with Martha Graham, Doris Humphrey, Hanya Holm, Charles Weidman, Louis Horst, even John Martin, the dance critic. He became interested in Rudolf Laban's work of movement notation and studied under Hanya Holm, who focused on the human body exclusively. She was a proponent of Mary Wigman and had that German insistence on purity. When she taught, she did not fill it with emotional motivations. This particularly appealed to Nik, who had seen Wigman perform in the 1930s and never forgot its authenticity of form. Everyone else's technique at the time brimmed with emotional diversions. Nikolais wanted the clarity of form and the performance of that clarity to make the motion come alive. His idea was to get the dancer to feel the form. Even though he had a dance company in his early years, he was not a dancer. When we met I was young and had nothing cluttering my mind. I immediately grasped his thinking. I realized all the physical things on the stage that he couldn't do. I was able to evidence his techniques and theories. I was able to push his thinking and he mine."

"Sounds like an incredible fusion of thought and application."

"It was a physical, mental, and emotional fusion. We were two minds in one body, like a two-headed creature. He understood theatricality and lit everything that I did. When the curtain went up, he sat back and I carried the ball. I danced our collaborative work. I consulted with him on movement construction because he knew what I was working toward. The work with Nik gave me a verbalization for what I was doing. I could teach it. I could talk about it. I could do it. It gave me independence and the ability to express myself, the way a painter does not have to describe the color red or green or yellow."

"Do you think you could have had this type of artistic collaboration if it were not also an intimate one?"

"Nik was sixteen years older than I. We lived together. We trusted each other and believed in each other. And he was always there for me. I don't think our creative work could have gone as far as it did if we'd had two different focuses. With a common focus we were able to completely enhance ourselves. We kept separate identities, but art was primary in our minds at all times.

"I've exhausted you with all this talk. How about a cup of coffee?"

"Yes, that would be great."

I followed Murray into his kitchen and kept him company while he ground the beans and filled the coffeemaker.

"Murray," I said as he poured me a cup, "I'm very curious about all the great dancers and choreographers I never got a chance to meet. You knew many of them personally. Can you give me some quick impressions of what they were like?"

"Sure. Who do you have in mind?"

"José Limón?"

"José was a wonderful guy who managed to live through the quicksand of all the females that surrounded him. They fed off him because he was so magnificent and kind. He was a wonderfully lusty Native American boy. I enjoyed him enormously. We got along extremely well."

"Hanya Holm?"

"Hanya was a Dutch housewife, clean to the bone. She was meticulous and fierce and possessive. She could make you do pliés until you wanted to die. I'm sure she knew she was torturing those kids."

"Eric Hawkins?"

"Eric was an erudite dancer. He was like a Greek scholar. He had a very strong philosophy about movement. He looked for the purity of action and the fulfillment of movement, which was very much like my work. We therefore got along very well."

"Rudolf Nureyev?"

"Rudolf left Russia to hang on to the lifeline of dance, and he did. He was an absolute slave to the dance and therefore a victim of his own profession. He couldn't get away from it. His regime and touring schedule were mind-boggling. That's all he knew, that's all he had. The stage was his everything."

"Martha Graham?"

"I never got to know Martha very well because I was not in her company. She represents the sacrifice an artist must have, the soul-searching an artist must do, and the work an artist must commit himself to. She represented integrity in the profession. She is the symbol of modern dance the way the eagle is the symbol of the United States of America.

"You can understand what a close profession this used to be. We all shared the same passion and problems, like the lack of money and space. We pondered the questions of art and pushed as hard as we could to break ground. Things are very different now."

I finished my coffee and thanked Murray for taking time away from yelling at his publisher to answer my questions. He told me not to worry, he planned on picking up the phone as soon as I left.

New York City, 1999, 2003

Servant of the Dance

"You can learn all the elements of choreography:

form, structure, and musicality. Beyond that, you've

got to have talent. Talent is a gift. It is God-given."

mary anthony

Mary placed her feet in a perfect first position, her arms and hands rounded as if conditioned through muscle memory.
She waited till the room fell silent and all heads were turned in her direction.

"Demi plié," she instructed, demonstrating a bend at the knees. With my lens poised, I weaved in and out through a row of students, clicking images of the eighty-three-year-old dance master. But sometime between the pliés and the *tendus,* I placed my camera against a wall, rolled my jeans above the ankle, and took second position. It had been twenty-five years since I had taken a modern dance class. Mary turned her head slowly in my direction and nodded as if to say, "Welcome home."

She guided us through grand pliés, leg brushes, Pilates mat exercises, and barre and across-the-floor work. My limbs and torso knew exactly where to go and what to do. Why had I stopped dancing? I couldn't remember.

I returned to Mary's studio the next day for our interview and removed my shoes at her request. She told me it was her way of keeping out the city dirt and shifting awareness from the ordinary to the sacred world of art. She invited me to sit down in her small kitchen and offered me sweet biscuits and hot tea served in china that had once belonged to her grandmother.

"Walking into your dance studio is like entering a temple or shrine," I said.

"I purposely create an environment where people can explore their relationship to their art. I encourage students to know who they are and why they are here. When they ask, 'Can I become a dancer?' I tell them no one can make you a dancer. But if you have that need, no one can stop you."

"Taking your class yesterday affected me deeply," I said. "Your reverential approach to the movement and your relationship with the students brought up feelings in me I haven't felt in years. You reminded me how wonderful it is to work inside the body."

"A teacher must be so sensitive to their students, she can hear grass grow. People often comment about my teaching. I tell them it's because I've been teaching for 100 years, even though it's been only a little over 65. When you've done it as long as I have, you develop a trained eye to see who needs to be loved and touched and who needs a swift swat."

"You are sensitive but also very respectful of your students."

"My approach is more a reaction to my own training than anything else. I was trained by Hanya Holm. She was very, very strict and very German. One could never do anything right—never. Then one day I saw George Balanchine rehearsing his dancers, and it opened my eyes. He never raised his voice, never shouted, and always respected his dancers. He'd say to them in a gentle manner, 'Try it this way, dear. If it doesn't work on this foot, we can change it.' I decided then and there that I wanted dancers to love what they were doing. I didn't want to beat it or shout it into them. If you want to dance, you're going to do it because you love it and for no other reason."

"When did you first discover dance?"

"I was about fifteen when my gymnastics teacher took a bunch of her students to see a dance concert. Martha Graham was doing a solo, with Louis Horst at the piano. Half the audience left at intermission, but I was absolutely stricken by the performance. I left Kentucky at the age of eighteen and came to New York to study with Martha. But when I arrived at her studio, I was told that she didn't give scholarships to women, only to men. I had very little money. So I went to the Humphrey-Weidman Studio and begged them to let me take class. 'I'll wash windows, I'll do anything,' I told them. Pauline Lawrence, one of their dancers, who would later become the wife of José Limón, laughed at me. She said, 'I'd like to see someone make it in New York on twenty-five dollars.' I didn't know what to do and started to cry. Charles Weidman came over to me and told me that he had heard that Hanya Holm was giving an audition and if I was chosen I could receive three years of free training. So I auditioned and Hanya picked me."

"Had you had any formal dance training prior to that?"

"No. I had to learn from the ground up, and Hanya was a strict disciplinarian, very tough. I'll never forget one day I came to her after having my wisdom teeth pulled; my mouth was packed with cotton. I said, 'Hanya, would it be all right if I don't take class today?' She looked straight at me and asked, 'Why?' That's how she was. I would eventually teach her technique and perform in her company. She was never the artist that Martha was, but had I ended up with Martha early in my training, I never would have developed my own individuality."

"Why? Was Martha's technique so all-consuming?"

"Martha's grip was very powerful and very sexual. Once you study her technique it takes ten years to get it out of your system. Through its constant repetition, it's very hard to find out who you are and discover how you really want to move. I often compare the two techniques this way: The Graham dancer does simple movement, repeat; more-complicated movement, repeat; more-complicated movement, repeat. The Holm dancer does exploration, exploration, exploration, exploration. Hanya did not believe in copying others. She believed that artistic growth came from exploration."

"When you speak of exploration, are you referring to improvisation?"

"Yes, but not like the kind of touch improvisation you see today. She would set a structure, and you would improvise within that structure. Hanya had a very strict technique, as strict as a ballet class. She might ask you to create a rhythm and then find a movement to go with that rhythm. We'd then be asked to perform it. With Martha's technique you became Martha. With Hanya's technique you became yourself. I will always be grateful to Hanya for that."

"So Hanya was your primary dance influence?"

"Oh, no. My greatest influence was Martha Graham. She's the reason I came to New York. I wasn't able to study with her until much later, but I learned her technique through Jane Dudley and Sophie Maslow, two of her most accomplished pupils. Jane Dudley finally said to me one day, 'It's time you go to the horse's mouth.' So I eventually took class from Martha in the late 1940s."

"You told me on the phone that you and Anna Sokolow also worked together."

"Yes. Anna taught choreography in my studio for twenty years. I observed every class she taught and learned from watching her. She had her early training with Martha and Louis Horst, and all that was present in her teaching and choreography. Together she and I explored the fundamental elements of form and content. I would have students explore choreography through very structured improvisation. She would have them state a theme, choose a piece of music, and develop that theme. Once a month I'd convert the studio into a performance space with black curtains and wings so that our students experienced the art of theater and the path leading to performance."

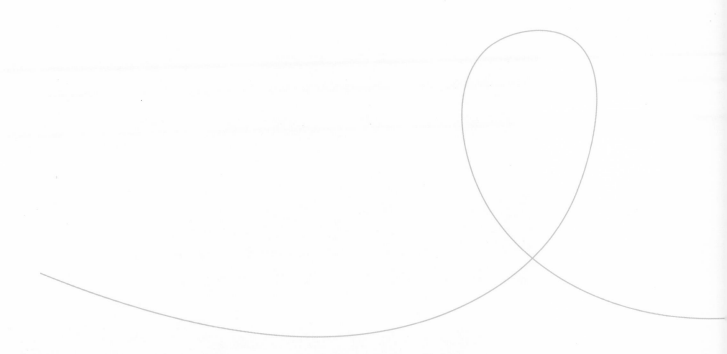

"I've always been under the impression that choreography cannot be taught."

"You can teach all the elements of choreography—form, structure, and music. Beyond that, you have to have talent. I've seen some wonderful performers attempt choreography but fail because they simply did not have the talent for it. I'm not critical of that. Talent is a gift. It is God-given."

"Is it possible to teach someone how to perform?"

"You can teach a dancer to go out on the stage, execute choreography, and understand the art of theater. But you can't teach a performer to communicate or connect with an audience. That comes inherently from within. The great dancers have this. I've known people with a wonderful instrument, but they failed as performers because they were not compelled to reach out to an audience. The true artist wants to give. That's why it's called 'giving a performance.'"

"Tell me about your company, the Mary Anthony Dance Theater."

"I modeled much of my work after the Greek concept of total theater, where there is no line between acting and dancing. If I have dancers they have to act, and if I have actors they have to dance. I'm drawn to dramatic presentation, and this is present in all my works, like *Threnody*, which is based on *Riders to the Sea*." (This one-act play is by Irish playwright John Millington Synge.)

"So many dancers coming through this studio. Do today's young dancers exhibit the same passion and commitment you had when you started out?"

"No, not at all. And it's not necessarily their fault. We are living in a very fractured age. Most young dancers, actors, and singers do not have the love and understanding of how hard you have to work for your art. If you are successful and receive a steady salary and benefits, then it's easy to be committed. It's much harder if you have to wait tables and walk dogs just for the privilege of dancing for virtually no pay. Today's young people do not want to be starving artists, and I don't blame them. Eventually they become physical therapists or Pilates instructors just to pay their rent."

"What's the secret to becoming a truly great dancer?"

"Some believe if you take enough classes it will make you a great dancer. But I can tell you that's not the case. A great dancer is one who sees movement and experiences it from the deepest part of their being. If you don't see movement, you don't see sunsets, you don't see stars, you don't see people. You have to train your eye to see the medulla oblongata—that's the last entrance of the spinal cord into the brain. It's what causes you to jump out of the way of a speeding car. It's pure and without thought. I'm talking about the animal part of your nature."

Mary suddenly leaned over and whispered, "This is what you dance with."

New York City, 1999

Socrates of Dance

bill t. jones

I met Bill T. Jones and his partner, Bjorn Amelan, outside the Aaron Davis Hall in Harlem, where

Bill T. Jones/Arnie Zane and Company was in rehearsals. We exchanged polite introductions and then walked to a nearby park for our photo session. With little time to spare, sixty minutes maximum, I positioned Bill between trees, on boulders, against a ledge—searching for the right composition the way a choreographer tries out new steps. My hope was that he might reveal something of himself, offer me an insight into how I might best capture him on film. He acceded to my direction with the ease of a fashion model. He showed no conceptual initiative, as if to acknowledge that the art of photography means more creatively to the one holding the camera than to the one in front of it.

"Turn a little more to the right and let your eyes rest on me," I instructed. As he did so, I sensed a subtle, almost imperceptible change in him. No longer was he just posing for the camera. He was looking through my lens at me. I took a few steps closer and refocused. When the sharp image appeared, Bill's eyes drew me in like an embrace. Held by the power of his gaze, I finished the roll and lowered the camera. Bill smiled at me as if to say, "I felt that, too." I asked him later what he had been thinking at that moment. He told me that I already knew the answer.

"We have about twenty minutes left," he said. "My dancers are waiting."

Bjorn helped gather my belongings and carried my camera bag back to the

"The artist should be the freest individual in our society.

theater for the interview. We entered the darkened hall and sat down in the back row. Bill's dancers were already onstage, stretching.

I began by asking him if the artist has a responsibility to serve anyone or anything beyond the self. Bill needed no time to think about his response.

"The artist should be the freest individual in our society," he said. "He should set an agenda for personal liberty and intellectual investigation. The artist should do what he feels he must and be as free as he dares to be. He should thumb his nose at all dogma, even his own. Artists are often full of self-deception and personal obsession, so a good dose of humility and serious self-appraisal is important. I would like my work to encourage people to live more freely in their bodies and explore the continent of their imagination.

"In my work I have a stage full of diverse bodies. I've tried to keep it that way as a metaphor for a world I want to live in. I hope that when young people see that, they say, 'Oh, all kinds of people can dance, and dance is an expression of freedom of the individual working out relationships to the culture.' I hope the work is at the service of presenting a broader vision of that world."

"How does your work inform you about yourself?"

"I think we understand something about what we love," he said. "I think we understand something about our will and our limitations. I am struggling with keeping a dance company, struggling with producing works and finding audi-

ences, and at the same time pleasing myself. I've learned that a good leader does not have all the answers. A good leader knows how to ask the right questions. I've learned this from my art."

"How do you move from one project to the next?"

"I'm sensitive to the winds of my life, inner and outer, and I try to use the winds to direct where the work goes. Circumstances, interests, music, individuals, new dancers, personalities, loves, economics, the business of art—all these things affect what I do next."

"What are the elements that make dance accessible to audiences?"

"Ah, this is a big question for our era. How do we take this thing, this art that we think is good for people, and present it to them so that they make it a part of themselves? Time, familiarity, and repeated viewing do wonders in closing the gap between an artist and his audience. Production values—how something is lit and costumed—go into attracting and seducing the eye. Articulate and open discussion on the edge of the stage, not to explain but to convince doubters of the passion that brought the work forth. Hopefully, audiences then begin to see themselves in that work."

"How do you explain passion?"

"You can't explain some things. How do you explain a dream or your love for another human being? You can talk about what it feels like. You can talk

He should set an agenda for personal liberty
and intellectual investigation."

about intention. And you can talk about the commonality you have as human beings. That's probably the most honest thing you can do."

"How do you know if your work makes a difference?"

"I don't. We're never really sure if we are moving forward, sideways, or backward. Everything is moving, so we don't know about our progress if we are moving in relation to something else. You will never know if what you do is valid. You will never know the truth about anything. You will only know the doing. That is a daunting but liberating idea. You will only know the doing."

"So what is it that you do know?"

"I know that faith, in its varied states of righteousness and order, can produce a positive outcome. A strong faith, well rooted in practice and action—not just dreaming—is probably one of the most important things in this life as an artist and a person. I know that the first obligation of the artist is to make the best work that he can make. As we know from history, oftentimes an artist may have created fantastic work and not a soul save a handful of people understands what that person was doing. Artists must always remember that."

New York City, 2001

Action Hero

elizabeth streb

Elizabeth arrived at the door of my New York sublet at precisely 10:30 a.m. She wore black leather pants and jacket and yellow-tinted eyeglasses, and her jelled hair was magenta. I invited her to have a seat at the kitchen table, poured her a cup of coffee with milk, and turned on my tape recorder.

"The dance community doesn't know what to label someone like you, who literally runs into walls and falls from high places."

"Yes, there are endless conversations about where I fit in. Is what I do dance or isn't it? But it's really not my job to define what dance is. I'm interested in a vigorous investigation of movement in its relation to time, space, and human body potential."

"Are your roots in dance?"

"I passed through athletics and was trained in dance. In high school I played varsity basketball and baseball and was an obsessive downhill skier and motorcycle rider. I started dancing at the age of seventeen when I majored in dance at the State University of New York at Brockport. My modern dance training was along the lines of Doris Humphrey, Charles Weidman, and José Limón. Through this and my history of extreme sports, I developed an interest in action. Action is what makes movement possible. This quickly became my passion, and dance was the only place in the arts that accepted what I was doing."

"So you began to explore action as an independent force?"

"Yes, I began to investigate time, space, and the body's ability to respond

"Go to the edge and peer over it and be willing to get hurt. . . .

But not so hurt that you can't come back again."

with force to physical exertion. I wanted to show what the body is capable of and, at the same time, identify an emblematic movement moment so powerful that it is undeniably true. I came up with what I do now, which is extreme action, or action that is pumped up with a lot of velocity and a lot of impact. Through my work I attempt to defy gravity, based on the belief that humans can fly. I attempt to demonstrate all that theatrically. I know it's wild and insane."

"Obviously humans cannot fly."

"Essentially, my work is an effort to highlight what ends up being a failure of flight. In other words, it's focusing on the other half of the parabolic curve, where your momentum and your will and your force end. Are you able to accept the hit and handle the crush without attempting to camouflage it the way traditional dance does through resistance and transitional moves?"

"What does the audience see?"

"A performance might include people running into walls, moving in different directions at varying speeds in hit-and-near-miss collisions, rebounding off immobile surfaces, diving through structures, falls and back-falls, trampoline work, and gravity-defying techniques. It's not like watching a dance presentation. It's more like witnessing people avoiding potentially devastating accidents. Once they get onstage it's all about survival. That's what makes it so compelling to watch."

"The work is stuntlike then, and potentially dangerous?"

"Yes. For me the point is to go to the edge and peer over it and be willing to get hurt while you're doing that. But not so hurt that you can't come back again. It's really about committing to a certain amount of bodily harm, realizing that's the price you pay to go into new territory. Come, let me show you."

Elizabeth stood up and walked over to the living room wall. I stood back and watched her slam against the wall three times with such force that the entire apartment shook as if an earthquake had just struck.

"Now it's your turn, Rose. I'll teach you my technique. You won't get hurt."

"Hey, wait a minute," I said, stepping even further back. "This is a bit too Evel Knievel for me. I'll have to take your word for it."

"I promise you'll walk away unharmed. Impact strengthens your bones. My recent bone-density test showed that my bone strength is off the charts."

"Well, I think I prefer to strengthen my bones the old-fashioned way: calcium tablets. It minimizes the chance of bruising. Besides, I'm interviewing you because you run into walls and I don't."

Elizabeth found my response—echo of Woody Allen—amusing.

Walking back to the kitchen, I asked her if her action concerts delivered a message or if she meant them as a purely visual experience.

"I take issue with the fact that story and message can be conveyed honestly through movement. If you want to tell a story, write a book. People only understand what they are watching through their own cultural lens. If people from Mars landed on Earth and went to a concert of *Sleeping Beauty*, they'd have no idea what it's about."

"So what do you concern yourself with if not message or story?"

"For me, action is the message. If you are true to the form, pure in your presentation of action, then the message lies within. I find information inside the invisible forces that cause movement to happen. I set up a condition of turbulence to examine velocity, momentum, rebound, and impact, rate of speed and distance."

"You must have had to invent your own investigative process and vocabulary. How did you do that?"

"It's taken me twenty-five years to research this vocabulary and develop my show ideas. If you're developing a new vocabulary it's very time-consuming. If you're using a vocabulary that already exists and personalizing it, then it's a lot quicker. I think I work very much like a scientist. I could spend two years on an idea and possibly find out that I went down the wrong track. Then I have to go all the way back to the fork in the road and go another way. It's a very zigzaggy path. It's all about setting up a structure that enables you to ask new questions, like why should gravity be camouflaged, and how does the hit inform us about the human body? The focus becomes how do you draw attention to that which has never been addressed or attended to?"

"You mean like how is it possible to engage the audience in an action experience when they are seated in a theater?"

"Yes. I'd like audiences to leave the theater with a physical memory of the experience, not just a visual memory. The sound of bodies on impact helps bridge the distance from the proscenium stage to the audience seated in their chairs. They come along with us on the ride and interpret what they see for themselves. My intention is to involve them and move them. They gasp, grab their seats, twitch, and do all sorts of things with their bodies during our performances. At the end of the show, I ask the audience to stand, and I teach them how to become a perfect vertical line, which you need to be to do my work—plus it's a sneaky way to get a standing ovation."

"Ah, very clever. Sounds like the proscenium stage might not be the best place to perform work that encourages physical action and reaction."

"I'm not sure it is, and that's why we are planning to perform at Coney Island and Central Park. I'm also thinking about some large open venues in Las Vegas. You want the audience physically, spiritually, and emotionally with you and not restricted by the physical environment."

"Do you have a target audience for your action-driven work?"

"I spent over two decades alone in a studio developing these ideas, desperate to be taken seriously in the art world, believing that art is meant for all the people, not just the elite. I want to give audiences an action experience that doesn't require a private invitation. One of the reasons I retired from performing is to get out in the real world and feel what the audience feels. Sitting in the theater with them is the best way for me to see if I'm proving my theories and to gauge my progress. You know what they say in the theater—if you really want to hear what people think, go eavesdrop in the ladies' room."

"That's a pretty good way of getting information," I said. "May I take some photos of you before you go?"

"Yes, of course."

I positioned Elizabeth back at the wall and photographed her slamming into it until the neighbors complained. She paused to rest. I clicked the shutter, catching her inside an idle moment.

"Oh, but I thought you wanted action shots," she said, surprised.

"I suspect there is information in a motionless moment too."

She smiled as if to say yes, of course there is.

New York City, 1999

Messenger

rennie harris

Rennie greeted me with a hug in the lobby of the community center in West Philly.

We had last seen each other two years earlier, when I photographed him for *Dance* magazine. I followed the six-foot-plus hip-hop dancer up to a huge empty studio on the second floor. It was decorated with tie-dyed wall hangings and African art.

"I'm thinking of a simple shot, something intimate," I said.

"That sounds fine."

I pulled up a chair and suggested that he sit facing the back of the chair with the mirror behind him. Rennie immediately began to play around on the chair as if it were something to ride. Balancing his huge frame on one or two of the chair legs, he tipped playfully from side to side, almost falling to the floor before catching himself. Later I asked him to dance for me, which he did happily. He stepped out into the big empty space and, as if possessed, flew into a fast-paced hip-hop rampage. I clicked like mad.

After the shoot we sat down for sandwiches and coffee at a local eatery.

"Since I last saw you, your company took *Rome and Jewels* on the road. How has it been received?"

"Overall—quite well. I did receive some criticism. I was accused of being misogynistic. 'Why weren't there any women in the piece?' The thing is, I came to this work from a male perspective. That's all I know about. Maybe I do have some issues with women. I do have to acknowledge that. But, honestly, I think all men have issues with women. I think we're conditioned to be sexist from day one."

"Inspired by Shakespeare's *Romeo and Juliet,* how does *Rome and Jewels* relate to 'our time' the way *West Side Story* did to the late 1950s and 1960s?"

"Jerome Robbins's *West Side Story* was definitely appropriate to its time. Our time is hip-hop. What that means is that its presentation should be straight up—not watered down just for mainstream audiences."

"So you're not changing the presentation to make it more accessible. You want to engage audiences on your own terms."

"That's right. I'm asking the audience to try and decipher hip-hop poetry and culture through the telling of the story. We're doing a kind of physical Ebonics. We didn't remove Shakespeare. We just adapted him."

"How did you do that?"

"We did a modernization of the text utilizing the language of hip-hop—the rapper's poetry. If you notice, rappers speak in rhythms. They speak indirectly and behind things. They switch words around or change their inflection, which changes the meanings of the words. That's called signifying. They take you in a roundabout way to say what they really mean. It's a decoding of the English language that stems from slave culture. Slaves created a way of talking to each other so that white people wouldn't understand what they were saying. It had the same grammatical structure as many traditional African languages. Professors and scholars have written about this. We've carried our language rhythms with us over time. But because America is a big melting pot, no one wants to accept the fact that people hold on to their original language or aspects of it."

"But if you want to reach a broad audience, how can you communicate if only a select group can understand what you're saying?"

"Hell, if I didn't care about reaching a broader audience, *Rome and Jewels* would have been entirely in Ebonics. I did keep in mind general audiences. That's why I retained a good portion of the Elizabethan text—so both communities could follow."

"How does what you do inform us about ourselves—and I'm not referring now to only the African American community. What are we gaining from your work?"

"I can put that in one word—humanism. Being universal. It goes beyond what you're seeing on the surface. If you are not equipped to look beyond what I'm presenting, then it's not your time to understand universality. We, unfortunately, are taught to look at things at face value. Words are always the last thing we should use to communicate with. The truth of the matter is that movement and action are the only things that really communicate. I can use words to say something to you, but if I don't include gesture and my body to support the words, then the words might not be believable."

"Do you ever manipulate your choreography—add a twist here or a jump there—so that the audience might grasp your meaning better?"

"No. Not at all. I just go in and I do it. When I'm creating, I'm not thinking about anything. I just do it. At the base of creation is improvisation. Improvisation leads me to a structure, and then I follow where it takes me. Without improvisation there would be no new work. I'd just be doing all the old stuff over and over. Most of my thinking about the actual choreography comes after a piece is done. Once I've created something I might look at it and say, 'This

other thing would be better here.' Like *Rome and Jewels*—I've been redoing it for the past year while touring it on the road. Since I've started cleaning it with new movement, it started to make even more sense to me."

"Do you feel you have the power to change other people's views and perceptions through your choreography?"

"I've recently started to feel that I can increase awareness through my dances, my teaching, and through discussion. In fact, I think I've become responsible for that power. My goal is to bring people back to the truth. We're trained to think linearly, and when we do that, somebody has to be first, second, third, and fourth. But if we are thinking circularly—like the shape of the earth, then there is no hierarchy, everyone's on the same level and everyone contributes."

"Rennie, you know I think you're inherently rebellious."

"Oh, yeah," he said with a laugh.

"Yes, I've seen how you deal with your students. You rile them up. You get them going. You create a spark in them and then encourage them to go out and do research, study history and philosophy, and be connected to their culture. You go way beyond dance steps. I heard you tell them that you can't teach dance without putting the experience into some sort of cultural context. It's rebellious because your students become proactive in their lives and expand their way of thinking."

"I think you're right. To gain knowledge is to be somewhat rebellious."

"How does someone from the outside, someone like me, come to understand your hip-hop culture?"

"You're not going to unless you understand my language, and you're not going to understand my language unless you live here. I grew up within a two-block radius of hip-hop culture. The music, with its heavy bass, was always grinding in my face—yeah, yeah, yeah, boom, boom, boom. It helped define who I am. You have to be in here with me to understand why I'm so pent up. As an outsider, the only thing you can do is develop sympathy for my culture and my experience. For example, I might want to be a Rastafarian, but I can't be a Rastafarian because I'm not living a Rastafarian life and I'm not living in Jamaica. I can appreciate and sympathize with them, but never project that I really understand what they're about. If I do, I'm just appropriating."

"What do you think are the most important lessons you've learned as a creative person?"

"I've learned to stand by my words and support them with action. When I've done that honestly, truthfulness is revealed."

"I think I'm beginning to understand. Well, let's say I sympathize."

Rennie threw me a smile.

Driving him home gave me a chance to see his neighborhood. I imagined him as a kid in dance battles on corners and in alleys.

"I can get out here. There's my building," he said, opening the car door. He leaned over, gave me a parting hug, ran down the street, and disappeared through a doorway.

Philadelphia, 2001

Man with the Moves

cholly atkins

I met Cholly while on assignment at the 1998 American Choreography Awards in Los Angeles.

He received that year's Innovator Award for having introduced "vocal choreography," a dance genre based on African American chorus line dancing of the 1920s–40s and designed as a technique to enhance the stage presence of vocal groups. Cholly coached more than a hundred groups and solo artists, including the Temptations, Smokey Robinson and the Miracles, the Supremes, Gladys Knight and the Pips, Marvin Gaye, and Aretha Franklin. Cholly's "moves" helped propel these and other artists to international stardom, even as he established a new performing dance style. He understood that audiences respond to the syncopated rhythm patterns in the music and move their bodies to the background music while the performer is singing in another rhythmic direction through the melodic line. Cholly taught his artists how to separate the vocal line from the background rhythmic pattern, to which the moves correspond. The singer's challenge was to coordinate body and voice during performance. Above all, the moves had to be true to the spirit of the song. He formatted different moves to accentuate the song's message and mood.

When I approached Cholly at the awards event, he was in conversation with media choreographer Russell Clark, one of the pioneers of music video choreography, who that year had choreographed and portrayed Cholly in a TV movie on the Temptations. I asked permission to take a picture of them together. They posed with arms around each other. I shot a couple of frames

and then asked them if they'd be in my book. Russell agreed to a portrait as well as an interview. Cholly agreed to a portrait, but declined the interview. As the subject of an upcoming biography, he was contractually barred from granting interviews.

"What about after the book's publication?"

"I don't want to think that far into the future."

"So when can we do the portrait?"

"Tomorrow morning at ten at my hotel."

I arrived at Cholly's hotel at the designated time only to find that he had already checked out. I was stunned that he had left without even leaving me a note. After a few days, I phoned him at his home in Las Vegas and brought up the missed appointment. He confirmed that he and his wife had left Los Angeles early but offered no explanations or apologies. When would I have another opportunity to photograph him? He wasn't sure. I offered to fly to Las Vegas. He was silent. I decided to back off.

About a year later, I heard that Cholly was coming to Los Angeles to rehearse the Temptations for their upcoming Las Vegas show. I phoned him again. This time he was more forthcoming.

"Come to the rehearsal in Studio D at the Debbie Reynolds Professional Rehearsal Studio in North Hollywood," he said. "I'll step out during the lunch break and pose for a quick photo. Do you know the place?"

"Yes," I said. "I've been there many times. I'll reserve one of the adjacent studios so all you'll need to do is walk out one door and in another."

"That would be convenient," he said.

The day of the rehearsal I arrived at the studio early, determined not to let Cholly give me the slip again. I asked at the front desk if Cholly was in Studio D and was told that he'd been there for hours. I began to unload my gear. Once I had moved everything inside, I put up a black backdrop, positioned a barstool in front of it, and set up a couple of lights. Now all I needed was Cholly Atkins. I sat down on a wooden bench just outside Studio D and waited for the group to break for lunch. After thirty minutes I grew impatient and knocked on the door. Otis Williams, the founder and the last of the original Temptations, came out wearing sweats, with a towel around his neck. He looked like he had just stepped out of a sauna.

"Yes?"

"Hello," I said. "I'm sorry to disturb you. I'm looking for Cholly."

"Hey, Pops," he called out. "There's a young lady here to see you."

I looked inside and saw Cholly working with four men in front of the mirror, all of them dripping wet.

"Yes, Rose, I'll be right with you. Just give me a second."

I returned to my makeshift photo studio next door. A few minutes later Cholly joined me. He was holding a brown lunch bag in one hand and a thermos in the other.

"I promise not to keep you too long."

"Oh, no problem. What would you like me to do?"

"Why don't you have a seat on the barstool and just face out toward me."

There he sat—the "man with the moves." How do you immortalize a living legend on his lunch break? Long before Cholly brought his talents to Motown in the mid-1960s he and Honi Coles had formed one of the greatest dancing duets of all time. After their debut at the Apollo in 1946, Coles and Atkins went on to dazzle audiences as headliners for Louis Armstrong, Duke Ellington, Count Basie, Cab Calloway, Dizzy Gillespie, and many of the other big bands of the swing era. Their showstopping dance number from the 1949 Broadway hit *Gentlemen Prefer Blondes* became legendary for its brilliance.

Searching for the right pose, I thought of a line from one of the Temptations' biggest hits, "The Way You Do the Things You Do."

"Cholly," I said, "snap your fingers as if you're keeping time to the music."

He looked straight at me with a natural smile and began to snap his fingers as he'd done a million times before. I could see he was absolutely fine with my unspoken idea to blend rhythm and tempo with the kind of stylized body movement he'd made famous. I kept him for about fifteen minutes, trying various poses, and then mercifully freed him to eat his lunch.

After a few minutes Cholly looked at his watch and said, "Gotta get back to work."

He shook my hand, wished me the best of luck on my book, and returned to Studio D.

North Hollywood, 1999

Assistant

alex romero

Alex Romero's story sounded like the opening lines of a Hollywood movie.

"I was born Alexander Bernard Quiroga in Mexico, 1913. My father was the wealthy general don Miguel Quiroga. But I never met my father. Shortly before I was born, he and thirteen of his sons were massacred by Pancho Villa's rebels. My mother, who was pregnant with me, made a narrow escape with the help of one of our servants. She managed to get us and my sister to Texas in a flatbed train. I was born in a mud hut in San Antonio. Eventually we were reunited with my nine surviving brothers."

"Wait a minute. How many brothers did you have?"

"My mother birthed twenty-three sons and one daughter."

"Wow!"

"Yes, we were once a very large family. They're all gone now. I am the sole survivor. But back then, several of my brothers were very good Spanish dancers, so they formed a group and began performing in vaudeville. The rest of us relocated to Los Angeles and lived in a poor Mexican neighborhood. From the age of six, I worked selling newspapers. I only went up to the fourth grade. I've always felt bad about that. We were so poor I didn't own a pair of shoes until I was twelve years old.

"On occasion my mother and I would accompany my brothers on tour. One day while we were in Chicago, I wandered into a neighboring theater and sat down in the third row. Out on the stage came three black performers. They called themselves King, King, and King. They started tap-dancing—hoofing. I'll tell you, I had never seen anything like it. That night I couldn't get it out of my mind. I came back the next day and secretly memorized their rhythms—*ta-ca-ta-ca-ta-ca-ti-ca-ti-ca-ti*. Then I started to make up steps to match those rhythmic taps. When my brother John spotted me playing around, he asked how I had learned those steps and if I could repeat what I had just done. To his surprise, I repeated the tap routine. So he had me teach it to him and to my brothers, and as soon as I was old enough I was made a member of the act. Ours was a fairly successful act and toured throughout the United States and Europe. The act broke up in 1939, just as the war was beginning."

"What happened next?"

"I returned to Los Angeles and auditioned for Jack Cole. He hired me to dance in his nightclub act and dance team for Columbia Pictures. His style was very unusual, sort of a combination of jazz and modern dance, flavored with Oriental motifs. I didn't think it would go over, but people liked it. He trained all his dancers in this technique and, boy, was he tough. His work at the ballet barre was like torture. He'd count one … two … three … four so slowly and drag out the counts for so long that your muscles would be on fire. You know what that does?"

"Builds strength," I said.

"Yes, that's right. When you work like that, you build muscle and power. His training enabled us to do those big jumps, like we did in the 'Sing, Sing, Sing' number. Jack Cole was an absolute perfectionist and could be very tough on his dancers. Everybody hated him. He would scream at us, he'd cuss us out. I even saw him slap Carol Haney across the face one day because she didn't do a step right. And she was an incredible dancer! But I didn't hate him. I understood him. He just wanted us to get it right.

"In 1947 I got a call from Robert Alton at MGM asking me to come and work as an assistant to the contract dance arrangers. He knew I had been a Jack Cole dancer and wanted to incorporate some of Cole's style into their musical numbers. Over the years, I would assist him, Hermes Pan, Nick Castle, Gene Kelly, Fred Astaire, Busby Berkeley, Michael Kidd, and others. I worked on dozens of films, among them *The Barkleys of Broadway, Seven Brides for Seven Brothers, An American in Paris, Show Boat, The Band Wagon, Small Town Girl,* and *Take Me Out to the Ball Game.* I also danced in many of them. Later I became a choreographer in my own right. You know, when we get back to my place, I'll show you some of my movies."

"Alex, I would love that. Tell me, what exactly does a choreographer's assistant do?"

"The way it normally works is you stand behind the choreographer, and every time he makes a move, you learn it. You have to be plenty sharp at picking things up because he doesn't know what he's going to leave in or take out. He throws out so much stuff that he doesn't always remember what he's done. He'll come back to you and say, 'What did I just do?' And you have to repeat whatever he demonstrated."

"You're like a human video recorder."

"Yes."

"Did the choreographers ever pick your brain for dance moves?"

"Oh, yes. I would make suggestions, but only when I was asked to. Let me tell you a story. One day I'm in the rehearsal room with Gene Kelly, and he's doing this number, you see, when suddenly he gets stuck. 'Alex,' he says, 'what can I do next?' I think to myself, 'Well, he never went in that direction and maybe we could add a turn over here,' and suddenly this thing is coming together. He says, 'That's great. Do a little more.' So I choreograph at least a quarter of the number, and he's applauding me, when suddenly the door opens and in walks the producer, Arthur Freed. Gene pushes me aside and says, 'Cool it, Alex.'"

"So what are you saying—that Gene Kelly didn't want anyone to see that you were helping him?"

"He didn't want anyone to know that he might need help. You have to understand that he had a huge reputation to maintain. I understood what was at stake. And I didn't care about getting any credit. I always felt that Gene Kelly respected me and appreciated what I did for him. I loved the man."

"What was it like assisting Fred Astaire?"

"Astaire had a different attitude. One day I was working with him on the 'I Want to Be a Dancing Man' number, and he says to me, 'Alex, I honestly don't know what to do here. Help me out.' So I get out there and do about twelve to sixteen bars when the door swings open and there's Arthur Freed. Fred leans back and says, 'Arthur, sit down. Look at what Alex just came up with.'"

"You've had some amazing experiences."

"Oh, Rose, I just loved those days. Back then I lived in Studio City and would drive to MGM by taking Coldwater Canyon up to Mulholland Drive and then down into Culver City. I'd pull up in front of the main gate, and it would hit me. How did I get here? I didn't remember driving the car. Had I run any red lights

"Dance makes me completely happy."

or driven through stop signs? Was I speeding? My mind had been on a dance step, not on the road. I loved dancing and choreographing so much. I'd do it before breakfast, after dinner, on my days off, and on Sundays."

When I told Alex it was time to step into my studio for the portrait, he immediately began warming up with a little soft shoe routine.

"How's this?" he asked. "Normally I would throw in a handful of pirouettes right here. I used to be able to do ten at a time. Now, at my age, I'm happy that I can still do one."

"Alex, whatever you want to show me will be fine."

Alex started clapping out a pattern—*ta-ca-ta-ca*—and launched into a classy tap number. I marveled at his carriage and grace.

After the shoot, I drove him back to his condo, where he showed me old movie stills of him with Gene Kelly, Fred Astaire, Robert Alton, and many of the actors and dancers he had worked with over the years. In his small loft-turned-tap-studio hung a signed portrait of Elvis Presley.

"I understand you worked quite a bit with Elvis."

"Yes, I choreographed several of his films. Come, let me show you one of my favorites—*Jailhouse Rock*."

Alex slipped a video into the player and went on to explain how he had conceptualized and designed the two-tier jail set. The inmates would dance in front and behind bars. Elvis would sing and travel in and out of the cells.

"Elvis could really move his hips, but he wasn't very good at repeating choreographed steps. I had a very hard time with him, especially when I wanted him to slide down the pole. He was afraid of heights. I worked with him on the platform, showing him several times how to hug his body to the pole and just spiral down. But he was very fearful. Watch, honey," he said, pointing to the TV.

"See how he virtually falls down to the floor? It's not supposed to look like that, but we had to leave it in.

"I choreographed Bob Fosse's first film. Would you like to see it?"

"Absolutely."

Alex ejected the *Jailhouse Rock* video and slipped in *The Affairs of Dobie Gillis*, forwarding it to the Fosse solo. The energetic young dancer seemed to jump out of the screen. One minute he was on top of a piano, then he went up and down a staircase, then did a duet with a jukebox—all in a single number. I thought to myself, this looks like Fosse's style, but he's performing Alex's choreography?

"Alex," I said, "are you in part responsible for Fosse's dance style?"

"No, no. I would never take credit for influencing Bob Fosse. This was the dance style of the time. The only thing I might have done was give him the idea to use a hat."

"I don't know, Alex, I think you might be a bit too modest. Everyone has seen *Jailhouse Rock*, but hardly anyone knows that you choreographed it. Your name is not even on the film credits."

"Rose, I was never interested in those things. I didn't look for fame or even care about making lots of money. I loved what I was doing. That was my reward. If I had to live my life over again, I'd make it a rerun. All I ever needed was just enough money to feed my family and put a roof over their heads. Even now, at eighty-eight, I don't need much. I only hope I have enough to get me to the end of my life. But it's been a great life."

Encino, California, 2001

167

Soul Man

kenny ortega

It was just around lunchtime when I arrived at Kenny's Southern California home.

"Rose, you look hungry," he said as I walked through the front door. "Do you like Mexican food?"

"Yes, but . . . "

"Just leave all your equipment here and let's go into the kitchen."

After a delicious lunch of quesadillas with salsa, he led me out to his lush backyard, where we sat poolside under an umbrella.

"Tell me the Kenny Ortega story."

"I grew up in Redwood City, California. When I was four my mother took me to watch my two cousins take dance class. I couldn't sit still, so the teacher came over and offered me a scholarship. By the time I was a freshman in high school, I was acting and dancing in community and professional theatrical productions in San Francisco. But my life changed dramatically when I got a part in the rock musical *Hair,* one of the most influential shows of the 1960s. *Hair* was so powerful that it inspired people to alter their thinking and change their behavior. I was eighteen when I landed the role of George Berger, the shy draft-card burner. Gerome Ragni, the show's writer, originated the role on Broadway. The minute I stepped into that character, he became part of me. George freed me as a person because the role was about listening to one's inner voice. The show's producers didn't want the cast to playact their roles, they wanted them to live them. *Hair* was all about breaking from convention and setting new boundaries. It was this experience that shaped my thinking, enlightened me, and gave me a process I have used to conduct my life from that time forward. I toured with the national company for almost three years."

"I imagine you learned a great deal from Julie Arenal, the show's choreographer."

"Julie is one of my great heroes. She had a unique method of working. She created an environment of absolute safety that enabled us to surrender completely to the work. Julie had a way of choreographing from the inside out. She inspired you to feel where the movement was coming from—as opposed to painting it on your body. Her choreography was specific in terms of steps and moves, but she also gave the dancers freedom to express themselves within that movement. It was a very generous and human approach. That's how I choreograph to this day. I got it all from her."

"What turn did your career take after *Hair*?"

"I met a San Francisco–based rock-and-roll group called the Tubes, which took me in a new direction. They were looking for someone to help design and stage their act for live performance. I ended up working with them for a decade, and it was during those years that I realized I had the skills and talent to be a choreographer."

"What happened next?"

"Toni Basil came into my life. She had seen the Tubes perform and came backstage looking for me. She wanted to hire me to help her put together a show called *Toni Basil's Follies Bizarre*. Working with her added another dimension to my development as a choreographer. She is one of the most animated and innovative artists around. She would do things like mix classical ballet with locking [West Coast hip-hop] and then combine the result with mixed media."

"Who would have the greatest influence on your career as a choreographer?"

"Gene Kelly. He mentored me on my first feature film."

"How did that come about?"

"Toni Basil was offered the job of choreographing a new roller-disco film called *Xanadu* (1979) but was unavailable. She recommended me for the job. I grabbed it, despite the fact that I had no formal training in choreographing for film. Olivia Newton-John, who had just come off of *Grease*, was planning to star in the film. Gene Kelly was considering acting in the film but insisted on meeting the choreographer before signing on."

"What was that meeting like?"

"The producers asked me not to come on too strong. They hoped Gene would volunteer to dance in the film, even though he was already retired. But ten minutes after we met, he asked me, 'If I were to dance in this film, what would you have me do? Show me a step.' So I got up and performed one of his signature tap steps. He laughed and said, 'I can do that blindfolded.' He got up and we danced around the office together. 'What about adding this?' he suggested. 'Yeah, that's great,' I said. When the meeting ended, he walked up to the producer, turned to me and said, 'I like you, kid, and I'm going to dance in your movie.' Suddenly at the age of twenty-seven I was choreographing a Gene Kelly movie!"

"What did Gene Kelly teach you?"

"Kelly was a master at filming dance. He didn't just choreograph a dance; he conceived it with the camera in mind. He told me, 'You'll never realize your full potential as a choreographer in film unless you learn how to design for the camera.' He insisted that I direct his on-screen dance and took that opportunity to teach me what he knew. On the day of rehearsal, Kelly banned the producers from the set and walked me onto the soundstage. Putting a viewfinder around my neck and a stopwatch in my hand, he said, 'Okay, get down on your knees.' He had me crawl around on the floor and measure the distance from the dance space to the camera, and time how long it would take for the camera to get from point A to point B. Kelly then invited me to his home to watch his old films and would freeze-frame sections and say, 'Do you know why I put the camera there?' or 'Why I added more movement here?' He gave me this incredible education. He said he believed in me and chose me to pass on his knowledge. It's one of the most significant relationships that I've ever had."

"How has all this inherited knowledge informed your work?"

"At the start of any project, no matter the medium, I try to gain the trust of my collaborators—the producers, writers, performers, assistants, and crew. Even when I choreographed 10,000 people for the Olympics ceremony in Atlanta, I tried to inspire each one of them to connect with the work. I tried to encourage them to show themselves through their performance."

"How did you do that on such a large scale?"

"By creating choreography that is precise. Everyone knows exactly what to do and how to hit their mark. Then you fuel it with your personality and your spirit, and it becomes contagious."

"With a space as vast as the Olympic stadium, how did you conceptualize the choreography? Did you do it on a computer, with pen and paper, see it in your mind?"

"Eventually you use those visual tools, but not in the beginning. Gene Kelly taught me a very important lesson. He said, 'Ask what's the purpose of this? Why am I doing this? Once you know why you're doing it—start at the beginning.' For me, the beginning is the concept, and that comes from a very internal place."

"Was choreographing the water ballet for the Bellagio Hotel and Resort in Las Vegas a huge departure for you creatively?"

"Yes, huge. You can't just look out at a vast lake and tell 1,200 nozzles to pirouette! You have to tell a machine in codes and numbers. The challenge was to figure out how to interpret music and tell a story with water."

"What process did you use to create the look and style for the film *Dirty Dancing*?"

"I drew much of it from my own high school experience. The music was hot back in the mid-sixties. Every time a new forty-five record came out, we'd run over to our best friend's house waving the vinyl disk in the air. 'Wait till you hear this new Martha Reeves and the Vandellas song. You're not going to believe how great it is!' We'd play it fifty times before the school dance on Friday night. I remember having all this sexual tension bottled up inside of me that couldn't wait to explode on the dance floor. It was not uncommon for our high school dances to be shut down because of all the gyrating and rubbing up against each other. The vice principal would routinely come out on the stage and announce, 'If there is any more dirty dancing in here, the dance will be canceled.' When I met Eleanor Bergstein, who wrote the screenplay for the film, I told her that I knew what to do choreographically because I had lived it."

"How did you translate that high school experience to film choreography?"

"We re-created the days of our youth in a large studio in the Blue Ridge Mountains of Virginia. My assistant Miranda Garrison and I blackened out all the windows, brought in the kids, put on these old songs, and took them back in time. We workshopped it by listening to all sorts of rhythms—Cuban, mambo, cha-cha-cha—until we found the essence of what we wanted. Miranda came from ballroom dancing, I came from partner dancing, and we just pooled our ideas."

"I love that final scene in the movie when Patrick Swayze comes dancing up the aisle with the dancers behind him."

"That's a combination of Cuban rhythm steps. Old Cuban salsa, old-style mambo, and the grind formed the basis for *Dirty Dancing*."

Kenny jumped up and demonstrated the grind—"hips two times to the left, hips two times to the right, hip grind one to the left, hip grind one to the right, and then pull up to center, repeat."

Sherman Oaks, California, 1999, 2003

Reporter

paul taylor

As I pulled into his driveway, Paul emerged from his weekend home on the eastern tip of Long Island.

I handed the tall, lean, blue-eyed legend a bouquet of sunflowers from a local farm stand. Commenting that his sunflowers had already finished for the season, he invited me into his house, where I was greeted by his black Labrador retriever, Emma. Paul's living room was artfully decorated with a large mirror outlined in seashells, framed butterfly and insect collections, antique blue bottles in a sunlit window, African masks he had purchased at a Paris flea market, and a large picture of a fearsome shark above the mantel. He offered me a cold drink, and we stepped out on his deck to a clean, panoramic view of Long Island Sound.

"Do you mind if I look around?" I asked as I pulled the light meter from my backpack.

"Please do," he said, sitting down on a wooden Adirondack chair washed in pastel blue and lighting up a cigarette. I scouted the grounds, carefully cultivated with a mix of perennials and wildflowers, and noticed a lookout point with a park bench. I then followed a dirt path down to Paul's private beach. I pictured him walking among the large rocks and pieces of driftwood with Emma running ahead of him. When I returned, he made a face at my suggestion that I photograph him at the water's edge.

"Annie Liebowitz took me down there and photographed me for over two hours. I don't want to do that again," he asserted.

"That's all right," I said. "Why don't we go to that little enclave overlooking the water?"

"Ever since I was a child, I hated having my picture taken," he confessed as we walked toward the bench.

"This will be relatively painless," I assured him.

Paul took a seat on the park bench with Emma at his feet and waited for my instructions.

"She's a very sweet dog," I said.

"Yes, she is. She was trained as a seeing-eye dog but flunked her final exam. Not assertive enough. That's when I got her. I take her to the studio with me every day. She lies down under the piano when we arrive, and she gets up just as we are about to finish rehearsal. Before I had Emma, I had this other dog that liked to nip the dancers' feet. They hated that. But Emma here, she's a great dog," he said, patting the top of her head.

After shooting a Polaroid and checking the exposure, I asked Paul to remove his watch, something I normally ask of my subjects.

"Really," he said, unstrapping his watch, "time is very important in the theater. One must be vigilant of time. If you're late in the theater, it can cost you enormous sums of money."

"Well, then, perhaps you should wear it," I said, realizing that it was probably out of character for him to be without it, even here, where he comes to decompress.

We then moved to Paul's unintended bamboo forest—he explained that bamboo is very hard to control, something he discovered too late. I noticed a cluster of bamboo illuminated by a shaft of sunlight.

"Paul, over here," I said, pointing to the spot. He stepped inside, the sun blinding him on one side and casting dark shadows under his eyes and across his face.

"You look like you're in prison," I said.

"Yes, well, artists are always in the jail of their art," he said matter-of-factly.

"The way the light is falling on you, your face is half light, half dark."

"From the beginning my dances have been both dark and light—positive and negative—with grays in between."

"So this mixed lighting and composition resonates with you?"

"Yes, very much so."

I slipped in another roll of film and concluded our photo session.

Back on the deck, I asked Paul how his country environment informs his work.

"I don't know exactly, except being out here with all this greenery keeps me relatively sane. It's a wonderful break from my work, which is often very tense. So I come out here to vegetate. I'm not really thinking about dance when I'm here, except just before going into rehearsal when I need to create a general plan and find new music."

"Do you come here to escape?"

"No, I don't really want to escape my work. I love my work. It's just a way of living two very different lives."

"Do you find that there is a common thread that connects your early work with your current work?"

"Probably, but I don't think about that too much. Once a dance is done, I put it out of my mind more or less, except once in a while when we do revivals. But even then, it feels like someone else made the dances. They are hard to relate to, mostly because so much time has passed."

"What about your choice of subject matter? Are you still interested in the same things?"

"Well, there has always been a good deal of variety in my work. I've never stuck with one kind of viewpoint. My pieces are not autobiographical. They're not about me. What I do is called reporting. I think that's what life is. I like to think that a dance is multifaceted and can be so many things. Dance writers like to put you in a category. I think they probably have a terrible time with me if they're familiar with my work over a period of time. I'm hard to slot," he said with a laugh. "Nobody likes to be a type. It's an American thing—labeling people."

"Do you feel Martha Graham's influence inside you?"

"Oh, yes, I think of her often. She used to say it takes ten years to make a dancer. I joined her company after two years of training. I guess she thought I was all right," he said, smiling. "She was a major influence on me."

"In what way?"

"Well, I've occasionally stolen things from her dances, and by looking closely at her work I could decide what I didn't want to do. When you narrow things down, you see what you don't want to do, and then you do what's left."

"Was Martha ever maternal toward you?"

"Maternal?" he said, looking at me as I were off my rocker. "Oh, she would be insulted at the accusation."

"I meant was she nurturing?"

"She was nice to me. She really was, but I don't think I ever thought of her as my mother, and I'm sure she would not have liked that. She didn't nurture, but she did come to my concerts, which was an encouragement in itself. The only thing I remember her saying to me after I had done a concert in which the audience left after ten minutes was 'You naughty boy.'"

"Was that the concert of *7 New Dances* in 1957—the one Louis Horst reviewed by signing a blank page?"

"Oh, yes, that was the one," he said, laughing.

"How did you react to it at the time?"

"Well, I was disappointed and mad that people didn't understand what I had done. But that review was a big help because it brought me great notoriety. No one had heard of Paul Taylor before that. I've never lived it down."

"I read that you were trying to incorporate gesture and natural movement into your vocabulary?"

"Yes, making something out of naturally found movement—like a light turn of the head or the drop of an arm. Then the Judson Group came along and stole everything, but they didn't do it as well. [The Judson Group emerged in the early 1960s in sharp contrast to traditional modern dance, abandoning conventional repertory, the proscenium stage, and dance technique.] I moved on to do dance steps, but I kept coming back to some of that material, like in *Esplanade* (1975). I never could have done that piece if not for *7 New Dances*, that early concept."

"What are some of the most important lessons you've learned?"

"Patience is very important when working with people. I think a healthy working atmosphere is just as important as steps. Morale is terribly important. Martha had another system. She'd get everybody screaming mad at each other, and that worked pretty well for her. She liked to twist the knife. It gave her energy. But don't misunderstand me—she wasn't evil, but she could be very difficult at times."

"I imagine she was a very complex person."

"Yes, complex and wonderful."

"Soon you will be celebrating your company's fiftieth anniversary. You've been all over the world with your company—touring for twenty years. How important was your relationship with the audience?"

"Honestly, as a performer I didn't pay much attention to the audience. I was too busy dancing. When the curtain came down and there was all this applause, it really didn't matter much to me. I wasn't doing it for them. I was doing it for myself. It sounds selfish, I guess, but I didn't want to just dance in an empty room. That's sort of pointless."

"So the audience was really a pretense to perform?"

"Yeah, in a way. I never felt required to do anything but what I wanted to do. I've also never had any kind of pressure put on me about what kind of dances I should make. People let me do what I want. Somehow I've had that license. I've been very lucky."

"We are living in interesting times, I think, when artists have the freedom to say pretty much anything they want."

"Yes, well, I think these are pretty uptight times. There is an awful lot of moralizing going on. I think it's time someone said something. The last couple of pieces I've made have been intentionally politically incorrect. I comment on things like being fat. Suddenly it's okay to be fat. People are suing hamburger places because eating their food made them fat. If you're a white guy these days, you're the villain. And if you smoke…" He burst into laughter and displayed his own lit cigarette. "So, I made a dance called *Dreamgirls*. Each of the girls has something wrong with her—one is too pushy, one is too fat. It's a humorous piece. I'm actually surprised people haven't complained about it. I suppose you can get away with all sorts of things if it's funny. I try not to preach. I try to make dances that will allow the viewers to draw their own conclusions."

"Do you ever get stuck creatively?"

"No, I can't afford to get stuck. I can't get writer's block. I can't … my imagination has always been there for me, and I trust it. Making dances can be a strain. I don't mean because you have to be physical and demonstrate. You must try many different things, and if something doesn't work, you've got to change it and find the right thing. That can be confusing."

"Is there something you would like people to know about you?"

"Yes, Rose, tell them that I'm wonderful. I'm so nice. I'm so handsome. I'm just a great guy," he said, and both of us broke into laughter.

Mattituck, New York, 2003

Triple Threat

lynne taylor corbett

The first time I met Lynne Taylor Corbett, she was in LA directing a play called A Rockette's Tail

at the Lee Strasberg Theatre Institute. She posed for her portrait while on her lunch break. A year later, I photographed her choreographing the Broadway musical *Swing*. Two years after that, I bumped into her at the Alvin Ailey American Dance Theater facility, where she was working on *Prayers from the Edge*, a piece commissioned by the dance company. But it wasn't until the summer of 2003, when I sat down with her at a Manhattan coffee shop at Seventy-second and Amsterdam, that I began to sort out her multivaried career.

"I've watched you direct a play, stage a Broadway musical, and choreograph a modern dance. You're all over the map. Are you creatively schizophrenic or simply multitalented?"

"Probably both," she said with a laugh. "I come from a very literary family, where the written word is sacred. I'm drawn to plays because of the power of words and to movement because of its expressive nature. I find there is a kind of purity in each of these. My preference is either to direct plays or to choreograph concert commissions."

"What about stage musicals, which combine words and dance?"

"Well, I'm a fairly serious person, and I have found that the books of musicals are not well written—they don't stand on their own as serious material. With the huge success of *Swing*, everyone thought I'd be dying to do another musical. But I really wasn't. I'm generally looking for work that runs deeper."

"Take me back to the beginning of your dance career."

"I knew at a very young age that I belonged on the stage. I studied acting, opera, and ballet, but dance was my first love. In 1967 I was accepted into the Alvin Ailey American Dance Theater. I had no previous experience with modern dance. I think they took me because I could do jazz fairly well and gave myself passionately to the movement."

"Were you the only white dancer in the company?"

"I was viewed as their white token. Most of the time I felt invisible, as if I were in a community of foreign-speaking people. It was sort of a culture shock for me. I kept thinking to myself, 'What are they saying? What did that joke mean? Are they speaking a different language?' We toured Africa and the Middle East in 1967, and civil war raged in just about every country we visited. It was a very violent time. A representative of the US State Department accompanied us on tour, and that gave us the illusion that because we were Americans we would be safe. But it was really like walking through the valley of the shadow of death—especially for me. As a white person I really stood out and was terrified."

"How did dancing Alvin Ailey's work affect you as a choreographer?"

"My choreography is very deeply informed by having danced the works of Alvin Ailey. He never took me aside and offered me pearls of wisdom. It had much more to do with the fact that his dances spoke of the depth of his soul. One can't help but be affected by that. His choreography was very brilliant, especially his early work. He incorporated many different techniques into his choreography—Lester Horton's technique, earthy African moves, ballet with its beautiful lines. Alvin saw that Horton alone, or Graham alone, was not the direction dance was headed in. He was one of the first to begin fusing and incorporating many different forms into one. But I think that by 1967 he was struggling to create new works. It seemed to me that he was trying desperately to produce another *Revelations*, and it wasn't coming. This stagnant period was probably complicated by the fact that even though he worked very hard and was very famous, he hardly ever made any money. I remember on a couple of occasions when he'd get stuck choreographically, he'd borrow from his previ-

ous dances. 'Let's take thirty-two counts from *Blues Suite* and insert it here,' he'd say. Back then, I didn't stop to think how difficult it must have been for a black man to find a place in the dance world. There were very few role models for him to follow. One time he was having a press conference—I forget what country we were in—and he was asked, 'Do you prefer to be called black or Negro?' He responded by saying, 'I prefer to be called Alvin Ailey, choreographer.'"

"When did you realize that you had the desire and the talent to choreograph?"

"Well, it sort of happened by accident. After I left the Ailey company, I got together with some friends and we formed a group called Theater Dance Collection. After we performed in a dance festival in Central Park, the director of Lisbon's Metropolitan Ballet approached us and offered to hire us to perform in his theater. I remember going over on the plane worrying that he would find out that I wasn't really a choreographer. Once we got there we were given studio space and plenty of time to prepare for the concert. I choreographed the piece, and my friends performed it. On opening night, as I sat in the audience watching the group onstage, it suddenly hit me. I don't belong up there. I belong down here. It was a pivotal moment for me. I realized that I was never going to be as great a dancer as potentially I could be a choreographer."

"Once you made the decision to become a choreographer, how difficult was it to get jobs and make a name for yourself?"

"I didn't think about it quite like that because around that same time my marriage fell apart, and I had to work to support myself and my child. Dance and choreography were all I knew how to do. I wasn't trying to become famous or track a career rise. I was just trying to survive. I never left a job patting myself on the back. I didn't have that luxury. I'd come home and say, 'Yes, now I can pay the bills and send Shaun to summer camp.' Even during that period, choreographing was a deeply satisfying experience."

"What was it like to be a choreographer in the late 1960s and early 1970s?"

"It was a time when the moderns were rebelling against traditional dance vocabulary. They found meaning in a more perceptual approach to movement.

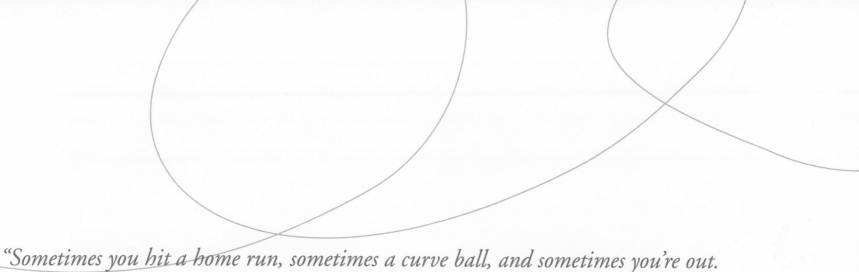

"Sometimes you hit a home run, sometimes a curve ball, and sometimes you're out. It takes courage to run the bases and realize that these are all parts of life in the creative field."

My sensibility and aesthetic were very far away from that way of thinking. I was literally out of step with the choreography of the times. I see now that we've benefited from the minimalism, negative space, and improvisation of that period. It taught us about tolerance and how to appreciate diversity in art. But I've always been more interested in work that is story-driven, theatrical in presentation, and composed of different movement styles and vocabulary—what audiences today want to see. So it's a wonderful time for me because, at long last, I identify with the aesthetic of the times."

"Tell me about *Prayers from the Edge,* the commission you did for the Alvin Ailey American Dance Theater."

"When Judith Jamison came to me in 2000, eleven years after Alvin's passing, and asked me to do a piece for the company, I felt it was a wonderful opportunity for me to contribute to the company that had meant so much to me. While trying to come up with a concept for the piece, I recalled an incident that happened to me in Israel when I was on tour with the Ailey company. It was a week after the Six Days' War, and my friend Enid and I decided to hitchhike to Jerusalem. It was a pretty dumb thing to do, considering the country was still in a war zone. Walking through Jerusalem, we entered a neighborhood where Jews and Arabs had congregated. They were talking to each other and really getting along. I remember saying to my friend, 'Isn't this great? I think they have finally found peace.' Obviously, history has proved me wrong, but the memory of these sworn enemies interacting peacefully stayed with me. I decided to use it as a theme for the work."

"Once you have an inkling of what a piece is going to be about, as you did with *Prayers from the Edge,* how does the movement unfold?"

"Typically I'll come up with a deep movement instinct and then try to create a vision to satisfy that instinct. I draw dance vocabulary from ballet, modern, and/or jazz, unless I'm doing a period piece, like *Swing,* for example. In that situation, I had to utilize swing dancing, with its emphasis on partnering and steps. Often I allow the music to help me find the movement. With *Prayers from the Edge,* I used a song called "Passion," by Peter Gabriel, and it inspired movement within me."

"How do you know if what you're coming up with is going to work?"

"I don't. If I'm heading in the wrong direction, a red flag will go up. When that happens, I can't choreograph a single step. But you never really know what's going to read to an audience. Sometimes you hit a home run, and sometimes you're out. Success and failure are just part of life when you play on a creative field. It takes courage to create."

New York City, 1998, 2003

179

Radical

eleo pomare

"You've been labeled an angry choreographer. Why?"

"Probably because I tell the truth. People who have refused to see the truth label what I do as angry. I talk about the human condition as I see it."

"Have you always been rebellious?"

"I have a rebellious nature. When I was young, I defied my family, who wanted me to be a doctor or a lawyer. I preferred the arts and attended New York's High School for the Performing Arts. I thought I would be an actor but soon realized that there would be few roles for me, unless I wanted to be stereotyped to do dark, moody parts. So I transferred to the dance department. I thought dance would allow me to be my own voice and demonstrate my own point of view. I was beginning to develop a deep political awareness. I wanted to be involved in the human experience, and I thought I could do that more easily through dance and choreography. It was also around that time that I met James Baldwin, who had a powerful influence on me and would affect the direction of my art."

"When did you first start choreographing, and what was the work about?"

"I formed my first company, the Eleo Pomare Dance Company, in 1958. I began to draw subject matter from real events and personal experiences. A few years later I received a fellowship to tour Europe. While in Amsterdam I lived next door to the Anne Frank House. I saw where she and her family hid and where the Jews were brought before being sent to concentration camps. It was

"I don't run

because I hear the train.

If I miss it,

it wasn't mine."

chilling and reinforced my commitment to speak about humanity and injustice. Jimmy Baldwin urged me to return to the States to attend the March on Washington when Martin Luther King Jr. gave his 'I Have a Dream' speech. The civil rights movement was in full swing, so I decided that my place was here, where the shit would fly."

"So your intention was to use dance to comment on the sociopolitical condition in this country, particularly the black experience?"

"Yes. Many of my works deal with black identity. What I read, what I hear on the street, what I get from conversations with people, and what I see all go into the work. *Blues in the Jungle* was a piece I first choreographed in 1962. It depicts ghetto life in Harlem. Through the choreography you experience various elements of black life. You see inside a prison or tenement window. You see junkies on the street, et cetera."

"How was it received?"

"Many thought it very powerful because it was truthful. I was immediately labeled angry or militant."

"How do you convey your sense of truth in a way that will enable audiences to understand your intention?"

"I'm not concerned about other people understanding my work. I make it, and it's out there. They can take it or leave it."

"If they leave it, how do you pay the rent? And don't you need to eat?"

"Artists don't need to eat," he said jokingly. "I don't care if the work makes money. I am a survivor, and I'm not afraid of anything. I've been down to six dol-

lars, the minimum to keep my bank account open. What I've learned as an artist is not to be afraid of the outcome of my life. Why do you need a whole wad of money? It just makes you want more and more and more."

"What about just living comfortably? Is that selling out?"

"A lot of people live comfortably but self-destruct because they're so bored."

"Do you think if you were financially comfortable it would make you creatively complacent?"

Stunned by my question, Eleo sat back and gave me a long, hard look.

"I think struggle is important. I think reality is important. I can't think of anything I want really badly that I can't make myself, that doesn't come to me naturally, or that I don't already have. I don't run because I hear the train. If I miss it, it wasn't mine."

"Does it bother you that you've been labeled angry?"

"Yes. I'm tired of being called angry just because I've shown the black man as he truly is rather than as folksy or exotic."

"How do you try to counteract this perception?"

"Periodically I craft commercially acceptable work just to get the critics off my back. It's lovely work that has no significance to reality. It's for people who don't want to think or be touched emotionally. I do it to protect my freedom to say what I want to say. It's a way of distracting certain people, and it gives me license to do the so-called 'other stuff'. Still, people will say to me, 'Oh, this work is so nice, why do you have to do that other work? Why do you have to do things like that, or say things like that?' I've been told by many regional companies who'd like me to choreograph on their companies, 'We love your work, but please don't do anything that will upset the community or our funding.' UPSET, UPSET, UPSET."

"That upsets you."

"Yes, because it's the colonialist attitude of bowing. I don't think it should be that way—to do things just to please or compromise your integrity. So when I'm confronted with these situations, I end up using my favorite phrase: 'I ain't doing it.' I walk away and tell them they might as well go find someone to stage *Swan Lake*."

"Are you still addressing the same civil rights issues you did in the 1960s, or have things improved for African Americans?"

"I think we're moving backward. I think the benefits from the battles we fought in the 1960s have been turned around. It's due to apathy and a preoccupation with me-ism. This generation has completely forgotten what happened in their parents' lives. They never hear the truth."

"How about the black dance artist? Has he made headway in recent decades?"

"I think very few black dance artists will make history. Very few will emerge in the forthcoming decades."

"Are you saying that only one Alvin Ailey will emerge in our lifetime?"

"Yes, that's right. It stopped with Alvin Ailey. It's not the intention of the arts establishment to have more than one great black choreographer in New York, regardless of how fine other choreographers might be."

"Why? Was Alvin simply the more 'brilliant' or did he surface at the right time?"

"Alvin was brilliant, but so was Talley Beatty. He is not as well known, but Talley's dances were not created to please anyone. He was not sponsored by Coca-Cola, and therefore he did not have to fear losing funding if he said or did the 'wrong thing.' Talley did not need to censor himself, so he could tell the truth in his work. When I saw his dances in the 1960s they inspired me, even though I didn't know where he was coming from. He taught me that I could go in my own direction, that I could be liberated by my own individuality, even if it meant stepping outside the dance mainstream."

"You strike me as a loner. Have you ever collaborated with another choreographer?"

"I find choreographing work to be a private experience. I'm not in favor of two people choreographing one work. It reeks of making a saleable product."

"Do you consider yourself an anarchist?"

"Yes."

"How would an anarchist advise a young aspiring dance artist?"

"Well, for that one I'd have to quote Shakespeare. 'To thine own self be true.' And then I would tell them, 'Be aware of tigers and monsters. There are people who suffer from jealousy and lurk in the shadows. Don't let them destroy you or push you to self-destruction.'"

"Do you make a distinction between yourself the man and yourself the artist?"

"I don't separate my art from who I am. I am purely intuitive. In fact, my biggest fear is that I'll wake up one morning and have lost my intuition. It's an ongoing nightmare of mine that I will lose my spark, that spontaneous thing that helps me create. You see, I never plan anything in advance. I might take a stack of books or CDs with me when I set out to create a work. I never know what I'm going to do until I do it. It is a spontaneous approach that comes naturally out of my relationship with the dancers, the music, and my imagination. The movement that I create comes from an organic place. I have managed to create a style and approach to movement that is uniquely mine."

"Do you feel you've been successful?"

"It depends on how you define success. I'm exactly where I should be in my life. I am successful because I've never tried to design myself after anyone else, and I am free to make statements I believe in. I'm a happy person, not bitter at all. I embrace life, experiencing different people, music, and cuisine. I have two beautiful cats that wake me every morning at sunrise. Together we look out at the extraordinary Manhattan skyline and the new day."

New York City, 1999

Balletomane

christopher wheeldon

The twenty-nine-year-old choreographer bounded up the stairs of the San Francisco Ballet School, a Starbucks cup in his hand.

"So sorry I'm late. I overslept," he said in a British accent. "I didn't have a chance to even shave. Is that all right?"

"Yes, of course. I want you to be yourself."

I directed him to the lighting setup in one of the small studios. We pulled up a couple of chairs and sat down to get acquainted.

"Chris, you seem to be addicted to dancemaking."

"Choreography is something I really have to do right now. It's become more than just a desire. When I'm in the studio with the dancers and the muse has struck, there is no other place in the world I'd rather be. When I'm not choreographing, I'm not happy. I feel completely at a loss and terribly unfulfilled. Ever since I stopped dancing a half a year ago, I've become much more aware of how disconnected I feel during the off times."

"I understand now how you've been able to create such a large body of work in so short a time."

"In the eight years that I've been in the States, I've created sixteen ballets, and I'm just now starting to form a style and find out what it is that I want to say in my work. I feel that the maturity of my work is in direct proportion to my maturity as a human being. I still think of myself as an apprentice. I don't really feel comfortable referring to myself as a choreographer. The true test of my talent will depend on whether or not my ballets stand the test of time."

"How do you spend your time when you're not in the studio with the dancers?"

"I hunt for music. I love classical music and draw readily from Renaissance to contemporary composers. When I go to the Philharmonic and hear a composition, ideas immediately start whizzing around in my head. I'm no longer hearing a concerto or a symphony, I'm envisioning a pas de deux or the corps dancing. It's taken a certain level of enjoyment away from listening to music, but I can't seem to help myself. I never choreograph prior to working with the dancers in the studio. I may spend days in my apartment completely immersed in the music, but only in the presence of the dancers, driven by the music, does the choreography emerge."

"So you create spontaneously—on the spot without any preparation?"

"Yes, that's right. If I choreograph staring at myself in the mirror, I'm not drawing anything of the personality, or the feelings, or emotions of my dancers. I want to look inside the souls of the people with whom I work. You see, there are no spoken words in ballet. The intent of the choreographer is to bring out the subtle nuances of the dancers through the steps and movements he gives them."

"What happens when the dynamics between you and the dancers are anything but dynamic?"

"That happened to me once. I walked into a studio and just felt like doing nothing with these people. They stood there with their hands on their hips, and I stood there with my hands on my hips, and we got nowhere. I think the problem was that I felt no connection to the commissioned score. If I lose confidence in the music, I lose rapport with the dancers, and the choreographic process takes a downward dive. I've since vowed never to accept a commission unless I feel truly passionate about the music."

"How would you describe your approach to ballet?"

"In the past couple of years I've learned a great deal about the shape and quality of movement, and I prefer to focus on that rather than production values like theatrics, scenery, and costumes. I'm more interested now in stripping away to the movement, to the purest dance. In the tradition of George Balanchine, I try to communicate to an audience without relying on spectacle."

"Do you try to impart personal messages or ideas through your choreography?"

"I don't try to convey a specific message. I'm not really interested in telling an audience what they should feel or think. I prefer that they decide on the message themselves. I might put a man and a woman together and create a pas de deux. It can be a literal telling of love or even the breakup of a marriage. I'm interested in letting their movement spark emotions and ideas."

"But in creating a piece you come in with a specific idea, don't you?"

"Yes, but none of that matters because the audience is free to interpret what's being presented in front of them. The only thing I know in advance is once I get into the studio with music and dancers that inspire me, something is going to be created—good, bad, or indifferent."

"You really trust yourself."

"Yes, I guess I do."

"You've obviously been greatly influenced by the work of George Balanchine. It must be an incredible feeling to have been appointed resident choreographer of the New York City Ballet, the company he created. Tell me what led to your appointment."

"For that I have to take you back. I fell in love with ballet at the age of seven while viewing a televised performance of Frederick Ashton's *La Fille mal gardée*. Then, after attending a live performance by the Royal Ballet, I asked my parents to enroll me in ballet class. My beginnings were not unlike the fictional character in the film *Billy Eliot*. I attended ballet classes at a small village school in Somerset, England. Amidst a sea of girls, I learned the positions holding on to the back of a chair. The girls got to use the barre. After a few months, my mother began driving me two and a half hours to London's Royal Ballet School. I would do my homework in the car and fill up on sandwiches and milk shakes to keep up my energy. By the age of eleven, I was accepted as a full-time student, which required that I leave home and reside in the school's boardinghouse. At first I was terribly homesick, but making dances kept me busy and relieved my anxiety about being so far away from my family. One of my first ballets was a complete rehashing of *Swan Lake*. I did a prequel. I had eggs hatching and swans emerging. In 1991, when I was eighteen, I was accepted into the Royal Ballet's corps de ballet. I hate to admit it, but I was a real 'bun head' back then. All I focused on was promoting my career. I dismissed anything that did not pertain to ballet. When a friend offered me a free airline ticket to the United States during a school holiday break, I took it. While in Manhattan, I had the opportunity to take company class with the New York City Ballet. The company's artistic director, Peter Martins, happened to be present and immediately offered me a job. I finished my contract with the Royal Ballet and by the following season was dancing in several NYCB ballets. In 1998 I was promoted to the rank of soloist. Jerome Robbins gave me my first principal role in *Dances at a Gathering.*"

"Did you know then that you wanted to become a choreographer?"

"Absolutely. My dream was to become choreographer of a major ballet company. I inundated Peter Martins with videos of short ballets I had created in my spare time. The videotapes would stack up on his desk. Eventually, he permitted me to choreograph small projects, like holiday programs and workshops. It didn't take too long before I convinced him to let me create a few ballets for the company. I decided to retire from dancing at the age of twenty-seven to devote myself to choreography."

"Tell me about your first couple of ballets for the company."

"*Polyphonia,* set to the piano music of Gyorgi Ligeti, premiered January of 2001. It was created along the lines of *Agnon or Episodes,* a plotless ballet with pure dance at its core. *Variations SerPeusus,* was a comedic, behind-the-scenes look at a dance company preparing for a performance. I used the music of Felix Mendelssohn."

"The critics have hailed your work as 'innovative,' 'daring,' and 'inventively unpredictable.'"

"Yes, I was really pleased with the response. I feel a responsibility now to go beyond mere entertainment and try to be more creative and to push the art form forward a bit."

Chris looked at his watch and reminded me that soon he would need to leave to resume his work with the San Francisco Ballet.

"Well, then," I said, "let's take that portrait now."

I suggested that he step up to the mirrored wall and play around with his own reflection until we came up with something interesting. He began sculpting shapes with his hands and body, and then leaned up close against the glass.

"What about this?"

"Yes, that looks very cool," I said, taking a Polaroid.

I handed it to him for an opinion. He looked at it, and his face turned pale.

"Chris, what is it? Are you all right?"

"This is too wild," he said, mesmerized by the photo. "I was born with a twin. He died at birth. This is too wild," he repeated.

He leaned against the mirror again and studied the double image on the Polaroid. "I'm all right," he said after a minute. "I'm sorry. That really took me by surprise. It's fine. Let's shoot it."

I re-created the image on film just before Chris was summoned to the adjacent studio. Before leaving, he invited me to come watch him work. He said it would help me understand his process. So I packed up all my gear, loaded another camera, and followed him into the large company rehearsal space.

To watch Wheeldon in action is to watch a skilled and confident artist. Once the work began to find its shape, he paced up and down like a basketball coach shadowing the players from the sidelines. Animated, energetic, and excited, he flipped interchangeably between technician and tactician as he moved the choreography along. Here and there he slipped in among the dancers, breathed them in, suggested a change, and then slipped out again. He sculpted the dancers into a shape and then slowly whirled them out of it, adding colorful dance motifs and dramatic arm gestures. After a good forty-five minutes, he stopped and covered his eyes with his hands.

The dancers stood silently. Only the music could be heard.

San Francisco, 2001

187

Man of Means

grover dale

I met the former publisher and editor of L.A. Dance and Fitness *magazine in 1995.*

After reviewing my portfolio, Grover Dale agreed to give me my first photo-journalist assignment—an article titled "Why the Dancer Needs the Photographer." We have since collaborated on numerous projects, but it was not until I interviewed him for this book, in the backyard of his Beverly Hills home, that he revealed to me the forces that led him to a life in dance.

"You've come a long way from your meager beginnings in McKeesport, Pennsylvania."

"Yes, today I am a millionaire. But I've never forgotten my past. Just the other day, I discovered an old photograph of my mother standing outside the gate of our house—a three-room shack on a dirt road. I was born into a dysfunctional family. My father, who was an alcoholic, abandoned us when I was very young. My future held no promise, no expectation for success. I spent my early years just trying to survive."

"Given your circumstances, how did you discover dance?"

"When I was nine years old, a neighbor came to my house and asked my mother if I would accompany her son to his tap dance lesson. In exchange, she offered to pay for me to take the class. Anything that was free was of interest to me, so I gladly accepted the assignment. If that woman had not come to my house that day, I don't think I would ever have stepped foot inside a dance studio."

"Can you recall what that first dance class felt like?"

"Yes, I remember that I really liked it and that the steps came fairly easily to me. There were no bolts of lightning or fireworks. I didn't realize until years later the significance of that first class. The dance teacher, Lillian Jasper, recognized that I had what she called 'natural talent' and refused to let me stop studying dance. By the time I was thirteen, the other kids at school were making fun of me, calling me names like Mr. Tap Toe. I almost quit. But Lillian Jasper said, 'Don't quit! I'll pay you to assist me.' If she hadn't put me to work and paid me nine dollars a week, I'm pretty sure I would have been out of there. I only understood in hindsight that those two women—the neighbor and my dance teacher—probably saved my life."

"Teaching dance helped you support yourself?"

"Yes. By the time I was fifteen, I had opened up my own little dance school and was earning anywhere from fifteen to thirty-five dollars a month, an impressive sum of money in 1950. I realized then that the dance profession could support me financially throughout my life. When I was seventeen, I acquired an Equity card, which enabled me to dance professionally. I took off for New York City and never looked back."

"You had your eyes on Broadway?"

"Yes. I made it to Broadway, all right—selling hot dogs on the corner of Forty-second and Broadway. It took another six months before I landed my first dance job."

"I've heard you tell your dance audition workshop students that you were clueless when you first came to New York, that you didn't know how to get hired."

"That's right. I thought all you had to do was check the Equity listings for jobs and just go dance your best. I didn't know that one needed to dress and behave a certain way. I didn't know that you needed to be taking acting lessons to boost your employability and to have an agent. I didn't know that you needed to market yourself in order to get noticed. It took months before I realized that in order to get seen by the casting people, you had to position yourself down front. Once I did that, I got hired by the June Taylor Dancers to appear on *The Jackie Gleason Show.*"

"How did you come to dance on the Broadway stage?"

"I auditioned for a part in *Li'l Abner* and was chosen by choreographer Michael Kidd to dance in the show. That was a very big break."

(I later asked Michael Kidd why he cast Grover Dale in the show, and he told me, "Grover had a youthful spontaneity and vigor that *Li'l Abner* required. I saw a twinkle in his eye and a colorful sense of humor. That was just the sort of enthusiasm I was looking for. Of course, he executed the oddball movements perfectly.")

"What happened next?"

"*West Side Story.* I was selected over hundreds of dancers to play Snowboy in the original Broadway production."

"What did it feel like to win such a sought-after part?"

"Rose, that was something like fifty years ago."

"Yes, Grover, but that role must have been a life-altering experience. Surely you must remember how you felt."

Grover was silent for a minute, and then he looked at me and said, "I was panic-stricken, absolutely terrified. The anxiety was enormous. I didn't think I could do it. I felt like running. And I was put to the test on opening night. During the drugstore scene, I was supposed to be doing push-ups as the curtain goes up and then switch to the 'Cool' number. Well, Chita Rivera's 'America' number preceded the drugstore number and brought the house down. But it threw off the timing. I was forced to start my push-ups early. I'm supposed to do just a few push-ups, but suddenly it's ten, then twenty, and now it's forty and I'm dying. I'm terrified that I won't have enough energy to perform the 'Cool' dance that follows. I decide I'd better do something, so I collapse on the stage. The audience loves it and sees the humor in it—and so does Jerry [Jerome Robbins]. After the show I felt very proud of myself—I was able to take the initiative and get a laugh."

"How did your career progress from there?"

"I danced in several Broadway shows, including *Greenwillow, Sail Away, The Unsinkable Molly Brown,* and *Half a Sixpence."*

"When did you become interested in doing your own choreography?"

"Joe Layton allowed me to make choreographic suggestions. In *Greenwillow,* he let me choreograph my own dance. While I was performing, I could see and hear that the audience loved it. Bells and whistles went off in my head—perhaps I could be a choreographer. In 1966 I sent a thirteen-page proposal for a dance show to a producer friend at CBS. To my surprise, I was invited to stage the project on national television, thus making my choreographic debut. In 1969 I received my first Broadway assignment, a musical called *Billy Budd."*

"Did you feel prepared to choreograph for the Broadway stage?"

"Well, a year prior to that I had worked with Jerome Robbins in his American Theater Lab. I knew his process of research that was incredibly thorough and deep, and I applied it to *Billy Budd.* I spent two days on an old schooner in Connecticut to see how it would move in water and how that would affect body movement. When people weren't looking I'd dance around on deck, climb the ropes, smell the air, and let that environment inform me about what I should do. It turned out that the show opened and closed the same night. *Billy Budd* received disastrous reviews, but the *New York Times* dance critic called my choreography 'brilliant.' I went into a numb state because here I had just received this wonderful review, but hardly anyone would ever see my work."

"Later you worked with Robbins again."

"Yes. In 1989 I served as codirector of *Jerome Robbins' Broadway.* During that time I had a major revelation. Jerry and I had worked together on and off for thirty-five years. He was my mentor, my idol. But while working on this show, I realized that the man who was the single most creative influence in my life was a man who gained his strength by pointing out the weaknesses of others."

"It is well known that he could be very cruel to his dancers."

"Yes, but there was something else. I patterned my entire creative life after his. I always wanted his approval and emulated him as an artist. I walked into rehearsals, and my behavior reflected the behavior I learned from him. One day it dawned on me that I was being cruel and heartless, just like Jerry. It was a devastating revelation. I knew right away that I would need to make some fundamental changes in my life and in my behavior. I dropped out of the profession for the next six years and devoted myself to community service."

"In recent years you've become a major authority and resource for aspiring young dancers. What do you see as some of the major pitfalls that they should avoid?"

"The struggles that were true for dancers back in the 1950s and 1960s, when I was dancing, still exist today. The road has taken on some new curves, but it's still a long, hard road. Passion and drive were not enough then and are certainly not enough today. The industry bar continues to rise, with choreographers giving two-counts-of-eight auditions and no second chances. Producers and choreographers look for well-trained dancers who can also sing, act, and shine their inner light—all without skipping a beat. I feel for dancers who don't have the tools or experience to cope with the stresses of a dance life and make informed career decisions. I'm in a position now where I can teach those with potential and assure them that their dreams are possible. For many, my experience offers strength and hope."

Beverly Hills, 2001

191

Blond Bombshell

mia michaels

"I started dancing when I was still in diapers," Mia said, straddling the ottoman in my Greenwich Village sublet.

"My father owned a dance studio, so I grew up with tap, ballet, and jazz. By the time I was seven or eight I was choreographing shows for the neighborhood kids. Dance has always been part of my life."

"And yet you've never had a performance career."

"No. When I first started out in this business, I couldn't get hired because I didn't fit the 'prescribed body type.' There's little room for the bigger woman in the dance industry. I decided that I would just have to do my own thing, create my own niche. As it's turned out, I don't think my choreography would have the same power behind it, make the same impact, if I weighed ninety-five pounds. I also think being a larger woman sends out a message that you don't have to be anorexic to dance. When I cast or audition dancers, I'm not thinking about their body type at all. I'm one of the few who like to blend different body types and different sizes and shapes. It's about the movement, not how big someone's thighs are."

"Your work strikes me as very organic, very individualistic. Do you think your not having danced the work of other choreographers has actually served you in your development as a choreographer?"

"I think if I had worked with other choreographers, I might have had a greater dance vocabulary. All I've had to draw upon was my own training, which was classical, contemporary street dance with jazz and a little modern thrown in. I was never someone else's instrument and did not experience diverse styles and individual techniques. So when I first started out, I asked everyone, 'How do you structure a dance? What are the guidelines?' I found out through my own exploration that there is no set structure. There are no guidelines. I realized that once you bring a preconceived structure to your art, it becomes formulaic. The idea is to get out of the way of formula and allow the creative impulse to find its own path. I eventually saw myself leaning toward the humanness of movement and allowed the changes in my life to direct and inform my movement."

"How difficult has it been to make a name for yourself?"

"It's been difficult at times. The concert world told me that they thought my work looked too commercial. The commercial world said I was too artistic. No one knew where to put me. I'd lose choreography assignments on both ends. I've just kept plugging along, and recently I have found that these two worlds have begun to merge. People are now looking at my work with very accepting eyes. It's almost as if the artistic appetite of the times has caught up with what I'm all about."

"How do you choreograph a dance?"

"Well, it depends on the circumstance. I recently finished choreographing the Celine Dion show for Caesars Palace in Las Vegas. I flew to Belgium, where I worked with sixty dancers for six months, and then had them for another six months in Las Vegas. They had been selected from all over the world and were widely diverse in their training. I couldn't just go in there and set 'Mia movement' on them. I had to find out what each one of them brought to the table as an artist. Because of the many different energies, techniques, and influences around me, I was inspired to create in a whole new way. Rather than just telling them what to do, I focused on their strengths and capabilities to showcase their talents. Franco Dragone, the show's director, who is also the originator of Cirque du Soleil, collaborated with me on much of the movement."

"How much of the choreography was intended to reflect Celine Dion's image as a pop icon?"

"We didn't focus on that. During the creative process we didn't even rehearse to Celine's music. We varied the music to blend different moods, styles, and energy. I ended up creating nine and a half hours of dance choreography. Then Franco and I went back and assessed all the work. We began pulling sections from here and there, in a sort of cut-and-paste process, until we had what we needed. I saw hours of choreography that I consider to be some of my best work go unused because it didn't fit into the nature of the show. Then, when we hit the stage in Las Vegas, which was half the size of a football field, we started lining up the choreography with her vocals. Our approach to the choreography turned out to be a very good one. Had we choreographed to each one of her songs, which are very pop-oriented, the dancing would have been too clichéd. Because it is so random, it works. We provided a new context for her music in a way people could relate to her."

"When you choreograph a commercial like your Coldwell Banker ad, in which you had real estate buyers doing the tango, how much control do you have over your work?"

"My experience has been that the clients—the people who hire artists to help them sell their product—get very nervous about an artistic approach. They want you to supply them with something that will make their product accessible to the consumer and lighten up their sales pitch without alienating anyone. Therefore you often have to hold back creatively, because if you go too far they simply won't use it."

"Do you put any judgment on concert work as opposed to commercial work? Does one have more artistic value than the other?"

"It depends on the project. If a commercial project allows you to really dive in and create, like I was able to do with the Celine show, then it's extremely valuable and becomes a launch-off point to one's next work. Some choreographic jobs are what I call gigs—jobs that are not particularly fulfilling but move you along. But even when it's a gig, I try to take something away from the job beyond the paycheck. I always want to stretch and challenge myself to new levels. I also want to impact the people I'm working with—help them see things a little differently. I don't consider what I do as just a job. It's part of my identity. It's really all I know how to do. It's the only constant in my life."

"What are the most important lessons you've learned, Mia?"

"One of the most important lessons I ever learned was taught to me by my good friend Gregory Hines. About two years ago I was premiering some of my concert work with my company, RAW. I was wracked with anxiety, fixating on every little detail, taking notes like mad. When I spoke with Gregory on the phone, he asked me, 'Mia, are you enjoying this?' 'No,' I told him. 'I'm so nervous. I can't get this one dance to work. I'm going crazy.' And then he said something that has stayed with me ever since: 'We work so hard in this business, so if you're not enjoying it, why do it?' I realized then that I needed to change my attitude. He was right. I was so preoccupied with the small details I forgot to see the big picture. I made a conscious decision to accept what I had created and stop being my own worst critic. That night I put the notepad away and sat down with the audience to watch the show. I found myself sobbing with joy at what I had created."

Mia looked especially beautiful as she related her story, prompting me to begin our photo session. She wore a black sweater and slacks, and her blond dreadlocks and fair skin glowed under my lights.

I positioned myself directly across from her at eye level.

"You just want me to sit here?" she said. "I'd prefer moving around or dancing. This is sort of a magnifying glass—isn't it?"

"Well, it is up close and personal," I said. "I've found if I refrain my subjects from dancing, they're forced to just be themselves."

"Oh," she said unenthusiastically. She looked at my lens as if it were an old boyfriend—guarded, uneasy. Avoiding eye contact, she looked away. After a few minutes she nestled her face in her arms and pulled her knees to her chest. Mia suddenly reminded me of Marilyn Monroe: blond, beautiful, full of depth and determination—and strangely vulnerable.

New York City, 1999, photo and interview
Las Vegas, 2003, interview

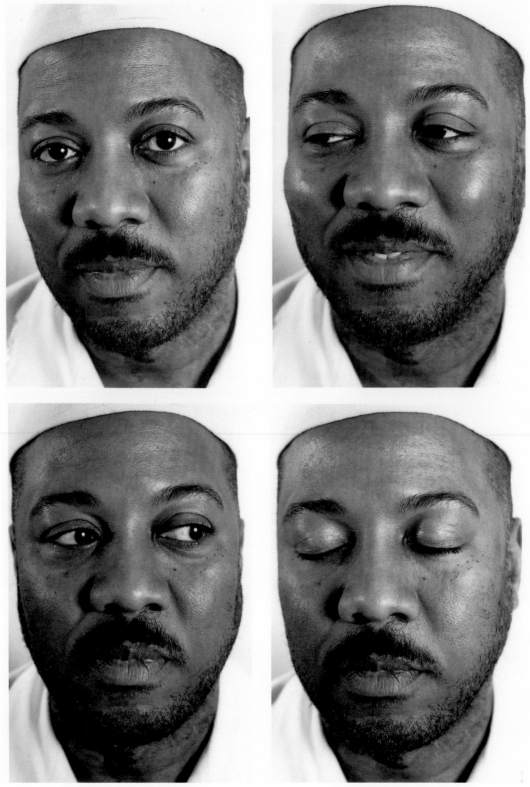

Dance Mystic

alonzo king

It was a clear, fogless morning. From Alonzo King's window I could see the entire San Francisco Bay.

While he dressed, I examined his spacious living room, furnished only with a sofa, a chair, and shelves of books on mysticism, Eastern religions, yoga, science, and art. I imagined him choreographing entire ballets in the outsized space.

"Sorry to keep you waiting, " he said, emerging from the bedroom. He was wearing only denim overalls.

"I appreciate your seeing me this morning," I said. "You must be exhausted from the concert last night."

"Yes, I'm beat. I hope you're not planning to photograph me today. Look at the bags under my eyes. I don't think I can deal with a photo just now."

"I understand," I said, although my camera was burning a hole in my bag.

"We will have to do it another day," he said, collapsing on the sofa and hugging a pillow to his chest. I joined him, pulling out my notes and tape recorder.

"Your ballets last night at the Yuerba Buena Performing Arts Complex gave me the feeling that the dancers were having a dialogue with the audience. What was your intention in creating those pieces?"

Alonzo closed his eyes and took a moment to collect his thoughts. Without opening his eyes, as if first needing to visualize the words, he began.

"What I'm interested in are the perennial truths, universal truths that we learn from living. I'm talking about truths we gather from science, literature, art, scripture, and having those ideas physicalized and communicated in dance.

"Dance is thought made visible."

Dance is thought made visible in the same way that music is thought made audible. I am obsessed with the discovery of who we really are."

"How does the human body facilitate communication of ideas?"

"The body is a symbol that we use as a reference for huge ideas."

His eyes closed once again, as if he were going into a meditation.

"We've been told that contemplatives who were watching the sun in its journey around the Earth got the information to create what is called the greatest invention of all time—the wheel. Whether we are talking about folk stories, aboriginal sculptures, or dances, their origin always points back to something primordial. If we look closely at classical ballet, we see that it too has been informed by elements in nature, the planets and stars and the world around us. Take, for example, the fouetté in ballet. The action is like a planet, an orb going around its axis, repeating itself. Much of dance technique has its origin in some natural or aboriginal idea."

"Do dance viewers really have to know the origin of a specific gesture or move to understand what they're looking at?"

"What's fascinating about art, if it has any depth at all, is that regardless of origin it yields many meanings. If a group of people went out together to view a sunset, some might look at the architecture and design of the perfect circle falling beneath the perfect straight line and how it decreases and disappears. Some might see metaphor—the close of the day—and think about the beginning on the other side. Some might focus on the colors and tones and marvel

at how that inspires them. And some might ask what's the big deal? Experience, familiarity, and capacity have everything to do with how we perceive information. You cannot recognize what is not within you. For example, someone who only knows a little about love and measures everything in terms of what they put out and what they get back will not understand selfless perpetual love. It's inconceivable to them."

"Isn't intuition also a factor in determining how we see and think and react to things?"

"Yes, intuition is one of the key elements in the artistic process. It has to do with trusting your instincts and following an impulse. Every person has it, but it's like a weak muscle if it hasn't been exercised. People tend not to trust themselves. 'Oh, I have a feeling I should take the umbrella today. Oh, that's silly.' And then it rains. We don't listen to ourselves enough."

"Along with intuition, when you create, how aware are you of your rational, thinking mind?"

"There is a part of dancemaking that is sheer construction. Whatever it is you make, you want it well made, and so you use craft and skill. If someone builds a house, and you open the front door and find yourself in the bathroom, well, that's poor design. If I cook a meal that has no nutritional value but looks pretty, then it's not going to be very satisfying. The artist is always aiming to create something of value. What animates the form is determined by what the artist is trying to reveal. Ultimately it is his spirit that drives things forward, but body and mind are participating simultaneously in a triumvirate of body-mind-spirit."

"Is it easier for an audience to see the value in a ballet if it comes in the form of a narrative?"

"Well, there are deep truths in spiritual fables like *Cinderella* and *Sleeping Beauty*. In *Swan Lake*, we are looking at a white bird that symbolizes spirit and a man who has to make a choice between reaching for a spirit that is unattainable or accepting the status quo: the marriage, the family, the kingdom. We face these life-altering decisions in real life all the time."

"In your quest for universal truths, do you lean toward a certain look or mood that distinguishes you from other ballet choreographers?"

"If you are asking me about style, I can tell you that style is an afterthought, not something that is preconceived. If I'm digging for diamonds in a mine, the maze that I've dug, which might look interesting, is just an aftereffect of all the digging, nothing more. The Buddhists say, 'Look.' But we get hung up staring at the finger instead of where it's pointing."

"So you're saying people sometimes get distracted by exterior factors and don't look deep enough into themselves?"

"So many dancers feel that what they look like is more important than who they are. This is a real danger for dancers who focus for years on appearances and think of themselves as merely a body. The choreographer can't work with them in the realm of ideas. It's a huge problem if they haven't been connecting internally. If they've decided that what's inside is of little value, they can only try to approximate some kind of look."

"What does dance teach you?"

Alonzo closed his eyes again. After a long pause he spoke.

"When I see great dance, I see fearlessness and selflessness. I see Gandhi, Helen Keller, Harriet Tubman. I see sacrifice and unfailing generosity. I see intelligence and intuition. I see humor and joy. I hear a voice guiding me: 'When you fall down, get up. You are able to do more than you think. When you feel you've given all you've got, give more.' I see how life can be lived."

We sat together in silence for several minutes. When Alonzo opened his eyes he looked refreshed.

"Rose, how about helping me bake a cake?" he said suddenly, completely shifting gears.

"Ah, well, sure. I have a plane to catch, but I think I can spare a little time before the shuttle gets here."

I followed Alonzo into his kitchen and watched as he mixed the ingredients in a large bowl with the deftness of an experienced chef. When the batter was smooth, Alonzo scooped up a spoonful and fed me a taste.

"Mmm, lemon chiffon."

San Francisco, 2001

Ambassador of Love

cleo parker robinson

"Okay, Sugar, you want to know about where my passion comes from?

Pull up a chair and get comfortable. Rose will be staying a while.

"I've spent my entire life trying to blend the opposing forces that make up my world. I was born to a white mother and an African American father. My experiences with racism run as deep as my commitment to overcome it. I grew up feeling more like an object than a human being. Dancing helped me feel better about myself. As a young child I would dance everywhere—in the living room and up and down the aisles of the market. I found I communicated better with my body than I did with words. In fact, I withdrew almost entirely from using language. When I was ten years old my parents separated briefly, and I moved with my mother to a segregated section of Dallas. It was during that time that I experienced full-blown racism. I had to drink out of the colored people's fountain, while my mother drank out of the white-only fountain. It was horrible for me, and even though I was a very healthy child, I suffered a near-fatal heart attack. I remember the journey—the feeling of dying and my organs shutting down. But I had a very strong will to live and came all the way back. That experience changed my life forever."

"Really, Cleo, I had no idea."

"Yes, that's right. The doctors said I'd be bedridden. But I fought hard and regained my strength. After the heart attack I remember looking in the mirror and seeing my reflection, but much more. Somehow I had a heightened aware-

201

ness about the things around me. I didn't know what to do with it. I couldn't talk about it. So I had to dance about it. I was struggling to find a way of living in a white world and a black world. My challenges throughout my life have been to bring these two together."

"So you chose to dance your feelings?"

"Yes. I started choreographing dances while in junior high school. I had a teacher in the PE department who familiarized me with modern dance. I started to use modern dance vocabulary to tell stories. My stories were intended to alter perceptions. Through my dance I explored emotions, content, texture, shapes, and sounds. No one around me was doing that sort of thing. My world was all about being in a black environment defending my white mother or in a white environment dealing with my blackness. Most people didn't understand what I was saying, but dance was the best way I knew how to communicate."

"When did you begin formal dance training?"

"I began my formal dance training much later, in college. I began to study with a woman named Rita Berger, a former dancer with George Balanchine. Rita had survived the Nazi death camps and really understood where I was coming from. As someone who had experienced racism firsthand, she helped me to understand the nature of prejudice. Through her guidance I was able to channel what I was feeling and use it expressively. After Rita, I began to study with Katherine Dunham, who had a major influence on me as an artist. She helped me project my artist's voice with resonance and volume. Her technique teaches you to make your movement and dance purposeful. Katherine Dunham didn't only affect me, she opened the door for all African American artists to express their creativity on the stage. It's only in the last thirty years that dancing has been acceptable for African Americans. If we look historically at dance and movement in this country, we see that our drums were taken away from us as soon as we got here. Dunham helped bring them back by celebrating our dance heritage and filling us with pride."

"How do you express this in your choreography?"

"I try to present dynamic works that speak of respect for all peoples and encourage us to feed our souls. We need our heart pumping a little faster in harmony with other folks. We need to find a spiritual language to communicate to one another. I tell the dancers in my company that they can use the tools of dance—pliés, *relevés*, and *développés*—in the service of something positive and beautiful."

"You speak through your choreography, but you're also an educator and a mentor."

"Yes. Education takes place in the studio, on the stage, and in the spirit. We want to see our children develop strategies to make this world a better place. Dance is much more than just entertainment. It is a means to self-discovery. And whether it's hip-hop, ballet, or modern dance, it isn't the form, it's the essence of the spirit that I'm after."

"Dance teachers traditionally teach steps and then ask their students to repeat them, but you ask for something else."

"Yes, there is a preoccupation with simply handing over steps and shapes for students to repeat. I think dancers dishonor themselves if they don't put a part of themselves into the experience. As a choreographer and educator I'm not worried about your steps, I'm worried about your relationships. I tell my dancers, 'Concern yourself not so much with what you look like, but with what it is you want to say. How you look will grow out of how you feel.'"

"So you're not as concerned with dance technique as you are with trying to convey messages and ideas?"

"No, I think dancers must be well trained if they are going to perform on the stage. Don't forget they have a responsibility to express the visions of the choreographer who supplied them with the movement. But I think there is too much time spent in the studio doing pliés at the barre. We've forgotten that knowledge can also be found in nature. Dancers have fallen out of touch with the energy and beauty that is all around us. There is a truth and discovery in our mountains, oceans, deserts, and natural environment. Dancers need to experience all their senses and apply that knowledge to their bodies and movement expression."

"You're saying that dance should not be something that just happens in the studio. It should reflect aspects of the dancers' real life."

"Dance is about the whole person and about every part of your life. When we learn how to integrate the dance with who we are, we elevate it to a whole other level. Let's not forget, dance technique is not an easy thing to master. It's time-consuming, painful, and challenging. So it's important to find a balance between the dancing life and the non-dancing life. I am guided by what I call synergy. It's a way of integrating the physical and the spiritual aspects of your life. I try to impart this thinking to my dancers and students, and share with them the things that turn me on. I hope it encourages them to investigate their own synergetic experience and find a balance. I want the dancer to become everything—the musician, composer, and storyteller. If the dancing doesn't have meaning to them, it won't matter to anyone else."

Three years later Cleo and I were having lunch at a picnic table on the grounds of Jacob's Pillow Dance Festival. While I had photographed Cleo on many occasions, I noticed that on this day she looked positively luminous. Dressed in an orange top and multicolored African fabric tied at the waist, she held her face up to the sun and soaked in its rays.

"Cleo," I said, "I hope you've put on sunscreen. This sun is very harmful."

"Oh, Sugar, don't worry. How often do we get to feel the warmth of the sun surrounded by God's green earth?"

I knew at that moment that the many photos I had taken of her on the stage, in the studio, and in her dressing room didn't do her justice. I invited her to take a walk with me into the woods and then pulled out my camera to capture her true nature.

Denver, 2000

Lee, Massachusetts, Jacob's Pillow Dance Festival, 2003

Tough Guy

donald byrd

Donald Byrd's reputation of toughness was confirmed during the two days I spent with him and his company, Donald Byrd's/The Group. In rehearsals, he believed he could get more out of his dancers by intimidation than praise. When the time came for me to take his portrait, I wanted to make sure that he did not use his bullying tactics on me. So as soon as he sat under my lights, I took charge.

"You're mine now," I told him. "Sit up. Pull in your stomach. Pay attention!"

He was stunned, as were his dancers, who broke into catcalls and applause. I gave them a wink and turned toward my prey. Donald immediately tuned out the dancers and turned his attention on me. I took about four shots and realized that I had his attention, but not much else. His true nature lay hidden behind a professional mask. How was I to draw him out?

"Didn't he come in with a hat?" I called out to his agent. The hat appeared, and the second Donald put it on, he found his face.

"Now show me who you really are," I demanded.

He offered me a variety of Donald Byrd impersonations: Donald the tough guy, Donald the clown, Donald the playboy. But midway through the first roll of film, his expression turned serious. Donald Byrd the man had surfaced.

Six months later we met for our interview at a hotel coffee shop in Orange County, California. Away from his dancers he was a patient and pleasant man.

"Your choreography is very controversial," I began. "You make statements in your work about sensitive issues like domestic violence and racial stereotypes."

"Well, I don't see any reason to add to the noise factor of this century unless I have something really important to say. I try to be honest with the work I put in front of the public and hope that my messages come across."

"You can be pretty harsh with your dancers," I said. "Is that because you want to ensure that they represent you correctly?"

"The movement that I give my dancers has to be authentic. If they start to interpret or paraphrase my movement, then they are not being true to my intention. The problem arises when dancers bring their own agenda, when they put themselves as performers or their insecurities about who they are onto the stage. When that happens, they are not authentic in their representation or communicating honestly to an audience. My job is to remind them to return to the original intent of the work, should they stray from it. I know I can be very demanding, unrelenting. But I want what I want, when I want it! I don't think that's being harsh with my dancers."

"Do you feel any sense of responsibility that they might end up crippled one day from performing your extreme dance vocabulary?"

"The dancers who perform my work can do it. If they tell me they can't do something, I don't force them. But the demands of ballet are what they are. The possibility for injury is great. There are a lot of crippled dancers out there as a result of this codified structure—turn out and point your feet. That's just the way it is."

"Yes, but you bend the boundaries of conventional technique to make extreme statements and explore new physical possibilities, don't you?"

"Anytime you challenge the body there is danger. When you challenge the mind, go on a spiritual quest, you might not come back. I think it's the same with the body. I also have an agenda. And that is to see how far I can push the body. I don't mean just the physical body, I mean the mind, too."

"My agenda . . . is to see how far I can push the body.
I don't mean just the physical body, I mean the mind, too."

"Does that require creating a new vocabulary of movement within your process?"

"I'm not married to a particular process or vocabulary, although those are the things that feed me. Craft can be a dangerous thing. You can hide behind it. You construct things that are so elaborate that you don't have to reveal anything about yourself as a human being. You don't even have to reveal a point of view. I've become less interested in dazzling the world with my fabulous technique and more interested in the substance or content of my work."

"How does your process sustain you?"

"Ultimately the process gives me a reason for being, makes me want to create again and again. The process is therapeutic, like a medication. Through it I discover what I really think, feel, and believe in. I don't really know until I get into the process who I am as an artist."

"What's it like for you when you're not in the process?"

"I get very anxious. I begin to fear that I might not know how to do it again. It's not about finding the inspiration for a piece, it's about thinking I may lose touch with the skill. Experience and my logical reasoning mind tell me, 'You've been doing it for a long time, you know how to do this, don't worry, just trust.' But the other part of me is saying, 'You've forgotten how to do it. Up until this point, it's just been luck.'"

"Have you had to make personal sacrifices for your art?"

"In my personal relationships, I have had to ask people to play second fiddle to my art. If they couldn't, then I wasn't interested. I realize it's an emotionally brutal way to live, giving up the gentleness and comfort of intimate relationships. Perhaps I'm too self-involved, too selfish. The commitment to my art comes first. I don't think you can have it both ways."

Orange County, California, 1998

Guardian of the Tradition

alan johnson

Alan Johnson decided to become a professional dancer at the age of eighteen after seeing Jack Cole dance in the film *The I Don't Care Girl*.

"'Oh, my God,' I said to myself. 'Now that's dancing. That's what I want to do and that's how good I want to be.' It was as if Cole were interacting with space—lifting it up, pushing it out. It was clean and precise and intoxicating."

"Once you made that decision, where did you go for your dance training?"

"I came to New York from Pennsylvania in 1955 and studied with two wonderful teachers, Matt Mattox and Peter Gennaro. I sought out Matt Mattox because he had been one of Jack Cole's featured dancers, performing his nightclub act and in his movies. I figured his Cole influence could rub off on me. Peter Gennaro was great fun and just danced from his soul. He didn't care if you made mistakes or if you were off the beat. He just wanted you to feel the music. 'I just want to see you boogie,' he would say. He drove his assistants crazy because he never gave counts. You'd have to figure them out for yourself, and just as you did, he would change them. I also realized at a certain point that I needed the foundation of ballet, so I went to Nanette Charisse. She was an incredible ballet teacher. All the gypsies went to her."

"While taking dance classes, were you auditioning for parts in Broadway shows?"

"Yes. I took dance classes at night and went to cattle calls by day."

"When did you get your first big dance job?"

"It was 1956. I got into the national traveling company of *Damn Yankees*, which, of course, had been choreographed by Bob Fosse."

"How did you get a part in *West Side Story*?"

"Seeing that show bowled me over. I had to go back and see it again and again and again. I went to every dancer-replacement audition, hell-bent on getting into the show. I was hired in 1958, a year after they opened, and was in rehearsal the week of their one-year anniversary. I became dance captain and danced in the first national company, its reopening on Broadway, and then I spent nine months with the European company."

"It's amazing how many dancers and choreographers refer to *West Side Story* as fundamental to their development as artists. Why was this show so significant?"

"It was the first time that dance told a story in such a dramatic and beautiful way. You weren't watching someone doing steps. You were seeing characters revealed and emotions expressed through dance."

"Wasn't Martha Graham emoting and revealing characters through dance?"

"Yes, but her expression was abstract and obscure. That's the difference."

"What was your relationship like with Jerome Robbins?"

"As a replacement I wasn't close with him. He would come by once in a while to keep the show clean, but by then he'd moved on to other things. I didn't have as intimate a relationship with Robbins as did those who were with him at the beginning, during the creative development of the show. But he trusted me, because eventually he granted permission to only five individuals, of which I was one, who were legally allowed to stage the show. I've been presenting *West Side Story* now all over the world for over thirty-five years. The show is foolproof. It works in every country, even if it's not in their language. Everyone can relate to Romeo and Juliet. People often ask me, 'Don't you want to change it, put something of your own in it?' I tell them there's no reason to change it. Every moment in the show was carefully thought out. Robbins did tons of preproduction work and had an unprecedented eight-week period to develop and rehearse the production. He found what worked best. It's funny, he phoned me to assist him when he was putting together *The West Side Suite* for the New York City Ballet. He kept screwing around with the ending of the 'Cool' number. He cut bars of music and added a knee slide and a position change at the end. Then he turned to me and said, 'Maybe after forty years I'll get it right.' I thought that was sort of sweet. While we all thought it was perfect, he thought it could be better."

"When did you start thinking about becoming a choreographer?"

"When I was around twenty-seven, I started to feel that I should do more than just dance in the chorus. I started to seek out a choreographer's career. It meant going back to zero, because if you have nothing to show, why should anyone hire you? I knew I had to build a body of work. It was just around that time that I got hired by Mel Brooks to choreograph the film *The Producers*. We had met socially through some mutual friends, and he told me about a movie he was working on. He wanted to call it *Springtime for Hitler*. Months later he asked me to choreograph the dance sequences for the film, retitled *The Producers*. I told him, 'Mel, it's your first movie. You don't have to do a friend a favor.' He said, 'No, no, no. I know the way you think about these dance numbers, and I want you to do it.' It was one of those fortuitous circumstances that started my choreographic career."

"What was it like creating those zany dance numbers?"

"It was easy because I had a dance arranger [pianist] and Mel in the room and we just said, 'What if we do this, how about a waltz, what about that?' I knew what I wanted to see. Mel came up with the swastika idea à la Busby Berkeley. You have to remember in the story Max Bialystock and Leo Bloom hire the worst director-choreographer they could find—Roger De Bris. How good could the number be?" he said with a laugh. "It wasn't going to be Jerry or Martha. It was Roger De Bris."

"So you choreographed for character?"

"Yes. Once you know your characters and what's going on with them, then you have a jumping-off point for the choreography. You're not just making up random steps."

"You worked with Mel again on *Young Frankenstein*. Tell me about choreographing 'Puttin' on the Ritz.'"

"We actually put that together very quickly. I would only get Gene Wilder and Peter Boyle for twenty minutes at a time, due to their shooting schedule. I had a mad scientist and his monster demonstrating dexterity in a musical number? We went for top hats and tails—reminiscences of Fred Astaire. What more did I need?"

"Alan, what do you think is so compelling about the art of choreography?"

"I think there is something deeply instinctual in some people that drives them to convey ideas or messages through movement and respond physically to music. I know that when I hear music, I see dancing. My happiest times are in a rehearsal studio with a music arranger and a group of terrific dancers. I've had a very diverse career—film, television, nightclubs, industrials [theatrical shows put on to sell commercial products], live performance. My favorite is the live performance. There is such an exciting dynamic that cannot be matched in any other venue. I love a live audience because you know how you're doing right at that moment. And you want to bring the audience to a point where they're going to say, 'Oh, my God' and stand up and applaud. You know immediately if you've been successful or not."

"Is that your endorphin rush?"

"It is. It is."

"What haven't you done?"

"I decided about two years ago that I wanted to do a ballet. After years of dancing other people's work and choreographing for other people's projects, I wanted to do something that afforded me creative freedom—to see all the work come from me and see it fulfilled. I'm pursuing that now. I realize that it's never complete freedom because you have an obligation to your audience. Your goal is to communicate. Jerry, of course, did this even with his concert work. His ballets were very abstract, but you say, 'Oh, that is so lovely,' and you are moved by it even if you don't understand what he was getting at. The obligation is to affect someone, not change them, just give them something—a feeling, an expression—something."

"How would you rate your level of self-confidence at this stage of your career?"

"Choreographers live with a lot of pressure. I never sign a contract for a job without thinking, 'God, I hope I'm good enough.' First you have that pang, then you get over it and get to work. Even with so many years of experience it still happens. I think it's because we so want to measure up. Basically, we know we can do it. But will the audience love us? I know some choreographers who fall in love with their own work. They go, 'Oh, God, that's so beautiful, that's wonderful. I did such a terrific job.' That's not me. I always ask, 'Is this good enough? Can I make it better? Have I gone in the right direction?' Self-doubt is terrific when you're an artist."

I asked Alan how he wanted to be immortalized on film and he said, "Moving." So I suggested that we reschedule our shoot and do it at my studio where he could move around. A week later we met again.

"Alan, step out onto the floor and let's see what you're about."

As he began to perform, I couldn't help but think of the men who had inspired him: Jack Cole, Peter Gennaro, Bob Fosse, Jerome Robbins. He embodied them all. And yet there was no doubt that the man before me was Alan Johnson—dancer and choreographer in his own right.

Encino, California, 1999

211

Connoisseur

glen tetley

Glen Tetley's midtown apartment reminded me of the great museums of Europe.

His spacious living room was filled with fine Renaissance sculptures, antique sofas and chairs covered in Italian silk, drawings and busts by Francois Gilot Picasso, Joseph Glasco, and Paul Klee, to name a few. A large, ornate mirror in the dining room caught my eye.

"That's from the Baroque period, over 250 years old," Glen said. "Very fragile."

"Would it be all right if we used it as a backdrop to your portrait?" I asked.

"Yes, of course."

I positioned Glen with his back to the mirror, facing the dining room table. He looked stoic before the camera, offering me no discernible clues to his character. I decided not to probe, to photograph him at face value. Perhaps insights would be revealed to me later, within the captured image.

"I read that you once planned to be a doctor. What could have been so compelling about dance to cause you to change the direction of your life?"

"While a pre-med student at Columbia University, I saw a performance of Anthony Tudor's *Romeo and Juliet* performed by Ballet Theater. I was absolutely stunned to learn that something without words could move me so profoundly. I knew in that instant that I wanted to be part of that world. But it was wartime, 1943, so I enlisted in the navy, and it wasn't until much later, and quite by coincidence, that I got my first job dancing. I landed a part in the show *On the Town*, choreographed by Jerome Robbins. I had come to the theater to borrow money from someone who was in the production, when Jerry Robbins walked out and said, 'Okay, come in and audition.' 'But I'm not here to audition,' I told him. 'Well, you look the type,' he said. The show was about three sailors, and I was still wearing my sailor's uniform. He demonstrated a few steps and asked me to repeat them, which I did to the best of my ability. The next thing he said was, 'Give him a job.'"

"Jerome Robbins gave you your first dance job without your having had any dance training?"

"That's right. He told me that I had a lot of talent and recommended that I study with his ballet teacher, Helene Platova, who was very Russian. While taking her class, I heard about a woman who was teaching contemporary dance in Greenwich Village and had an extraordinary ability to explain movement. Her name was Hanya Holm. I went down to meet her and immediately fell in love with her technique. Having come from pre-med, I understood what she was talking about. She wouldn't just say, 'Use your legs,' she'd name them by muscles—quadriceps, hamstrings, gluteus maximus. She had a wonderful way of teaching preparation for plié, relevé, and movement into the air. I became her assistant and performed in her musicals, the original Kiss Me Kate and Out of This World."

"So Hanya was very instrumental in your development as a dancer?"

"Yes. She used to say you have to find your own unique quality, and you do that by going into the subconscious and tapping into the deepest core of your being. She taught us how to do this through improvisation and various self-exploratory exercises. This was invaluable to me as a dancer and later on as a choreographer, particularly because my father taught me to always keep a poker face. 'Never reveal what you're thinking,' he used to say. Hanya also had a deep understanding of the science of movement, which was based on the laws of physics—of gravity and the release of gravity and the relationship of the individual to space.

"I studied with many great teachers. It was a golden period of dance and theater. We had the American pioneers at their prime, Hanya and Martha Graham, Doris Humphrey and Charles Weidman, and I worked with all of them. At the same time, we had all these marvelous émigré Russian teachers that Balanchine had brought over to teach at the School of American Ballet, like Pierre Vladimoroff, Anatoly Obukhov, Muriel Stuart, and wonderful Felia Dubrovska. I studied with all of them."

"Wasn't it unusual to be studying both contemporary dance and classical dance at the same time? What did Hanya say about that?"

"Well, I never told anybody that I was studying with anybody else. They always thought they were the only ones teaching me," he said with a sly laugh. "At that time each one of these artists was closed off from one another. If you were a Martha Graham dancer, you did not work with Hanya Holm or vice versa. There were also major barriers between classical dance and modern dance. Because I came to dance at the age of nineteen, I saw no logical reason to accept barriers. I wanted to go to the essence of these techniques and saw real connections between them. A plié is a plié in any style, and there is only one way to do it correctly—with opposition of the muscles. In classical dance you learn to find your center and escape gravity. In contemporary techniques you are working to fall off that center and accept gravity. I viewed them as separate parts of the same whole."

"How did you integrate these opposing views as a dancer and later as a choreographer?"

"I decided that I was not going to choose between them. Classical training is a very difficult, beautiful technique and almost impossible to master. I always loved something that was pushed to the edge of impossible. I loved also the emotional freedom of contemporary dance with its deep sensual nature. When I danced as a classical dancer I did not dance as a modern dancer doing classical steps. I danced as a classical dancer. When I danced in contemporary technique, I danced it not as a classical dancer trying to dance contemporary. I think I was one of the first to cross these barriers."

"You were bilingual?"

"Yes, exactly. Both felt natural to me. It was exciting to run, do a preparation, and soar through the air. It was equally exciting to run, drop, and slide clear across the stage on the knees, going into gravity."

"You were one of the founding members of the Joffrey Ballet. What was that experience like?"

Glen hesitated. "It was the most restrictive experience I've ever had as a dancer. I felt as though I had been placed in a straitjacket and could not wait to bust my way out."

"Really? What happened there?"

"I didn't come into dance to have things neat and tidy, definitely not. I wanted my soul to be in everything I was doing. I didn't want to be put in a candy box. I wanted to be explosive and original. I didn't want to look like everybody else. Bob [Robert Joffrey] didn't understand this. He was a sort of a quiet tyrant. I returned to New York after nine months of touring with the company, but when I arrived at the studio for the next season's rehearsal, I simply could not walk through the door. I had my hand on the doorknob, but I couldn't turn it. I could not go in. I walked out onto the street, got onto a subway, and got off at Fifty-ninth Street and Lexington. I found myself walking three blocks and through the doors of the Martha Graham School of Contemporary Dance. Coming to her at this time in my career just restored me as a person. God... it was wonderful. It was deep. It was sensual. It was mature and concerned with the deepest part of one's being. A year later Martha asked me to dance in *Embattled Garden*."

"When did you feel the impulse to begin choreographing?"

"I was asked by Lucia Chase to join American Ballet Theater. Martha was against it and told me if I did, I would be ruining my life. I did it anyway. My first performances were in the Tudor ballets, *Pillar of Fire* and *Lilac Garden*, partnering with the famous Nora Kaye. It was a great experience, but American Ballet Theater at that time was just a repertory company. Very few new works were being created. In a way Martha was right; she warned me that I'd be wearing clothes made for other people. Once again, I felt very restricted. I started to hear this voice within me saying, 'You've got to find your own individuality. You've got to take this big jump and see if you have your own creative voice.' I turned down all contracts, which was living dangerously, as I had no money, and spent a year choreographing *Pierrot Lunaire* for my own small company. Using a score from Arnold Schonberg, I totally identified with the work—the figure of the outsider, the one caught between heaven and hell, earth and sky. It became one of my signature works and is still being performed today."

"*Pierrot Lunaire* launched your career as a choreographer. Why did you take your choreographic voice to Europe rather than remain here in the United States?"

"John Martin's review in the *New York Times* brought me great notice and an invitation from a very young Netherlands Dance Theater to set the work on their company. Once in Europe, it was quite a revelation to learn that there was virtually no contemporary dance being done. So I took it upon myself to show them how to move in this other world of modern dance. I believe I was the first to teach Martha's technique there. Ballet Rambert in England also wanted to change from a company that performed *Giselle* and *Coppelia* into a contemporary dance company. Suddenly it all just clicked for me. In Europe I could bring these two worlds of movement together—contemporary dance and classical ballet. And there were also practical reasons why staying in Europe made sense. The struggle of existing economically in New York City was prohibitive. One had to find a studio in New York City, pay rent, find salaries for dancers, pay musicians if you wanted live music, and cover the costs of sets, costumes, and a lighting designer. I knew in Europe dancers, musicians, designers—as well as studios and theaters—were in abundance and affordable. I could create freely without limitations. But it was a tough decision to leave the familiarity of the United States. It was also around that time that I came into contact with the Book of Changes—the I Ching. I read a passage that said, 'It furthers one to cross the great water.' I took that to mean that I should cross the Atlantic Ocean and go over to Europe and chart a new course."

"After so many years, what have you learned about the art of choreography?"

"Choreography is something that one has to do with other people. You can't pre-create. I know as a dancer, I never wanted something that was stamped on me, pre-planned with closed boundaries. I was looking for a magical spontaneous act and the collaborative experience. As a choreographer, I try to bring this to the dancers I work with."

"You've been creating ballets now for forty years. Does the choreographer ever feel he's created enough work? Is it ever enough?"

"No, it's never enough, because one has to come to terms with the fact that you spend your whole life creating something that is brilliant, exciting, on the edge, but exists only during the physical act of performance. I've worked all my life, and where is it? The curtain goes up, the dancers dance, and the curtain comes down. You might revel a bit in its afterglow, but it doesn't remain. You can't hang it on the wall, or pull it from your bookshelf. It's the most quicksilver, precarious, and volatile way of creativity. And because of that, you are compelled to create again and again and go on to the last breath."

New York City, 2003

215

Man of Emotion

doug varone

"Your choreography is known for its exploration of emotions. How do you translate emotion into physical movement?"

"I study how people move and gesture. I then try to translate what I've observed into dramatic movement. I am observing you right now—how you're holding your body and tilting your head as we're talking. All of that information stays with me subconsciously and then finds its way into the big stew of dance ideas."

"Are you conscious of your own dancemaking style?"

"I think in terms of a choreographic style as well as a movement style. I approach choreography stylistically the same way each time. In terms of movement style, I'm interested in how the back, the limbs, and the hands can be used to create space. I usually begin with a piece of music that sparks my imagination. I respond to music emotionally, and that gets my motor running. I then experiment with my dancers and we generate ideas together, sometimes exploring a different restriction of space or using the body in a new way. The tools of dancemaking are always within us."

"Tell me about your shift from dancer to choreographer."

"As a dancer I was in the Limón Company for a while, and then with Lar Lubovitch for eight years. I knew that I wanted to make dances and thought I might have the capability. Did I have anything significant to say? At first I wasn't sure. It took me three to five years to figure out that I did. I think one has to mature as a human being before growing into an artist. The two are finely wedded. When I began making dances, they were very well crafted and based on generic or learned steps. I wasn't exploring a true movement capability until a few years later, when something just exploded out of my brain."

"You mean you had some sort of breakthrough?"

"Yes. I suddenly understood that there was a greater sense of what I could accomplish and that I was holding back. From that time forward I made a conscious decision to exclude any steps I had used in the past. If it looked familiar, I wouldn't use it. Only when I stretched into new territory did I feel myself becoming a choreographer."

"Do your dances have a theme or a message?"

"Very rarely do I create a work that is linear in its dramatic content. I strive to create images that can elicit an emotional response. It will be different for everyone who sees it. Some will enjoy the abstract nature of the work, while others may see something very specific. As long as they are affected by it in some way, then I feel I've reached them."

"In photography I've learned that one should never need to explain a photograph. Does the same apply to dance?"

"We live daily with photographs. We are bombarded with photos in newspapers and on billboards. Basically, we know how to look at them. But dance is a completely different experience for most people. Lately, I have begun to believe that in dance it is important to educate people about what they are seeing. My motivation comes out of love for the art form. I want to ensure that if people go to see one dance performance, they'll want to see another."

"Sounds like you're on some sort of mission on behalf of the art form."

"Yes, that's right. I'm interested in enlightening people about dance. Five years ago I wasn't interested in answering people's questions. Now we hold pre- and post-performance discussions. If someone comes to a show early to hear me speak because they are afraid they're not going to get it, then I'm happy to shed a little light on it for them. That kind of dialogue gets people to the next place."

"How do you respond to the notion of the obsessed artist who has no life outside the studio or stage?"

"I am passionate about dance, but I'm not like many artists who have no life outside of dance. For them it's only about making dances, being on the stage, or teaching the next workshop. I'm not interested in having an apartment in New York City that I never see. That sort of full-time obsession is not for me. I see films, visit museums, and spend time reading. Those things fuel my imagination and help me in my art."

"What do you reveal about yourself in your work?"

"My work is introspective, exposing how I see the world and myself in it. I used to be under the impression that to be taken seriously I had to make dark pieces. I've since learned that humor and playfulness can be equally powerful.

"The tools of dance making are always within us."

The more I grow, the more my work changes, and I hope I'll continue to evolve. I don't want to wake up ten years from now and have nothing left to say."

"Lessons learned thus far?"

"Dancers have their own point of view and identity, and we choreographers need to respect them and know how to treat them as equals, as collaborators. The choreographer finds himself in a difficult place because he has this idea in front of his eyes and has to find a way of actualizing it through the dancer's body. When it's not transferred properly, it can be very frustrating, and easy to forget that the dancer is not just a tool to be used."

"Have you ever been treated as someone's tool?"

"Yes, absolutely! And it is because of that that I have learned not to mistreat people, to create a positive environment that dancers want to be a part of. The relationship between the dancer and the choreographer can be a very tenuous one, but it can also be very supportive. I want them to feel that they are there not only for me but for themselves, so that they feel comfortable contributing to the art of dancemaking."

"How do you preserve your dance creations and keep them vital?"

"Dances are not like paintings that you can just hang on the wall and look at whenever you want. Dances move into storage. That's the heartbreak of the choreographer. I'm beginning to believe that the works that we make are their most potent at the time of creation and live only in the moment. They are created for specific dancers, and even though they can be shared with other dancers, the original impetus will never be the same. It will never be the same identical drawing. There is something very sad about that."

Six months after my session with Doug, I received a call from his business manager asking me to join him in New York to photograph the making of Doug's next piece, *Neither.* Doug's intention for this project was to resurrect the spirits of the occupants of an abandoned building inside the Lower East Side Tenement Museum in Manhattan. My role was to bring the photographer's eye to the choreographer's vision. Inside the musty, haunted rooms of this crumbling old building, Doug and I exchanged perspectives throughout the composing process, using our bodies to experiment with movement phrases in an effort to imagine emotions and dramatic relationships of those who had inhabited these rooms a century earlier. His seven dancers re-created our movement ideas with little guidance. Doug's communication with his dancers bordered on telepathy as they simulated various emotional states—loneliness, fear, helplessness, confusion, determination. *Neither* had its premier on November 28, 2000, to critical acclaim.

New York City, 1999, 2000

Storyteller

ronald k. brown

Evidence was in the middle of its Joyce season when I phoned to request an interview with Ron Brown.

He agreed to meet with me for an hour at my Greenwich Village sublet. The shy dancer arrived noticeably tired. I offered him a cup of coffee, which he declined in favor of a power drink he had in his backpack.

"Why don't we do the interview first?" I suggested. "Then perhaps we can walk down to Washington Square, which is only a block away, and I can take your photo there."

"Sure," he said, taking a seat on the sofa.

"Ron, I was very moved, very elevated by the concert last night. In fact, I couldn't sit still. The music had me bouncing around in my seat and into the person sitting next to me. How did you develop your choreographic skills?"

"I started my formal dance education at seventeen with Mary Anthony. She believed in teaching her students not only how to dance but how to teach and create. After two years with her, I realized that there were things I wanted to talk about and a certain way I wanted to move. I felt I could tell stories and inspire awareness through the language of dance."

"Is this desire to tell stories through dance what motivated you to start your own company?"

"Yes. I asked a good friend if he thought I should create my own company. He said to me, 'You have to. Who else is going to tell your grandmother's stories?' It was that push that made me feel that I had a responsibility to create work about African American people. I want to help young people connect with their spirit, their elders, and those things that hold our society together."

"If you wanted to tell your grandmother's stories, why not write a book?"

"I came to believe that I could create a dance folklore for the African American community through kinetic storytelling. Dance is nonintellectual; so when you see movement and hear music, it becomes an emotional and visceral experience. I think that's what touches people."

"Your movement reminds me of rich batik fabric with vibrant colors, complex patterns, and powerful images. How did you develop it?"

"It's been fourteen years since I started my choreographic journey. My dance style has grown out of all my various influences. I had studied the techniques of Martha Graham, José Limón, and Alvin Ailey. I experienced many different styles of West African dance, traveling to Senegal and the Ivory Coast. I've also been very affected by popular dances that I've experienced in nightclubs. When I look back, I can trace my own creative evolution. When I first started choreographing I was interested in capturing gesture. Then I wanted to be as physical as I could, bringing in explosive flips and leaps. After that, I felt it was important to add words to my work to give the dances context. By 1994 things started to jell, with the integration of text with large powerful movement and gesture and the fusion of traditional West African dance with modern dance."

"It can be tricky borrowing influences from other traditional dance styles. How did you deal specifically with African dance?"

"It was a challenge, because I never wanted to be held accountable for presenting authentic West African dance. I don't romanticize it the way a lot of African Americans do. I believe that tradition is extremely important and should be honored, but that dance is always evolving and moving forward. Perhaps I'm one of those who's moving it forward."

"So like Katherine Dunham did with Caribbean movement, you've fused West African movement with contemporary modern dance to create your own movement style."

"Yes. For a while I toyed with the idea of living in the Ivory Coast. I thought I'd have schools on both continents and teach traditional dance and contemporary dance. And then I realized that my work was here, as a storyteller."

"What issues of concern to the African American community do you address?"

"What my dancers and I try to do is create strategies through dance, to talk about real-life behaviors and events and engage in discussions of race, class, gender, and assimilation. I want audiences to understand my stories and messages. I want to stir them, move them, and inspire them to feel good about themselves, warm with each other, and share a sense of community. I want them to have the desire to have their spirits set free. I want to free the soul and the physicality of the person. I want the work to be evidence of these perspectives. This is, in fact, why I named my company Evidence."

"Do you feel you can improve the human condition through your work?"

"Well, I see man in search of two basic pursuits—material attainment and spiritual attainment. Maybe that's why God is on the dollar bill—it brings both into view. There is no doubt we need money to pay our rent, eat, and have a decent life. But the push for material attainment has gone way beyond basic needs and is somewhat out of control. We are bombarded with advertising and commercialism to have more—more money, more cars, more this, more that. And technology feeds this drive. The compassion for people and culture and spirit has become secondary. I'd like to see things more in balance."

"If someone wanders into the theater and sees your choreography for the first time and is not privy to what inspired you to create it, would they understand it?"

"I think everyone perceives the work from wherever they're coming from. For example, last night at the Joyce, one of the guys on stage crew came up to me and told me that he loved the show. He said that to him it represented a celebration. Well, when I created that work I wasn't thinking 'celebration,' but if he sees freedom of the body and the spirit, then that's beautiful. But I am not

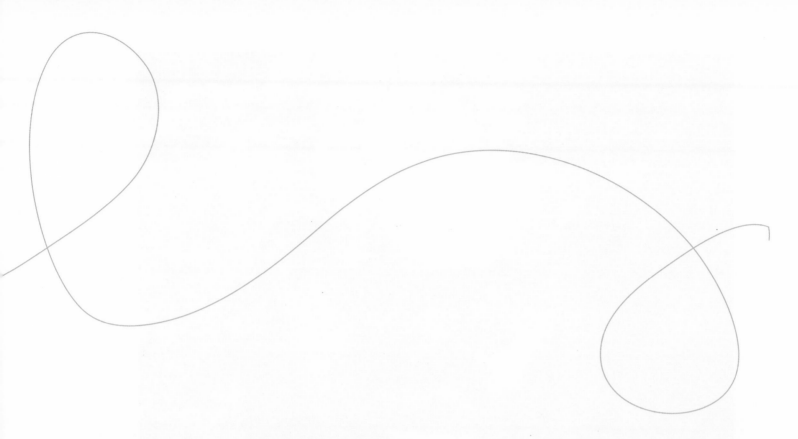

one of those choreographers who says, 'I don't care what you get from the work.' I prefer that people understand my intention and my message."

"You strike me as someone not comfortable with the business end of dance—you'd much rather just dance. But do you concern yourself with those lesser noble tasks of marketing and self-promotion?"

"Funny you should ask that. I am very uncomfortable with those issues. People in my organization have accused me of wanting to be invisible. Part of me doesn't want the company to even have an image. I just want the experience of dancing and creating, and simply letting the work be evidence of all these perspectives we've talked about."

"What's next for you?"

"Well, I'd like to have audiences come see dance in the same way that they go to see theater."

"What's the difference?"

"Somehow we've been trained to go to the theater and come away with an emotional and dramatic experience. With dance, people expect to simply be entertained. I'd like to change that expectation. I think by offering the work differently, I may be able to do something about this. I'm planning to create a fall season of pure dance and a spring season devoted to a more theatrical presentation. We'll just have to see what happens there."

"Do you think you could ever stop making dances?"

Ron smiled and began to shake his head slowly from side to side. "No, I don't think so. I just love crafting dances too much. Sometimes I fantasize what it would be like if I didn't dance or choreograph. I imagine myself running a fruit stand. I'd be selling melons and grapes, apples and bananas—all kinds of delicious fruits and also vitamins. Inside the stand, I'd have a massage table and would offer massages to my customers. Then I begin to picture a small dance studio attached to the fruit stand where I'd put on dance performances. And before I know it, I'm a choreographer again."

"Ron, you're hopeless!"

I grabbed my camera bag and suggested that we head out to Washington Square. The park was crowded with people walking their dogs, sitting on benches, throwing Frisbees. I spotted a quiet little corner and asked Ron to sit down and just let the sun warm him. While I loaded my Hasselblad, he closed his eyes. I wondered what he was thinking about.

"I'm ready," I said. "But no need to look at me. I don't want to disturb your thoughts."

New York City, 1999

Free Spirit

daniel ezralow

On assignment for the 1998 American Choreography Awards show and heavily doped up on cold medicine, I had the audacity to approach Daniel Ezralow while he was in conversation with some people and announce, "I am a talented photographer and would very much like to photograph you. Do you think that would be possible?"

He replied, "I'm sure you are, and I'd be happy to work with you." To my surprise, he reached into his pocket, pulled out paper and pen, and jotted down his private phone number. "Call me," he said, "and we'll set something up." He told me later that anyone as bold as I was that night deserved to be taken seriously.

A month later the international dance star and I drove out to a secluded section of Malibu, California, where I photographed him on the beach. Dressed in a white suit designed by Ermengildo Zegna, he danced in and out of the surf, scaled cliffs, and jumped gracefully to the sand. His energy seemed boundless. By the time the sun went down I was soaked from head to toe, but he and I had established an unspoken trust that would come to define our relationship from that point forward. Danny and I would become good friends and over the years have many conversations about career, life, and art. I would later do a cover story on him for *Dance Teacher* featuring my Malibu photos.

"Danny, since I've known you, I've discovered that it is very hard to put any label on you or the kinds of things you do."

"Rarely in my life have I fit into a mold. I'm both wonderfully happy and sadly exasperated about that. I've done operas, films, videos, television, concert

"There is no manual, no road map to a successful dance career.
   You have to write your own.
I'm still traveling an unmarked road with its detours and blind spots."

dance, and special events. I have a huge appetite for creative work. I'm never comfortable settling for just one form of expression. I might go over to Bucharest and Vienna and choreograph for the circus, then I'll do *Eros,* a full evening for the Romanian Olympic gymnastic team, in collaboration with Moses Pendleton and David Parsons. Or, I'll choreograph a Broadway musical, as I did with Julie Taymor for *Green Bird.* Next I might take on a Hollywood movie, like I did when I worked with Ron Howard's *The Grinch Who Stole Christmas.* I've done music videos for U2, Sting, Andrea Bocelli, and Ricky Martin, and live shows for David Bowie and Josh Groban. Because I work in so many arenas, people don't know how to classify me. That can be a curse and a blessing. But the truth is that this can be a very creative way to live. Why should there be any limitations on creativity? It's very exciting to be eclectic."

"What do you think is the source of your seemingly boundless creativity?"

"I think the idea that I can do anything in this world comes from my family and my Jewish heritage, which encourages creativity and curiosity—the asking of questions. My own curiosity is what drives me and at the same time feeds me. If I weren't constantly asking questions, I wouldn't be choreographing. I'd be living a much simpler life," he said with a laugh.

"How did you discover dance?"

"I stumbled upon it in my freshman year at Berkeley. I was a pre-med student when I took a dance class from former Martha Graham dancers Marni and David Wood. They instilled in me a love and passion for movement. Dance infected me with an incredible spirit. It spread through me like a virus or a fever. I could take three dance classes in a row, survive on a single milk shake all day, and still not get enough movement. I had been captain of my high school football team and a competitive track athlete. I saw that my football coach and my dance teachers had a lot in common. It surprised me that people learned dance with the same intensity and discipline that I had experienced on the football field. The difference was that with dance, you could express emotions, relationships, and concepts. I loved the idea of using the body for something other than just scoring points."

"So you abandoned your idea of becoming a doctor?"

"Yes. I was under a lot of pressure to stay in school, but my drive to become a professional dancer was stronger. I left school, moved to New York City, and immediately received scholarships from the Ailey and Joffrey companies. Within three months I was performing on the stage."

"Did you really have a sense as to how to navigate your career?"

"I was twenty years old and asked everyone I met, 'How does one succeed as a professional dancer?' Each person I asked told me something different. I began to realize that you have to choose your own road, and it will never be the same as someone else's. There is no manual, no road map to a successful dance career. You have to write your own. I'm still traveling an unmarked road with its detours and blind spots."

"After dancing in various companies, including those of Lar Lubovitch, Paul Taylor, and Pilobolus, you set out to create your own."

"Yes, in 1987 I cofounded ISO and later Momix with Moses Pendleton to express a new sense of dance as physical theater. I wanted to give viewers a more conceptual and surrealistic dance experience."

"Tell me about your one-man show *Mandala*. I sensed it was your way of really exploring the self."

"The story behind *Mandala* is loosely based on Hermann Hesse's book *Siddhartha*. I woke up one morning around the age of forty and said, 'This is my life now. What the next forty years are going to be about are my choices—not fulfilling what I had to do for my parents, society—but my choices.' It became an eyes-wide-open journey in which I realized that what I do with the rest of my life is up to me. *Mandala* was initially an experiment using multiple film footage running simultaneously from different projectors while I imposed myself within those projected images. It brought a different dimension to the live-action stage show. I shot the footage and edited every frame. I looked through the lens. I was in the helicopter. I was on the edge of the boat going through the tunnels of the Roman Aqueduct. I experienced the feelings. I understood subconsciously that the soul sees in images. As a dancer, I'm always searching for the emotions that can create a dance. I felt the emotions firsthand and understood them. I chose in this work to be informed by subconscious thought. That's where *Mandala* is me."

"Why haven't you formed your own company?"

"I don't need a Daniel Ezralow Dance Company to be creatively fulfilled. I've come to realize that opportunities in life choose you as much as you choose them. You sense what's good for you, and you go there. My spirit aspires to be a creator, someone who originates a vision and sees it realized. I can do that even when I'm working with a singer like Josh Groban or directing and choreographing an opera in Italy. If I'm able to share my vision with the people I work with, be true to myself, and translate my ideas, then the context of the work does not become an issue."

A couple of years after our rendezvous on the beach, I phoned Danny and asked him if I could photograph him on a winding mountain road. I reminded him of his comments about dancers creating their own road map to a successful dance career. "Perhaps we can illustrate that in a photograph," I said. Danny agreed to meet me early one Saturday morning on the road leading up to Will Rogers State Historic Park in Pacific Palisades, California. Barefoot, this time in a black designer suit, he positioned himself in the middle of the road and began to experiment with off-balance layouts and leans. I placed my camera on a tripod and tried to catch him in mid-action with a slow shutter speed. Later I panned him as he came toward me or ran sideways into the brush. He even lay down in the middle of the road, as if listening to the earth. Suddenly a truck came rumbling down the road, barely missing him. He suggested that we relocate and that I photograph him running through moving traffic on San Vicente Boulevard.

"Next time," I told him.

Pacific Palisades, California, 2000, photo
Italy, 2003, telephone interview

Forest Nymph

anna halprin

Anna looked slim and youthful for a woman of seventy-eight. She led me to an outdoor patio of her home in the hills of Marin County, California. We were to have our interview under the shaded canopy of tall redwoods and other indigenous trees. The air was cool and fresh. Anna handed me a glass of apple juice and sat down.

"I think you were courageous to leave New York and the established dance scene to settle here in the woods," I began, gesturing toward the forest that surrounded us.

"It's true that when my husband and I moved to Northern California, I was totally isolated from the modern dance scene. But I don't think that took courage. I've always been passionately involved in my own things and interested in pursuing the work I did with my teacher, Margaret H'Doubler at the University of Wisconsin. She looked at movement from an anatomical and kinesiological point of view, with a strong emphasis on creativity. You see that dance deck down there," she said, pointing to a wooden platform several hundred yards from the house. "My husband built that for me, and that gave me a wonderful opportunity to start from scratch. Away from Broadway, the commercial scene, and modern dance, I was able to investigate what dance meant to me."

"What did you discover?"

"I began to find inspiration in the way nature works. I observed its inner operation and then transferred that to the way my body works as a natural phenomenon."

"How did they relate?"

"All things in nature are interconnected, and each shapes the other. Wind, sun, and soil shape a tree. The tides shape the waves. What happens ecologically in one part of the country or the world might determine flight patterns in another. There is a total interconnection in all aspects of life. I think of my body in relation to the air I breathe. Nature is not a backdrop to life but a dynamic influence. Our natural environment brings out emotions and psychological associations. So, when applied to movement, this interconnectedness between elements leads to awareness, creativity, and regeneration."

"When you chose a more naturalistic approach to movement over stylized dance, wasn't it difficult to unlearn years of dance technique?"

"It was hard at first because you do get patterns imposed on your nervous system. They become almost automatic reactions. I had to go back to the biological aspects of movement and start all over. If you go into my studio you will see a hanging skeleton, along with muscle charts. I began to work my body kinesiologically and became aware of the feeling states associated with specific qualities of movement and actions like flexion, extension, and hyperextension."

"How did your kinesiological approach affect your creativity?"

"I found the work I was doing to be very freeing and a continuous source of inspiration," she said. "Through my process of connecting body and spirit, I discovered a series of road maps that guided me creatively."

"These road maps told you where to go?"

"Yes, but not how to get there. The first road map consists of the three levels of awareness that link movement, feeling, and associations. The second is collective creativity, the process of teaching, training, and producing performance work. The third is the five stages of healing: identifying the issue, confronting it, release, change, and assimilation or integration into one's life. Lastly there is movement ritual."

"How does 'your style' manifest itself when the intention of the work stems from a response to the mechanics and emotions of the body?"

"I feel that everyone has their own story, and that story impregnates one's movement. What I encourage is a technique of personal awareness. As a teacher, I don't demonstrate anything to my students. I don't want anyone to imitate my style. How can they? They don't have my body or my mythology. I teach them the principles of movement and then set up situations for them to discover their own natural movement inclination."

"How does this process translate into repertoire?"

"I've created what I call scores. Scores are designed to generate creativity in others by mystifying the creative process. A score is a set of activities that you design over time and in a specific environment. The activities are then collected and performed."

"Your process goes way beyond dance as entertainment and into the realm of real-life issues that can be transformative."

"I have a process of working that allows me to apply dance in many different venues. I can take dance out to nondancers and into communities. There is a therapeutic component to it, but it's not therapy. I'm not a therapist. I do it to create change in people, in their lives."

"Your work has drawn some criticism."

"I don't want anyone to imitate my style.

How can they?

They don't have my body or my mythology."

"Yes, but I'm not worried about what dance critics will say or that Alma Hawkins, the former chairperson of UCLA's Department of Dance, once said I've thrown dance back a hundred years because I use improvisation and natural movement freely rather than adhere to a formalized approach to dance. What I'm doing is based on the ancient concept of ritual. All I've done is give it a modern twist and new terminology."

"Working outside the conventional performance scene, how do you know where to present your work?"

"I allow the material I'm engaged in at the moment to direct where I should go. It can be performed on the concert stage, or it can go into an environmental experience, or be exploratory in a laboratory, or go in a hospital or prison. It can lead communities in ritual, like my Planetary Dances, which are now performed worldwide. I want whatever I do to be useful to others, and being on the concert stage isn't necessarily the only way to be useful. It's one way."

"How do you renew yourself, charge your creative batteries?"

"I always go back to nature to refuel. This is my natural habitat. I need the stability and constancy of the trees. Here I see new life coming up against trees that have died. I watch the earth replenish itself with old leaves falling and new ones beginning to bloom. It sustains me to see myself as part of the life process."

After the interview I asked Anna where she'd like to be photographed. Without hesitation she said, "I'd like to be photographed nude, here among the redwoods."

"That would be perfect," I said.

Anna walked into the house and returned about ten minutes later wearing a robe and sandals.

"I know a nice spot," she said and led me down a dirt path into the forest. She moved through the brush with the ease of a forest animal. I followed, stumbling over rocks and branches.

"What do you think of these hollowed-out logs?" she asked when we came to a clearing.

"I think we can incorporate them into an interesting composition," I said.

She stepped out of her robe and sandals and molded her body into the hollow of a charred tree stump. I was thinking about film speeds and how to avoid spiders when I noticed an immediate change in her demeanor; she grew serious and contemplative. Looking through my Hasselblad, I felt her absolute oneness with the environment. I shot a couple of rolls, speaking to her only when necessary. We then moved to a formation of trees with their roots aboveground. As Anna was nude, I lay down first to make sure nothing would poke or scratch her. Cradled by the tree's roots, I felt the sun's warmth on my face. This was a perfect spot.

Almost immediately Anna found a comfortable pose and closed her eyes. Her consciousness seemed to drift to some inner space. I walked back several yards to get a good look at the scene. Composition, lighting, visual perspective were in perfect balance. All I needed to do was press the shutter.

Marin County, California, 1999

231

Dance Alchemist

russell clark

Two years after I photographed Russell Clark in my Los Angeles studio, he phoned to tell me that he'd been diagnosed with terminal cancer.

"Rose, we never completed our interview," he said. "I don't have much time left, so I think we need to do it now, right away. And … I was wondering, would you mind chronicling my last days? I have so much I'd like to express before I leave, and I trust you to be my best voice. Maybe one day you could write a story about me."

I assured him that I would tell his story to the very best of my ability.

When I arrived at the intensive-care unit of Cedars-Sinai Medical Center I found Russell paralyzed from the waist down, gaunt and hairless. He looked nothing like the handsome man I had photographed two years earlier.

"Come in, Rose," he said, noticing me in the doorway holding a bouquet of flowers. I came around to the side of his bed and put my hand on his.

"I hope you're not in a lot of pain, Russell."

"I'd rather have some pain and be lucid than just lie here mindless on morphine. Thank you for coming."

I clipped my tape recorder microphone to his hospital gown, careful not to dislodge any of the tubes or monitoring wires.

"Have you come to terms with all this?" I asked.

"Yes, but only just recently. This body-mind split has made me feel very desperate. Once my body stopped functioning I wanted to jump ship, find a hole to escape through. I couldn't think of anything except, 'I've got to get out, got to get out, got to get out.' And then I realized I can't get out. There is no escaping this. The only thing left to do is embrace it. I remembered the most successful times in my life were those when I had brought all of my energies into a single focus. I was still fearful because I didn't know where this would lead, but suddenly I felt this envelopment, like being wrapped in a cocoon of peace and serenity. I began to feel like it's going to be all right. I heard a voice saying, 'I have you, don't worry.' It's been like that for a month."

"What brings you comfort now?"

"I dance in my dreams." He lifted an emaciated arm and posed it over his head. "And you know what? I'm fabulous!" he said with a mischievous smile. "I look like Desmond Richardson, only better! For the first time in my life, I have good feet and an incredible extension. And . . . my choreography, it's stunning!"

We both laughed loudly, and I felt like hugging him. Despite all he was going through, he had not lost his sense of humor.

"Russell, does knowing that you've spent your life doing creative work give you solace?"

"My journey as a dancer is so vivid to me, and I have no sensation that so much time has passed. Did I really do all that, choreograph a hundred music videos, umpteen TV shows, movies, and commercials? I literally chased myself up the ladder. I worked for thirty consecutive years and was between jobs no longer than three weeks at a time."

"You started a music video trend that changed popular culture. Did you expect to leave this sort of legacy behind?"

"We didn't know. We were just busy dancing. In the early 1980s MTV didn't even know what a music video was. There was no precedent and no resistance to new ideas. It was the most creative situation I'd ever been in. We had an amazing inside crew, and everything we wanted was at our disposal. I'd look at a stage and say, 'I need a staircase that goes like this with neon lights on the side, or a turn-of-the-century table lit with shafts of light,' and by the next day it was already built. The creative juice was hot. And I always embraced the rebels, the dancers that other choreographers didn't want because they had too much energy. I knew if you put a camera on this one or that one, this thing was going to jump. Then I'd go over to the dancer and say, 'Honey, just breathe and take your Bible over there, read Psalm whatever and then dance!' Nobody held back, and we just raged and rocked and filmed and filmed and filmed. I left a video trail of the music industry's most talented artists, like Marvin Gaye, Smokey Robinson, Michael Jackson, Gloria Estefan, Herbie Hancock, and David Bowie. The nineties saw a whole new scene, with rap music. Artists would come on the set high on drugs and exhibit bizarre behavior, so that's when I split for the world of feature films. I had no interest in amplifying that kind of behavior."

"Russell, what did dance teach you about life?"

"Dance offers us an approach to life—a methodology for living. It's not just about steps and moves. It's about humanity. It's about energy. It's about intellect . . . and heart. It has the power to elevate people to a higher level. Dance helps us dream bigger dreams and understand our connectedness. When we close our eyes and dream, we are all brothers. It's only when we open our eyes that we become aware of race, class, economics, and the things that separate us. We all want the same things out of life. What you and I feel, everyone feels."

"How does the discipline of dance inform us beyond performance?"

"Once you've been a dancer, you can go into any field or profession and be successful if you make the transference properly. Just think how difficult it is to build a perfect second position or execute an extension properly. When your strength, balance, and perception coalesce into a fabulous movement, it shows you that this is how things come together. You work on them, you commit to them, you desire them, and you have them. You must learn to put all your stuff on the same plate and manipulate it as an artist does. The artist is also an alchemist. I want people to comfortably transition their art into an engine that will fuel the rest of their lives."

"How do you come to trust and believe in yourself?"

"Ultimately it must come from deep inside of you. When someone says to you, 'Hey, kid, what can you do?' you've just been handed an incredible opportunity to show what you're made of. You should say to yourself, 'Stand back, I'm building a body of work.' Use that situation to become more confident with yourself, professionally and emotionally. This can only happen when there is no fear. If you operate from fear, it's blinding. Once you start with 'Was that good enough?' you become your own roadblock."

"How do you turn off fear and insecurity?"

"You gut it. You disempower it. You step in front of it and bully it away. That's how you protect the creative artist within you. When you do that, your creative powers get stronger and deeper, your eye gets sharper, and you challenge yourself to greater heights. Before long you hear yourself saying, 'Okay, I know that was good, but wait till you see what I do tomorrow.'"

"How did you become so fearless, Russell? So confident?"

"Maybe because I equated work with play. I've always had a strong connection to my inner child and an understanding that play leads to creative thought. When you play, you create energy, and that energy leads to productivity."

"Are creative people inherently different from noncreative people?"

"I've always felt that creative people have a resilience and a deep strength that other people don't enjoy. Take for example my father and my uncle—the Clark Brothers. They were one of the most successful tap-dancing teams of the 1950s. They played the big hotels and opened for Frank Sinatra and Peggy Lee in Las Vegas. Because they were black they'd have to go back through the kitchen and sleep outside the city. But they didn't need to drink from the colored people's fountain. They received standing ovations every night. In the back of their minds, they were saying, 'These people really get me. They think I'm fabulous. They paid to see me, and I'm going to give them all I've got.' This reinforcement builds self-confidence. It builds belief in oneself."

"What advice do you have for choreographers working in feature films?"

"Don't be the dummy on the set."

"What do you mean?"

"If you have the opportunity to do something in film, make a mark. Don't jeopardize your chances of doing something really important because you were lazy to get educated about the art of choreographing for film. Realize that you have an obligation to uphold the craft and a responsibility to the artists that came before you. Understand why Fred Astaire and Hermes Pan insisted that everything be shot from head to toe—so that arms and feet don't get cut off. Do your homework. Visit the film archives and learn how shots are lined up. Be prepared. Have an understanding of the language of the medium, including the jargon. If someone says, 'We are going to pan right,' know what that means; otherwise what you're doing is lessening the impact of dance, making it less appealing. You don't want to do that. You have an opportunity to present your work in the twenty-first century. Your name is going to be on that work and live longer than you do. If you come from anywhere less than that, then you're the dummy on the set."

"How difficult is it to maintain your creative integrity when working for large corporate production companies?"

"The artist/choreographer is at a disadvantage. Corporate people who hire talent have no artistic vision or point of view. They want to see another *Flashdance* or *Dirty Dancing* because those films made millions of dollars. Understand that they are interested in your art for the singular purpose of making money. They want to measure their pie chart by your creative output. All the artist really wants to do is keep his creative juices hot. All he wants to do is give his heart."

"How in such an environment does the artist create work that feeds him creatively?"

"You have to take the view that 'This is my movie and here is where I do my thing.' Remember, you're building a body of work. You make your dance so amazing, so breathtaking, so important that if it were to end up on the cutting room floor, the movie would not hold together. Your thirty seconds or three minutes, whatever it is, advances the story line in such a profound way that the editor would not dare cut it out. And here's what else you do. If they ask you for three minutes of dance footage, don't give them five. Don't give them ten. Don't give them an opportunity to edit your creativity. Give them the best three minutes you have in you."

During our fourth session, which took place in the bedroom of Russell's apartment, I could see that he was beginning to really struggle with the pain. I wondered how he could focus his thoughts so clearly.

"Would you like to stop now, Russell?" I asked.

No response. He closed his eyes and was motionless. I was deciding whether to run for the home nurse, when he said, "Ask me one more question."

"Are you afraid, Russell?"

With his eyes still closed he said, "The last thing I will accept into my world is the idea of being a victim. How do I survive this cancer—this experience? I do my best and take it now day by day, minute by minute. I have to win. For me winning is finding peace and love without fear. I've oriented my perception to whatever is in store for me. I'm thrilled that I have found some level of enlightenment and peace in my lifetime. I am now prepared for whatever eventuality."

Russell then opened his eyes and stared at me. I stood up and hugged him. "I'll be back tomorrow."

Walking out of the bedroom, I glanced back and saw him looking toward the window. At that moment a breeze came through and lifted the curtain. The room filled with bright sunlight.

When I phoned the next day, his mother informed me that Russell was not expected to make it through the day.

"Oh, I must see him one more time. It's urgent!" I told her. "May I come by just for a second?"

"No, Rose, I don't think that will be possible. This is a time for his family."

"But I have to see him one more time," I insisted.

"Why is it so important that you see him?"

"I need to reassure him that I will tell his story. I made him a promise."

"I'll tell him for you, dear. He knows you will. He knows you will."

Russell died two days later.

Hollywood, California, 2000, 2002

235

Russell Clark

Dee Dee Wood & Marc Breaux

Murray Louis

Donald Byrd's/The Group

Edward Villella

Patricia Birch

Ronald K. Brown

236

Mary Anthony

Ann Reinking

Rennie Harris/PureMovement

Doug Varone and Dancers

Lar Lubovitch

Toni Basil

Katherine Dunham

Tommy Tune

Christopher Wheeldon

Onna White

Cleo Parker Robinson

Daniel Ezralow

Gregory Hines

Anna Sokolow

Bill T. Jones

Garth Fagan

Vincent Paterson

Mark Morris

Grover Dale

239

Debbie Allen

Cholly Atkins

José Greco

Fayard Nicholas

Susan Stroman

Moses Pendleton's Momix

Rob Marshall

Pilobolus

Bella Lewitzky

Judith Jamison

Alan Johnson

Carmen de Lavallade

David Parsons

Dwight Rhoden

Eliot Feld

Sophie Maslow

Anna Halprin

242

Glen Tetley

Luigi

Alex Romero

Eleo Pomare

Michael Kidd

Alonzo King

Helgi Tomasson

Mia Michaels

Donald McKayle's *Games*

Elizabeth Streb's *Action Heroes*

Paul Taylor

244

Gus Solomons with Dudley Williams

Lynne Taylor Corbett rehearsing *Swing*

Graciela Danielle with dancers

Meredith Monk

BIOGRAPHIES

debbie allen

Debbie Allen danced in several Broadway shows in the 1970s, including *Raison*, for which she received a Drama Desk Award, as well as *West Side Story* and *Sweet Charity*, for which she earned Tony nominations.

Ms. Allen won two Emmy Awards and a Golden Globe for her role as passionate dance teacher Lydia Grant in the hit television series *Fame*. Her work in this show established her as one of Hollywood's most respected choreographers. She went on to stage the Academy Awards for five consecutive years during the mid-1980s.

In 1992 Ms. Allen was awarded an honorary doctorate from the North Carolina School of the Arts, as well as one from her alma mater, Howard University. In recent years she has made a name for herself as a producer and director in television, on the concert stage, and in feature films. Ms. Allen produced the film *Amistad* in 1998, which was directed by Steven Spielberg for Dreamworks. In 2001 she established the Debbie Allen Dance Academy in Los Angeles, which offers youngsters classes in classical ballet, modern, African, jazz, hip-hop, and special workshops. Her latest project is a new TV version of *Fame*, which she produces, choreographs, and hosts.

mary anthony

Mary Anthony is one of the most respected of the second-generation moderns. Through her teaching and dedication to the art of dance, she has helped establish modern dance as we know it today. She trained with modern dance pioneers Hanya Holm and Martha Graham. She also worked closely with Anna Sokolow for more than twenty years.

In 1956 Ms. Anthony founded the Mary Anthony Dance Theater and continues to offer performances in and around New York City. As a dedicated teacher, she has for more than sixty years inspired countless dancers and choreographers. Ms. Anthony has taught in universities throughout the United States and abroad and at the age of eighty-six continues to teach and run her school in New York City. During her dancing career she appeared on the concert stage, on Broadway, and on television. Her Broadway credits include *Up in Central Park*, *Rip Van Winkle*, and *Touch and Go.*

Her choreographed works appear in the repertories of the Pennsylvania Ballet and the Bat Dor Company in Israel.

Her signature works are *Threnody*, *Songs*, *Blood Wedding*, and *In the Beginning.*

cholly atkins

Cholly Atkins began his dance career in the 1920s, performing tap dance in nightclubs, traveling shows, and vaudeville. In the 1940s he and his partner, Honi Coles, established themselves as one of the most successful tap dance teams of the big band era, headlining for jazz greats Louis Armstrong, Cab Calloway, Lionel Hampton, and Count Basie.

In the early 1950s, while coaching singing groups, Mr. Atkins developed a technique he called "vocal choreography" to enhance performances through rhythmic steps and gestures. He coached some of Motown's most successful groups, including Gladys Knight and the Pips, the Four Tops, the Supremes, the O'Jays, the Temptations, and Smokey Robinson and the Miracles. He also worked with many solo performers, among them Sammy Davis Jr., Marvin Gaye, Stevie Wonder, Dionne Warwick, and Gregory Hines.

In 1989 he won a Tony Award for Choreography on the Broadway production of *Black and Blue.* The National Endowment for the Arts awarded him a choreographic fellowship in 1993, and he was honored with an Innovator Award by the American Choreography Awards in 1998.

Cholly Atkins continued to coach artists until his death in 2003.

toni basil

Toni Basil, a classically trained dancer and proficient in African dance, Afro-Cuban dance, tango, flamenco, and salsa, has been at the vanguard of dance and music for the last thirty years as performer, choreographer, director, and producer. Her choreographic credits include the films *American Graffiti, The Rose, That Thing You Do, Peggy Sue Got Married, My Best Friend's Wedding*, and *Legally Blond.* Her television work includes specials and television shows for Bette Midler, David Bowie, Rosie O'Donnell, the 46th Annual Emmy Awards, the MTV Awards, and *The Smothers Brothers Comedy Hour*, for which she earned an Emmy nomination.

Ms. Basil has choreographed shows and music videos for Bette Midler, David Bowie, Mick Jagger (coach), Tina Turner, Enrique Iglesias, Manhattan Transfer, and others. Her choreography for David Bowie's Diamond Dogs and Glass Spider tours is believed to have started the "rock theater" genre. She has choreographed and staged televised commercials for Toyota, Miller Lite, and Southwest Airlines, and ads for the Gap, which earned her an American Choreography Award nomination. She has received Grammy nominations for her own music videos, *Word of Mouth* and *Mickey*, which are now part of the permanent collection of the Museum of Modern Art. Ms. Basil is recognized as a seminal influence in bringing street dance to wider audiences as one of the original members of the legendary dance group the Lockers.

patricia birch

Patricia Birch began her early training with Merce Cunningham and Martha Graham. She later became a leading soloist in the Martha Graham Dance Company, as well as one of its directors. She appeared in *West Side Story* in the role of Anybody's and danced in several of Agnes de Mille's Broadway revivals.

She has created the musical staging for more than a dozen original productions on and off Broadway, including *You're a Good Man, Charlie Brown, The Me Nobody Knows, Grease, A Little Night Music, Candide, Pacific Overtures, They're Playing Our Song, Zoot Suit*, and *Parade.*

Ms. Birch choreographed several stage shows also, among them *On the Town* with Michael Tilson Thomas and the London Symphony, as well as the San Francisco Symphony, the Maurice Sendak/Carole King classic *Really Rosie, Salome, The Mikado, Elvis—A Multi-Media Celebration,* and *The Mass.* Her films include *Grease, Grease 2, Big, Working Girl, Sleeping with the Enemy, Stella,* and *Awakenings.* She has also created several television shows, including *Celebrating Gershwin, Dance in America,* and *20th Anniversary of Great Performances,* as well as music videos for Natalie Cole, Cyndi Lauper, the Rolling Stones, the Oak Ridge Boys, and Carly Simon.

Pat Birch's talents have earned her two Emmy Awards and four Tony nominations, as well as Drama Desk, Outer Critics Circle, Barrymore, Fred Astaire, Billboard, and MTV awards.

marc breaux *and* dee dee wood

Marc Breaux and Dee Dee Wood created some of the most memorable and well-crafted dance sequences in the history of dance on film. Their "Chimney Sweep Dance" with Dick Van Dyke and Julie Andrews in the movie *Mary Poppins,* and their "Do Re Mi" number in *The Sound of Music* are considered masterworks.

Breaux and Wood met while appearing in and assisting choreographer Michael Kidd on his Broadway show *Li'l Abner.* They moved on to feature films, choreographing *40 Pounds of Trouble, Mary Poppins, The Sound of Music, The Happiest Millionaire,* and *Chitty Chitty Bang Bang.* Television variety shows with Jack Benny, Jimmy Durante, Judy Garland, Dick Van Dyke, Andy Williams, Lucille Ball, Bing Crosby, Carol Burnett, and Debbie Reynolds

would serve as another showcase for their talents.

In addition to their collaborative work, Mr. Breaux choreographed and directed dozens of television specials and films such as *Huckleberry Finn, The Slipper and the Rose—The Story of Cinderella,* and *Sexette.* Ms. Wood's film credits include *In God We Trust* and *Beaches.* She has also choreographed numerous live spectacular events, including the XXIII Olympiad opening and closing ceremonies, many Super Bowl halftime shows, Pope John Paul II's visit to America, and the USA Olympic Festival opening.

In 1998 Dee Dee Wood and Marc Breaux were honored with the American Choreography Awards' Career Achievement Award.

ronald k. brown

Ronald K. Brown received his early dance training from master teacher Mary Anthony and later worked closely with Jennifer Muller: The Works, Judith Jamison, and Bessie Schonberg and Ann Carlson.

Since the birth of his company in 1986, Mr. Brown has changed the landscape of contemporary dance with a new genre of movement vocabulary—a fusion of modern dance technique and West African traditional dance styles. In addition to choreographing for Evidence, he has done commissions for the African American Dance Ensemble, Philadanco, Cleo Parker Robinson Dance Ensemble, Dayton Contemporary Dance Company (in collaboration with Donald McKayle), and the Alvin Ailey American Dance Theater.

Mr. Brown has received numerous awards and fellowships, including a

John Simon Guggenheim Memorial Foundation Fellowship in Choreography, a National Endowment for the Arts Fellowship, and a New York Dance and Performance Award (Bessie).

His signature works include *Water, High Life, Walking Out the Dark, Grace,* and *Come Ye.*

donald byrd

Donald Byrd has developed a movement style that integrates black vernacular dancing with classical ballet and modern dance techniques. His choreography is high-powered, direct, and highly technical. His works typically deal with controversial subjects such as racism and sexual abuse.

Mr. Byrd received his early training at the Ailey School and with ballet teacher Mia Slavenska. He danced with Twyla Tharp, Karole Armitage, and Gus Solomons Jr. Since 1976 Mr. Byrd has created more than 100 works for his own company, as well as for the Alvin Ailey American Dance Theater, Dayton Contemporary Dance Company, Philadanco, Cleo Parker Robinson Dance Ensemble, Dallas Black Dance Theater, Pacific Northwest Ballet, Oregon Ballet, Concordanse, and Aterballetoo in Reggio Emilia, Italy.

Other works created by Mr. Byrd include *Harlem Nutcracker, Carmina Burana, Aida, Prodigal, The Minstrel Show, Bristle, Jazz Train, The Beast,* and *Life Situations.*

He has received fellowships from the New York Foundation for the Arts, the Metropolitan Life Foundation, and the National Endowment for the Arts. In 1992 he received a Bessie Award for *The Minstrel Show.*

russell clark

A visionary and a pioneer, Russell Clark set the standard for the music video. Known for his strong visual sense and affinity for dancers with robust energy, he choreographed 100 videos for a wide array of artists, including Michael Jackson, Gloria Estefan, David Bowie, Grace Jones, George Clinton, Herbie Hancock, Marvin Gaye, and Smokey Robinson.

He choreographed more than thirty national commercials for products such as Diet Coke, Levi's, Clothestime, Taco Bell, and Miller Lite. He worked with some of the industry's most successful directors, including James Cameron, Ridley Scott, John Carpenter, Joe Pytka, Sean Penn, and Gregory Hoblit. His film credits include *Blade Runner, Devil in a Blue Dress, Major Payne, Why Do Fools Rush In, How Stella Got Her Groove Back,* and *The Banger Sisters.* He also choreographed for television, including episodes of *Coprock, Murder She Wrote, Red Shoe Diaries,* and The Temptations and M. C. Hammer miniseries.

Mr. Clark was honored with a Career Achievement Award at the 2002 American Choreography Awards. He died in October 2002 at the age of fifty.

lynne taylor corbett

Lynne Taylor Corbett studied at the School of American Ballet, the American Ballet Theater, and Harkness House of Ballet Arts. She danced with the Alvin Ailey American Dance Theater, Anna Sokolow, Dance Theater Collection, and numerous other companies. She appeared on Broadway in *Promises, Promises, Seesaw, Oklahoma!* and *A Chorus Line.*

Since the mid-1970s, Ms. Corbett has choreographed works for the American Ballet Theater, New York City Ballet, Pacific Northwest Ballet, Hubbard Street Dance Company, the Carolina Ballet, Alvin Ailey American Dance Theater, and many others.

Her Broadway credits include *Titanic* (1997) and *Swing* (1999), for which she received Tony nominations for both direction and choreography. Among the films that Ms. Corbett has choreographed are *Footloose* (1984), which became a huge box office hit, and *My Blue Heaven* (1988). She has also directed numerous plays and shows, including *Mona Rogers in Person, Boy's Breath, Darlene Love: Portrait of a Singer, Ballad of You and Me, 20th Century Pop, Natural Selection,* and *Opal* for the Dallas Lyric Theater, to be premiered in Hong Kong's 2,000-seat theater.

grover dale

Grover Dale made his Broadway debut in 1955 when Michael Kidd cast him in *Li'l Abner.* In 1956 Jerome Robbins cast him as Snowboy in the original Broadway production of *West Side Story.* Mr. Dale later became Jerome Robbins's assistant, and their collaboration continued on and off for the next thirty-five years. Mr. Dale appeared on Broadway in *Greenwillow* (1960), *Sail Away* (1961), *The Unsinkable Molly Brown* (1963), and *Half a Sixpence* (1965) before directing his own show, *Billy Budd,* in 1969. He codirected *Jerome Robbins' Broadway,* for which he won a Tony Award in 1989.

In later years Mr. Dale took on the role of dance advocate, establishing a dance foundation, programs, and scholarships. He was instrumental in the creation of the American Choreography Awards for dancemakers in film, television, music video, and commercials, paying tribute to teachers and others who have made significant contributions to the art form. In 1991 Mr. Dale founded *Dance and Fitness Magazine,* a monthly publication intended to serve the greater Los Angeles dance community. His workshops and Answers for Dancers Web site have become important resources for aspiring dancers.

graciela daniele

Graciela Daniele began her ballet training at Teatro Colón in her native Buenos Aires, Argentina. In 1963, while living and dancing professionally in Paris, she attended a performance of *West Side Story,* which she credits for changing her life. She moved to New York to study with Matt Mattox, Merce Cunningham, and Martha Graham. She made her Broadway debut in 1964 in *What Makes Sammy Run?* and went on to perform in several other shows, including *Here's Where I Belong* (1968), *Promises, Promises* (1968), and *Chicago* (1975). Her career as a choreographer began as an assistant to Michael Bennett. She went on to choreograph *The Milliken Show* (1976) and a number of Broadway shows, among them *The Pirates of Penzance* (1981), *The Rink* (1984), *Ragtime* (1997), and the revival of *Annie Get Your Gun* (1999). Her film credits include *Beatlemania* (1981), *The Pirates of Penzance* (1983), *Bullets over Broadway* (1994), *Mighty Aphrodite* (1995), and *Everyone Says I Love You* (1996). Her ballet pieces include *Presley Pieces* for the American Ballet Theater, *Cado Noche Tango,* and *El Nuevo Mundo* for Ballet Hispanico (1992).

Ms. Daniele has received numerous Tony and Drama Desk nominations, and an LA Critics Award.

carmen de lavallade

Carmen de Lavallade is regarded as one of the most beautiful dancers ever to grace the stage. At the age of sixteen she won a scholarship to study with Lester Horton, one of the pioneers of modern dance, and she was mentored by the great ballet dancer Carmelita Marracci.

She made her Broadway debut in *House of Flowers,* choreographed by Herbert Ross. She starred in *Carmen Jones,* also choreographed by Ross, and danced a duet with Jack Cole in *Lydia Bailey.* In New York she performed in numerous companies, including the Metropolitan Opera, American Ballet Theater, John Butler Dance Company, and Alvin Ailey American Dance Theater. Her performance credits include *The Four Marys,* choreographed by Agnes de Mille, and several works by John Butler, including *Carmina Burana* and *Portrait of Billie.*

Ms. de Lavallade has staged and choreographed several stage productions, including *A Midsummer Night's Dream, The Creation, Les Chansons de Bilitis,* and *The Earrings of Madame D.* She continues to perform as a guest artist in some of this country's most respected companies. She is a member of Paradigm, a performance ensemble with Gus Solomons Jr. and Dudley Williams.

At Yale University Ms. de Lavallade trained as an actor and became a member of the Yale Repertory Theater. She has appeared in numerous films, television specials, and stage performances. Her role in *Othello* won her the Clarence Bayfield Award, presented by Actors Equity.

katherine dunham

Ms. Katherine Dunham is credited with opening stage doors across America for African American dancers, choreographers, and entertainers, including Alvin Ailey, Cleo Parker Robinson, Talley Beatty, Eartha Kitt, Vanoye Aikens, Walter Nicks, Janet Collins, and scores of others. Her influence in encouraging black dancers and choreographers to live and work with pride is one of her greatest achievements.

Ms. Dunham was one of the first African American women to receive a master's degree in anthropology. In 1936 she traveled to the West Indies to study the dances of Martinique, Jamaica, Trinidad, and particularly Haiti. She used the research data gathered for her thesis, *Dances of Haiti,* to help her create future stage performances such as *Tropics, Le Jazz Hot,* and *From Haiti to Harlem.* In 1940 she appeared in an all-black Broadway show called *Cabin in the Sky.* From Broadway she moved to

Hollywood and appeared in several films, including *Star Spangled Rhythm* (1941), *Stormy Weather* (1943), *Casbah* (1948), *Pardon My Sarong* (1952), and *Green Mansions* (1959).

The Dunham technique, which provides dancers and choreographers with a vocabulary of movement to more fully express themselves, is considered one of her greatest contributions to the dance world. Her technique is still widely taught in schools and universities and continues to play an important role in the development of modern dance.

daniel ezralow

Daniel Ezralow has distinguished himself as a multitalented dancer and choreographer whose creative appetite knows no bounds. As a freelance choreographer for more than two decades, he is one of only a few in his field to work across a wide range of media—from the concert stage to feature films, music videos, live-action performances, Broadway, and commercials.

Mr. Ezralow studied with David and Marni Wood, who were both former Martha Graham dancers. He danced in the companies of Lar Lubovitch, Paul Taylor, and Pilobolus before becoming codirector with Moses Pendleton of ISO and Momix.

He has created works for Hubbard Street Dance Chicago, Paris Opera Ballet, Batsheva Dance Company of Israel, London Contemporary Dance Theater, Maggio Musicale Florentine, Helsinki City Theater Dance Company, and numerous others. His work in television includes the 1998 Academy Awards show; the Ricky Martin Live

special; *To Live: America* Celebrates Israel's 50th; and *A Tribute to Sarajevo*.

He has choreographed shows and music videos for David Bowie, Andrea Bocelli, Sting, U2, Pat Metheny, and Josh Groban. His one-man show, *Mandala*, toured the United States, Europe, and South America to sold-out houses. He is the recipient of two American Choreography Awards, an Emmy Award and nomination, the Positano Award (Italy), and the Nijinski Award (Poland) for choreography.

garth fagan

A native of Jamaica, Garth Fagan has been called one of the great reformers of modern dance. He blends ballet and modern dance with Afro-Caribbean movement. He began his career when he toured Latin America with Jamaica's national dance company and was influenced by legendary artists Pearl Primus and Livinia Williams. In New York he studied with Martha Graham, José Limón, Mary Hinkson, and Alvin Ailey, all of whom were influential in his development as a choreographer.

In 1970 he established his own company, Garth Fagan Dance, in Rochester, New York, and continues to serve as its artistic director and choreographer. In 1998 he choreographed the Broadway hit *The Lion King*, for which he earned numerous awards, including a Tony Award for Best Choreography, the 1998 Drama Desk Award, the 1998 Outer Critics Circle Award, and the 1998 Astaire Award.

Mr. Fagan choreographed works for many dance companies, including the Dance Theater of Harlem, the Alvin Ailey American Dance Theater, the José

Limón Dance Company, and the New York City Ballet.

A distinguished university professor at the State University of New York at Brockport, Mr. Fagan has received numerous grants and fellowships, including a Fulbright, a Guggenheim, and a fellowship from the National Endowment for the Arts. In 1998 he received Jamaica's highest honor, a Special Gold Musgrave Medal for his "Contribution to the World of Dance and Dance Theater."

eliot feld

Eliot Feld has remained a strong dance presence ever since his performance as the Child Prince in George Balanchine's original production of *The Nutcracker* at the age of twelve. As a youngster he danced in the companies of Mary Anthony, Pearl Lang, Sophie Maslow, and Donald McKayle. At sixteen he joined the Broadway cast of *West Side Story* and appeared as Baby John in the movie version. He also appeared on Broadway in *I Can Get It for You Wholesale* and *Fiddler on the Roof* and with the American Ballet Theater, the American Ballet Company, and his own company—Feld Ballets/NY.

He created his first ballet at the age of twenty-four. Since 1967 he has choreographed 115 ballets, among them such noted works as *Play Bach* (1981), *The Jig Is Up* (1984), *Echo* (1986), *Kore* (1988), *Paper Tiger* (1996), *Yo Shakespeare* (1997), and *Cherokee Rose* (1999). In addition to creating works for his own company, he has choreographed works for the Joffrey Ballet, Royal Danish Ballet, Royal Winnipeg Ballet, San Francisco Ballet, London

Festival Ballet, Atlanta Ballet, Richmond Ballet, Boston Ballet, New York City Ballet, and many others.

In 1995 he established the New York City Public School for Dance, which auditions more 35,000 students annually from 450 schools in the five boroughs of New York. Mr. Feld also is one of the cofounders of the Joyce Theater in Manhattan.

josé greco

José Greco popularized Spanish and flamenco dance worldwide. He became an international star, appearing on stage and screen, in television and films, and at nightclubs and stadiums. Embodying the machismo of the male Spanish dancer, he excited audiences wherever he and his troupe performed.

Born in Italy in 1918 and raised in Brooklyn, Mr. Greco studied Spanish dance with Helen Veola and first performed publicly in *La Traviata* at the famed Hippodrome. In 1942 he began performing with the legendary La Argentinita, considered one of the purest stylists of Spanish dance. He founded his own company in 1949 and toured for the next thirty-five years. He made numerous television appearances on *The Ed Sullivan Show* and *The Tonight Show with Johnny Carson*, and on Bob Hope specials. His films include *Around the World in 80 Days* and *Ship of Fools*.

Throughout his career, José Greco received numerous awards and honors, including the Cross of the Knight of Civil Merit in recognition of his worldwide contribution to the culture and performing arts of Spain, three honorary doctorates, the Silver Bowl

Award from the American Platform Association, and a fellowship from the National Endowment for the Arts.

In his later years he served as a visiting professor of dance at Franklin and Marshall College in Pennsylvania, where he lived with his wife, Dr. Ana Borger-Greco, until his death in 2000 at the age of eighty-two.

anna halprin

Anna Halprin, who began her dance career in the late 1930s, is celebrated for her innovative approach and exploration of movement for personal healing and community building. She strives to create an environment where "more of us will call ourselves dancers and work together to make art concerned with the primary issues of life." She envisions a future in which people will celebrate the beauty of nature and each other, regardless of race, culture, or spiritual practice.

Ms. Halprin attended the University of Chicago, where she studied with Margaret H'Doubler, who headed the first dance department at a major university. Ms. Halprin also studied with the psychologist Fritz Perls. After a brief stint working in a Broadway show choreographed by Doris Humphrey and Charles Weidman, she moved with her architect husband, Lawrence Halprin, to the West Coast and established the San Francisco Dancers' Workshop in 1955 and Tamalpa Institute in 1978, both dedicated to the expressive healing arts.

She later created and led "Circle the Earth," a contemporary community dance ritual, and her world-famous Planetary Dances.

Ms. Halprin has created many full-length dance theater works, which are extensively documented in photographs and on film. She is the recipient of numerous awards, including a Guggenheim Fellowship, a National Endowment for the Arts grant, a Sustained Achievement Award from the Isadora Duncan Hall of Fame, and San Francisco's Bay Guardian Lifetime Achievement Award.

rennie harris

Rennie Harris, the artistic director and choreographer of his Philadelphia-based company, Puremovement, has brought street dance/hip-hop to a new level of respectability as an art form. For more than a decade he has choreographed and taught hip-hop and has brought it to the concert stage. He organized the first hip-hop tour in America, the Fresh Festival, featuring the genre's leading stars.

Mr. Harris has had no formal dance training. He learned various hip-hop techniques by entering street competitions with friends. At the age of fourteen he was hired by the Smithsonian Center for Folk Life and Cultural Heritage to lecture and demonstrate hip-hop around the country and the Caribbean. He supported himself for the next fourteen years with the mission of educating and validating this dance genre.

Mr. Harris has used hip-hop dance to make cultural statements in such pieces as *Students of the Asphalt Jungle, Endangered Species, Lorenzo's Oil, Rome and Jewels,* and *Facing Mekka.*

Since 1992 Puremovement has received broad support through generous grants from such organizations as the National Endowment for the Arts, the Philadelphia Dance Alliance, the Pew Charitable Trust, the William Penn Foundation, and the Independence Foundation. It has also been recognized with the Herb Alpert Award in the Arts and the Bessie Award.

gregory hines

Gregory Hines did for tap what Bob Fosse did for Broadway and what Balanchine did for ballet. He revived a dance tradition and redefined it for a new generation. Mr. Hines revolutionized the look of tap, making it sexy, athletic, and downright hip. Always in search of the new step, he shifted the perception of the tap dancer from entertainer seeking applause to respected dance artist with skills, craft, and a choreographic voice.

Mr. Hines was not yet three when he began his show business training under the tutelage of tap master Henry Le Tang. By the age of five, he was performing with his brother, Maurice, in nightclubs and theaters all around the country. Backstage at the Apollo Theater in Harlem he was exposed to the great hoofers of the day: Honi Coles, Sandman Sims, the Nicholas Brothers, and Teddy Hale.

As a young adult he received multiple Tony nominations for his performances in *Sophisticated Ladies, Comin' Uptown,* and *Eubie!* From Broadway he went to Hollywood, acting and dancing in *History of the World—Part I* (1981), *The Cotton Club* (1984), *White Nights* (1985) with Mikhail Baryshnikov, *Running Scared* (1986), *Tap* (1989), *Waiting to Exhale* (1995), *The Tic Code*

(1998), and *Bojangles* (2001).

A beloved showman, Mr. Hines left an indelible mark on the worlds of dance, stage, and screen. He died on August 9, 2003, at the age of fifty-seven.

judith jamison

Judith Jamison made her debut with the American Ballet Theater in 1964. A year later she became a member of the Alvin Ailey American Dance Theater and would go on to dance with the company for the next fifteen years. Her tour de force performance in *Cry,* choreographed by Alvin Ailey in honor of his mother, brought Ms. Jamison wide recognition as one of the most powerful dancers of her generation.

After leaving the company, she appeared with dance companies worldwide and starred in the hit Broadway musical *Sophisticated Ladies.* She formed her own company in 1988, the Jamison Project, but disbanded it a year later after Alvin Ailey, nearing death, asked her to succeed him as artistic director of his company—a position she has held since 1989.

Among the numerous works she has choreographed for the Ailey company and others are *Diving* (1984), *Rift* (1991), *Hymn* (1993), *Riverside* (1995), *Sweet Release* (1996), and *Echo: Far from Home* (1998).

Ms. Jamison has received many awards and honorary degrees, including a Prime Time Emmy for Outstanding Choreography in the PBS special *Dance in America: A Hymn for Alvin Ailey* and a lifetime achievement award from the Kennedy Center.

alan johnson

Alan Johnson began his professional dance training at the age of eighteen with Matt Mattox, Peter Gennaro, and Nanette Charisse in New York City. He landed his first professional dance job in 1955 with the national tour of *Damn Yankees*. He would go on to perform in *West Side Story* (1957), *No Strings* (1962), *Anyone Can Whistle* (1964), and *Hallelujah Baby* (1964).

In 1964 he began his choreographic career at the Camden Fair, where he created dances and musical numbers for its production of *Damn Yankees*. His big break came when Mel Brooks invited him to choreograph his first film, *The Producers*. Mr. Johnson went on to choreograph several more Mel Brooks films, including *Blazing Saddles*, *Young Frankenstein*, *To Be or Not to Be*, and *Dracula: Dead and Loving It*.

Mr. Johnson's television specials include *Anne Bancroft "Women in the Life of a Man"* (1970), Shirley MacLaine specials (1974, 1976), *Every Little Movement* (1979), The 54th, 55th, and 60th Academy Awards shows (1981, 1982, 1987), and dozens more. His stage shows include *Ann Reinking—Music Moves Me* (1984), *Legs Diamond* (1988), *Can Can* national tour (1988), and *The Chita Rivera Show* (1991). He has also choreographed nightclub shows for Peter Allen, Ann-Margret, Bernadette Peters, Leslie Uggams, and Pia Zadora.

Mr. Johnson was selected by Jerome Robbins to serve as one of the guardians of *West Side Story*, allowing him to restage the landmark show worldwide. He has received numerous Emmy and Tony Awards and nominations, including the American Choreography Awards' Career Achievement Award in 2003.

bill t. jones

Bill T. Jones uses his dance company, Bill T. Jones/Arnie Zane and Company, to intelligently and artfully converse with his audiences. He has created more than fifty works for his own company and has received many commissions from the Alvin Ailey American Dance Theater, Lyon Opera Ballet, Boston Ballet, Berkshire Ballet, Berlin Opera Ballet, and many other companies.

Mr. Jones began his dance training at the State University of New York (SUNY) at Binghamton, where he studied classical ballet and modern dance. In 1973 he formed the American Dance Asylum. A little less than a decade later, he created Bill T. Jones/Arnie Zane Dance Company with his late partner, Arnie Zane.

His television credits include *Fever Swamp*, *Untitled*, *Last Supper at Uncle Tom's Cabin/The Promised Land*, and *Still Here*. His stage works include *Degga* (a collaborative work with Toni Morrison and Max Roach commissioned by Lincoln Center), *D-Man in the Waters*, *The Table Project*, *The Breathing Show*, and *How! Do! We! Do!*

Mr. Jones has received numerous prestigious awards, including the 2003 Dorothy and Lillian Gish Prize, a MacArthur Fellowship, and a Choreographic Fellowship from the National Endowment for the Arts. In 2000 the Dance Heritage Coalition named Bill T. Jones "An Irreplaceable Dance Treasure." He has received honorary doctorates from Juilliard, the Chicago School for the Arts, Bard College, and Swarthmore College.

michael kidd

Michael Kidd, one of the most influential creators of dance in the past half century, is best known for his staging of Broadway shows and Hollywood musicals. He was instrumental in launching the careers of Onna White, Dee Dee Wood, Marc Breaux, and Grover Dale.

Abandoning a career in engineering for one in the arts, Kidd began his dance training in the mid-1930s and began performing shortly thereafter with Lincoln Kirstein's Ballet Caravan. From there he moved to Eugene Loring's Dance Players in 1942 and after that to Ballet Theater—the forerunner of the American Ballet Theater. During his years as a ballet dancer he performed the works of Eugene Loring, Jerome Robbins, Agnes de Mille, Leonide Massine, Michel Fokine, Anthony Tudor, and many others.

Mr. Kidd choreographed his first ballet in 1945, which led him to a string of successful Broadway shows, including *Finian's Rainbow*, *Li'l Abner*, *Guys and Dolls*, and *Can Can*, all of which won Tony Awards. In Hollywood he choreographed such hits as *The Band Wagon*, *It's Always Fair Weather*, *Guys and Dolls*, *Seven Brides for Seven Brothers*, *Breakfast at Tiffany's*, and *Hello, Dolly*.

In 1997 Michael Kidd was awarded an honorary Oscar for Exceptional Contributions to the Making of Motion Pictures. He is also the recipient of the Career Achievement Award, presented at the 1996 Fosse Awards.

alonzo king

Alonzo King is one of America's leading ballet choreographers. His San Francisco–based company, Lines Contemporary Ballet, formed in 1982, has received international recognition for its innovative choreography and performance virtuosity. His choreographed works can be found in the repertoires of more than fifty dance companies, including the Frankfurt Ballet, Hong Kong Ballet, Dresden Ballet, Alvin Ailey American Dance Theater, Ballet Met, Joffrey Ballet, Washington Ballet, and Hubbard Street Dance Chicago.

Mr. King received his early training at the School of American Ballet, American Ballet Theater School, and at the Harkness House of Ballet Arts. As a dancer he has worked with a large range of choreographers and companies, including the Dance Theater of Harlem, Bella Lewitsky Dance Company, and Harkness Youth Company, and also with choreographers Donald McKayle and Glen Tetley.

A gifted dance teacher, Mr. King has been guest ballet master for numerous companies, including the National Ballet of Canada, Les Ballets de Monte Carlo, the San Francisco Ballet, and Ballet Rambert.

Mr. King has received numerous honors, among them the NEA Choreographer's Fellowship and the National Dance Residency Program, as well as four Isadora Duncan Awards.

bella lewitzky

Bella Lewitzky distinguished herself as an important modern dance activist on the West Coast. Choosing to ignore the New York dance scene, she offered Los Angeles a modern dance presence and an opportunity for dancers to explore movement "among the orange groves and freeways."

Lewitzky studied with legendary teacher and choreographer Lester Horton, who is believed to have used her body to develop his technique. She danced the title roles of *Salome, The Beloved, Sacre du Printemps*, and *Tierra y Libertad*. In 1946 she and Horton founded Dance Theater of Los Angeles—a storefront studio that would become the launching pad for artists like Alvin Ailey, Carmen de Lavallade, Joyce Trisler, James Truitte, and others.

In 1951 she formed the first of three dance companies that she would direct until her retirement in 1997 at the age of eighty-one. Her best-known works are *Ceremony for Three, Spaces Between, Gamer Plan Scintilla*, and *Confines*.

Lewitzky served as impresario to many LA dance events, including the Olympic International Dance Festival in 1984 and the American debut of Europe's best-known modern dance choreographer, Pina Bausch. She was a powerful advocate for dance education in the elementary schools.

She has received numerous awards, including the National Medal of Arts. Lewitzky died on July 16, 2004, at the age of eighty-eight.

murray louis

Murray Louis established himself during the late 1940s as one of the most kinetically intelligent dancers in the modern dance genre. In collaboration with Alwin Nikolais, Louis articulated a new dance voice based on the artful presentation of pure movement, unencumbered by story or conventional entertainment values.

In its heyday, the Alwin Nikolais and Murray Louis Dance Company toured worldwide and set a precedent in the presentation of modern dance by integrating the elements of theater, lighting, sets, and staging with dance to broaden the scope of performance.

Mr. Louis has choreographed hundreds of works for his own company as well as for others. He has worked closely with dancers Rudolf Nureyev, Eric Bruhn, and Patrick Dupond, and jazz great Dave Brubeck scored several of his dances. He has also authored several books on dance, including *Murray Louis: On Dance, Inside Dance*, and *The Unique Gesture*.

During the course of his career, Mr. Louis has received numerous awards, including two Guggenheim Fellowships, the *Dance Magazine* Award, and the Knight of the French Order of Arts and Letters Award.

lar lubovitch

Lar Lubovitch is one of the most prolific choreographers of his generation. His work is renowned for its musicality, beauty, and rhapsodic style.

Mr. Lubovitch attended the University of Iowa and Juilliard, where he studied with Louis Horst, José Limón, Anthony Tudor, Anna Sokolow, and Martha Graham. He danced briefly in the companies of Pearl Lang, Donald McKayle, Glen Tetley, and John Butler, among others, before forming the Lar Lubovitch Dance Company in 1968, which has performed in every state of the Union as well as in thirty nations abroad.

He has since choreographed more than sixty dances. His works are included in the repertories of the New York City Ballet, Paris Opera Ballet, Alvin Ailey American Dance Theater, Royal Danish Ballet, Stuttgart Ballet, Netherlands Dance Theater, White Oak Dance Project, and many others.

Mr. Lubovitch's signature works include *Whirligogs* (1969), *Les Noces* (1976), *Brahms Symphony* (1985), *Fandango* (1989), *Othello* (1997), *Meadow* (1999), and *Men's Stories* (2000). His Broadway credits include *Into the Woods* (1987), *Salome* (1992), *The Red Shoes* (1993), and *The King and I* (1996). He has also choreographed for television and for ice-skating events.

Mr. Lubovitch has received numerous awards, including an International Emmy, a Cable ACE Award, an Astaire Award, and a Tony nomination, as well as Guggenheim and NEA Fellowships.

luigi

Luigi (Eugene Facciuto) is best known for his innovative jazz style and teaching technique. Discovered by an MGM talent scout in Los Angeles and then hired by Gene Kelly, Luigi danced in many of the greatest films of the Hollywood musical era, including *On the Town, Singin' in the Rain, The Band Wagon, Annie Get Your Gun*, and *An American in Paris*. He worked with Hollywood's biggest names, including choreographers Michael Kidd, Hermes Pan, Robert Alton, and Eugene Loring, as well as actors/dancers Judy Garland, Cyd Charisse, Bing Crosby, Vera Ellen, Danny Kaye, and Donald O'Connor.

Luigi's "feeling from the inside" method of dance has made him one of the foremost jazz masters in the world. He has taught master classes in schools and colleges all over the world. Alvin Ailey, Patricia McBride, Jacques D'Amboise, Liza Minnelli, Christopher Walken, Ben Vereen, Ann Reinking, Susan Stroman, and John Travolta have all studied with Luigi.

In 1999 he was honored with Jazz Dance LA Foundation's Lifetime Achievement Award, and Dance Teacher honored him with its Lifetime Achievement Award in 2003.

rob marshall

Rob Marshall's long list of successes places him among the top Broadway choreographers working today. As director of the film version of *Chicago*, he has also left a permanent mark on Hollywood, with his film winning an Oscar for Best Picture in 2002.

Rob Marshall grew up listening to show tunes and watching musicals on television in Madison, Wisconsin. He knew he was destined for the stage. His first big break came at the age of nineteen when he auditioned for Michael Bennett and got a part in the touring company of *A Chorus Line*. He would later win roles in *Zorba, The Rink, The Mystery of Edwin Drood*, and other shows. When Rob was twenty-eight, he sustained an injury while performing in *Cats* that ended his dancing career. He turned next to choreography.

Marshall calls Graciela Daniele his greatest mentor. As her dance captain during the making of *The Rink*, he learned from her how to direct and tell stories through dance. Over the next few years he would choreograph *A Funny Thing Happened on the Way to the Forum, Kiss of the Spider Woman, She Loves Me, Petrified Forest*, revivals of *Damn Yankees* and *Cabaret, Little Me*, and *Victor/Victoria*. He has earned numerous Tony Awards and nominations, Drama Desk Award, Outer Critics

Circle Awards and nominations, and a Drama-Logue Award. His movies for television—*Cinderella* and ABC's *Wonderful World of Disney*—earned him Emmy nominations. His TV movie adaptation of *Annie* won him an Emmy Award in 1999.

sophie maslow

Sophie Maslow became a member of Martha Graham's first company in 1931. She, along with Dorothy Bird, Anna Sokolow, and Martha Hill, was among the dancers who helped Graham develop her famous technique. Ms. Maslow performed many of Graham's signature works, including *Primitive Mysteries* (1935) and *American Document* (1938). Ms. Maslow began to compose her own dances while still in the Graham company and working with Louis Horst during his famous lecture-demonstrations. From the early 1940s until 1954 she danced with Jane Dudley and William Bales in the Dudley-Maslow-Bales Dance Trio.

Her dances include *Folksay* (1942); *Champion* (1948), based on a story by Ring Lardner; *The Village I Knew* (1951), inspired by the stories of Sholem Aleichem; and *Prolouge* (1959), based on the Prologue to Boccaccio's *Decameron*, with music by Carl Orff. In 1964 she created *The Dybbuk* and in 1980, *Voices*.

In 1984 Ms. Maslow was awarded an honorary doctorate from Skidmore College.

donald mckayle

Donald McKayle became a dancer after seeing Pearl Primus perform. He would later study with Pearl Primus, Martha Graham, Sophie Maslow, Mary Anthony, Merce Cunningham, Paul Draper, Jean Erdman, and Louis Horst.

Mr. McKayle has choreographed more than seventy works for numerous dance companies including the Alvin Ailey American Dance Theater, Cleo Parker Robinson Dance Ensemble, Ballet San Jose Silicon Valley, Dayton Contemporary Dance Company, and Lula Washington Dance Theater. For the Broadway stage he choreographed several shows, including *Golden Boy* (1964), *Raison* (1974), *Doctor Jazz* (1975), *Sophisticated Ladies* (1981), and others, for which he earned multiple Tony nominations. His film credits include *The Great White Hope* and *The Jazz Singer*. His classic works include *Games* (1951), *Rainbow 'Round My Shoulder* (1959), *District Storyville* (1962), *House of Tears and Death* (2000), and *Eros* (2000).

Mr. McKayle is a master teacher, having served on the faculties of many prestigious institutions, including Juilliard, Bennington College, and the University of California at Irvine. He holds numerous distinguished awards, including a Tony Award and an American Dance Guild Award, and has been the recipient of an NEA Fellowship and an Irvine Fellowship in Dance.

mia michaels

Mia Michaels began choreographing local shows and performances at the age of eleven. She trained classically with the Miami Conservatory and in modern dance at the Performing Arts Center (which later became the World School of the Arts). In 1989 she formed her first company, the Miami Movement Dance Company, and she followed that with a second company in the mid-1990s called RAW (Reality at Work). She has also choreographed for other companies, including the Miami City Ballet, Joffrey II, Kirov II, and Jazz Theater of Amsterdam.

Ms. Michaels gradually moved into commercial choreography, creating music videos, national commercials, and live-action shows. She has created works for Prince, Ricky Martin, Gloria Estefan, Jimmy Ray, and Madonna. Her commercials include Coldwell Banker, Ziploc, Lady Luck Casino, and MTV's *Hot Properties*. In 2003 she collaborated with Franco Dragone, the creator of Cirque du Soleil, in choreographing the Celine Dion show at Caesars Palace in Las Vegas.

Ms. Michaels is the recipient of the Dance Educators of America's President's Cup and Leo's Dance Award, and she was also nominated for an Emmy Award.

meredith monk

Meredith Monk, a composer, singer, filmmaker, and choreographer, is known for her "interdisciplinary performances" integrating music, movement, visual image, light, and sound. She is one of the pioneers of site-specific performance and is responsible for creating the "extended vocal technique."

Ms. Monk graduated from Sarah Lawrence College in 1964 and quickly established herself as one of the most innovative avant-garde artists of the 1960s. Her works include *Juice: A Theater Cantata in 3 Installments* (1969), *Merce Cunningham Events #118* (1975), *Duet Behavior* with Bobby McFerrin (1987), *Offering for His Holiness, the Dalai Lama* (1999), and *Voice Travel* (2000). Her first orchestra piece, *Possible Sky*, was commissioned by Michael Tilson Thomas for the New World Symphony and premiered in the spring of 2003.

Ms. Monk is the recipient of numerous awards and fellowships, including a MacArthur "Genius" Award, two Guggenheim Fellowships, three Obies, a Bessie, and two Villager Awards. She has been awarded honorary doctorate degrees from Juilliard, the San Francisco Art Institute, and the Cornish School of the Arts.

mark morris

Mark Morris has been called "the Mozart of Modern Dance" for his musicality, devotion to classical music, and movement versatility. Since the early 1980s he has distinguished himself as a ballet, modern dance, and opera choreographer, creating works for his own company, the Mark Morris Dance Group, and for other companies throughout the world.

Mr. Morris began dancing and performing at the age of thirteen when he joined the Seattle-based company Koleda Balkan Dance Ensemble. Seeking a professional dance career, he moved to New York City in 1976 at the age of nineteen. Over the next few years he danced with various East Coast companies, including the Eliot Feld Ballet, Lar Lubovitch Dance Company, and Hannah Kahn Dance Company. Critics and audiences quickly embraced his choreography, establishing him as one of the more important postmodern dance choreographers.

From 1988 to 1991 he served as the director of dance for Théátre Royal de la Monnaie in Brussels, the national opera house in Belgium. It was during those years that he created some of his signature works, including *The Hard Nut, L'Allegro, Il Penseroso ed il Moderato,* and *Dido and Aeneas.*

Mark Morris has created more than 100 works for his own company and others, including the San Francisco Ballet and the Metropolitan Opera. He also cofounded the White Oak Dance Project with Mikhail Baryshnikov. He has received numerous awards, among them the Laurence Olivier Award, and was named a Fellow of the MacArthur Foundation in 1991.

fayard nicholas

Fayard Nicholas and his younger brother, Harold—the Nicholas Brothers—were the most accomplished tap dance duo of all time. From their childhood act at Harlem's Cotton Club to nightclub acts and Hollywood movies, their elegant style meshed with classic tap and acrobatic splits and double tours has never been surpassed.

Fayard and Harold, the children of vaudeville pit musicians, practically grew up in the theater, mostly in Philadelphia and New York, where they were exposed to all forms of entertainment, including tap dancing. Fayard worked up a routine, taught it to his brother, and the Nicholas Kids (later the Nicholas Brothers) was born. Fayard, who choreographed most of the numbers, incorporated the moves of ballroom dancing with the daring of flash acts and dance challenges, to the complex rhythms of jazz. The

Hollywood musical brought them great exposure, and although they were on the screen for only a few minutes, their numbers in *Down Argentine Way* (1940), *Sun Valley Serenade* (1941), *Orchestra Wives* (1942), and "Jumpin' Jive" from *Stormy Weather* (1943) have become legendary. At Twentieth Century Fox they worked collaboratively with choreographer Nick Castle.

The Nicholas Brothers enjoyed international fame for the next several decades. They received Kennedy Center honors in 1991. In 1994 they were given a star on Hollywood Boulevard's famous Walk of Fame and in 1998 a Carnegie Hall tribute and a Lifetime Achievement Award from the American Dance Festival.

kenny ortega

Kenny Ortega has created some of the most memorable dance sequences ever recorded on film, television, music video, and in legitimate theater, live events, and concert tours. His career has spanned thirty years of dancing and dancemaking.

Mr. Ortega began his early dance training in Northern California and landed his breakthrough role in the hit musical Hair. His staging and choreography for the rock band the Tubes led him into a full-time choreographic career. Ortega was one of the pioneers of the music video, creating works for Madonna, Cher, Elton John, Rod Stewart, Billy Joel, Fleetwood Mac, and many others.

During work on the film *Xanadu,* he met Gene Kelly, who mentored him on choreographing for the camera. His subsequent film Dirty Dancing became a huge box office hit. His other films

include *Ferris Bueller's Day Off, Newsies,* and *Hocus Pocus.*

Mr. Ortega has directed many large-scale dance events, including Michael Jackson's Dangerous and History world tours, the 1996 halftime show featuring Diana Ross, and the 1996 and 2000 opening and closing ceremonies for the Olympics. He also created the world's largest water show for the Bellagio Hotel and Resort in Las Vegas.

Kenny Ortega is the recipient of many distinguished awards, including several American Choreography Awards, the Golden Eagle for outstanding choreography, and the National Academy of Dance Award.

david parsons

David Parsons's boundless energy, creative risk taking, and charming wit have made him one of the dance world's most successful choreographers. The Parsons Dance Company, which he formed in 1987, has toured five continents and given more than 700 performances to an estimated combined audience of more than half a million people in 225 cities.

Mr. Parsons grew up in the Midwest and became attracted to dance after attending a summer camp led by Cliff Kirwin and Paul Chambers. They invited him to join their small performance company, where he danced for the next four years. It was during those years that he created his first dance. Later Parsons won a scholarship to the Ailey School, where he studied the techniques of Horton and Graham. In 1987 he became a leading dancer with the Paul Taylor Dance Company; he remained with the company for ten years before stepping out on his own.

Parsons has created more than forty works for his company, the most highly acclaimed being *Caught* (1982), *The Envelope* (1986), *Nascimento* (1990), *Ring Around the Rosie* (1993), and *Bachiana* (1993).

vincent paterson

Vincent Paterson's choreographic work in music video, television, commercials, and on stage and screen is among the most highly regarded in the entertainment industry. He emerged from backup dancer and assistant to Michael Peters, in Michael Jackson's *Beat It* and *Thriller* music videos to an impressive choreographer in his own right.

Paterson's *Smooth Criminal* video for Michael Jackson launched his choreographic career and led to his working with the biggest names in music, including Madonna, Paul McCartney, George Harrison, Van Halen, Leann Rimes, and David Lee Roth. He has choreographed more than 125 national ad commercials for IBM, Nike, Sony, Levi's, Coca-Cola, Pepsi, Mercedes-Benz, Anheuser Busch, and American Express. Paterson's television work includes *South Pacific, Elvis Lives, American Country Music Awards, Comic Relief VII* and *VIII,* the Blond Ambition Tour and *In Search of Dr. Seuss,* a body of work that earned seven Emmy nominations and five ACE nominations. He has choreographed numerous stage shows as well, among them *Blacklight Theater, A Salute to Three Carols, Oklahoma—Alzheimer's Benefit, Smoky Joe's Café—Alzheimer's Benefit,* and *Commitment to Life VI.*

Mr. Paterson's film credits include *Havana, Truth or Dare, Hook, The Bird*

Cage, *Evita*, and *Dancer in the Dark*, which won the 2000 Cannes Palme D'Or.

Among Mr. Paterson's many awards are two Drama Logue Awards, for *Kiss of the Spider Woman* and *Gangsta Love* on Broadway, American Choreography Awards, and others.

moses pendleton

Moses Pendleton is among the most inventive and conceptually articulate dance choreographers of the twentieth century. In 1971 he cofounded Pilobolus Dance Theater with five of his former Dartmouth College friends. The company would go on to receive world acclaim for its blend of acrobatics and imagination.

In 1980 Mr. Pendleton began working outside the company and choreographed the closing ceremony for the Winter Olympics at Lake Placid. He performed a solo work called *Momix*, which a year later became the name of the company he cofounded with Daniel Ezralow. For the past twenty years Momix has been celebrated for its stunning presentations using the elements of imagery, props, lighting, humor, and the human body. Momix has toured worldwide, with performances in the United States, Canada, Europe, South America, and Asia.

In addition to stage performances, Pendleton has worked on special projects in film and on television, including five Italian features that were broadcast to fifty-five countries, PBS's *Dance in America* series, *Homage to Picasso*, and a work for the San Francisco Giants that was the forerunner of *Baseball*, one of the company's most popular pieces. Mr. Pendleton has been a creative force

for other companies and projects, including the Joffrey, Milan's La Scala, Deutsche Opera, the US Spoleto Festival, and the Metropolitan Opera.

Moses Pendleton has received a Guggenheim Fellowship, the Governor's Award from the Connecticut Commission, and a Positano Choreographic Award.

pilobolus

Pilobolus is a world-class dance company deeply committed to its collaborative creative process and varied repertory of movable body sculptures. Named after a sun-loving fungus that grows in barnyards and pastures, Pilobolus, after thirty years, continues to mystify audiences on the stage and through television broadcasts around the world.

The company grew out of a dance class at Dartmouth College in 1971. The group's singular focus was to create something new and innovative that could reach a broad audience. Its founding members include Moses Pendleton, Jonathan Wolken, Robby Barnett, Michael Tracy, Martha Clarke, and Alison Chase. The company is based in Washington Depot, Connecticut, with four of its founding members choreographing for six dancers. The company is a self-sufficient organization, with its founders managing and publicizing its own programs. The works that it performs are drawn from codified dance movement but go through a reinvention process during intense periods of improvisation and creative play.

The company's works are also represented in the repertoires of other major dance companies including the Joffrey,

Feld, Ohio, and Hartford Ballets, Ballet National de Nancy et de Lorraine in France, and Italy's Verona Ballet.

Among the many prestigious honors that Pilobolus has received are the Scotsman Award for performances at the Edinburgh Festival, the Berlin Critic's Prize, the New England Theater Conference Prize, the Brandeis Award, the Connecticut Commission on the Arts Award for Excellence, and the 1997 Prime Time Emmy for Performance.

eleo pomare

Eleo Pomare formed his first dance company in 1958 after graduating from New York's High School for the Performing Arts. Four years later he received the John Hay Whitney Fellowship and the opportunity to travel to Europe, where he studied with legendary choreographers Kurt Jooss and Harold Kreutzberg and began defining his artistic voice. Upon his return to the United States, he revived the Eleo Pomare Dance Company, and also choreographed works for the Alvin Ailey American Dance Theater, Maryland Ballet, Dayton Contemporary Dance Company, Cleo Parker Robinson Dance Ensemble, National Ballet of Holland, Australian Contemporary Dance Company, and others.

Three of Mr. Pomare's works—*Blues for the Jungle* (1965), *Missa Luba* (1965), and *Las Desenamoradas* (1967)—have been reconstructed as classic works for the American Dance Festival, made possible by a grant by the Ford Foundation. Other signature works include *Hex* (1964), *Plague* (1993), *A Horse Named Dancer* (1995), and *Raft* (1996).

His company has performed at the Kennedy Center for the Performing Arts, New York's City Center, Alice Tully Hall at Lincoln Center, the Joyce Theater, Montreal's Theatre Maisonneuve, and the Adelaide Festival in Australia.

Mr. Pomare received numerous grants from the National Endowment for the Arts from the mid-1970s through the 1990s. He is also a Guggenheim Fellow and has received many awards, including the New Voices of Harlem Award in 1988, the International Association of Blacks in Dance Outstanding Achievement Award in 1994 and 2002, the SANKOFA Award: Living Legends from Florida's A&M University, and many prestigious certificates of recognition.

ann reinking

Ann Reinking is regarded as the foremost interpreter of the Bob Fosse style, having been his protégée during the 1970s and 1980s. In addition to dancing in his shows, she also appeared in his film *All That Jazz*.

Ms. Reinking began her ballet training in her birthplace, Seattle, Washington. Robert Joffrey, recognizing her talent as a singer and actor, advised her to set her sights on Broadway. She landed a part in the chorus of *Cabaret*, which led to other shows, like *Over Here!*, *Goodtime Charley*, *Chicago*, and *Dancin'*.

In 1996 Ms. Reinking restaged Fosse's *Chicago* and shortly thereafter created *Fosse*—a Broadway dance musical show in tribute to her late mentor. Both shows earned Tony Awards for Best Musical.

She went on to choreograph the Broadway show *The Look of Love* (2003) to the music of Burt Bacharach and Hal David. Ms. Reinking is also the director of the Florida-based Broadway Theater Project, which has become one of the most highly respected dance theater workshops in America.

In addition to receiving Tony Awards and nominations, Ms. Reinking has been honored with lifetime achievement awards from the Drama League, the Musical Hall of Fame, and the Elan Awards.

dwight rhoden

Dwight Rhoden blends technical virtuosity with emotional vulnerability in his highly visual choreography. He began his dance career at the age of seventeen in his hometown of Dayton, Ohio, where he joined the Dayton Contemporary Dance Company, founded by the legendary Geraldyne Blunden. Next, Rhoden danced with Les Ballet de Montreal, before becoming a featured performer with the Alvin Ailey American Dance Theater. Alvin Ailey would become one of Rhoden's most important mentors and supporters.

In 1994 Rhoden and his partner and muse, Desmond Richardson, left the Ailey company and formed the highly acclaimed Complexions Dance Company. Rhoden has choreographed more than fifty works for the company as well as works for the Alvin Ailey American Dance Theater, Phoenix Dance Company, Pennsylvania Ballet, Joffrey Ballet, Aspen/Santa Fe Ballet Company, and others.

His best-known pieces include *Ave Maria* (1995), *Global Warming* (1996), *Solo* (1998), *Please, Please, Please* (1999),

Higher Ground (2000), and *Lament* (2000).

Mr. Rhoden has lectured and served as "Artist in Residence" at universities around the country. In 1998 he received a New York Foundation for the Arts Award, and he was honored in 2001 with the Choo-San Goh Award for Choreography.

cleo parker robinson

Cleo Parker Robinson formed her Cleo Parker Robinson Dance Ensemble after graduating from Denver University in 1970. She has since collaborated with many leading choreographers, including Katherine Dunham, Donald McKayle, Talley Beatty, and Eleo Pomare, as well as author Maya Angelou and photographer Gordon Parks. Ms. Robinson's opera collaborations include *Aida, Salome, Samson and Delilah, Carmen, Porgy and Bess,* and *Dream on Monkey Mountain.*

Ms. Robinson's company has toured Africa, Asia, and the Middle East. In the United States the group has performed at such famed venues as the Kennedy Center, Lincoln Center, Jacob's Pillow Dance Festival, and the Joyce Theater.

Ms. Robinson has received fellowships from the National Endowment for the Arts, the Pew Charitable Trust, the Colorado Council on the Arts, the Lila Wallace Foundation, and others. She has also been honored with Colorado's Governor's Award for Excellence in the Arts, the Denver Mayor's Award, and an Honorary Doctorate of Fine Arts from the University of Denver. Ms. Robinson has served as a panelist for the National Endowment for the Arts and the

National Foundation for Advancement in the Arts. In 1999 she was appointed by President Clinton and confirmed by the Senate to the National Council on the Arts.

alex romero

Alex Romero began his Hollywood career as a dancer and went on to become a dance assistant and choreographer. At MGM, with Gene Kelly, Fred Astaire, Hermes Pan, Robert Alton, Michael Kidd, Nick Castle, and many others, Mr. Romero developed his own choreographic style, assisting in the creation of *The Belle of New York* (Robert Alton and Fred Astaire), *Annie Get Your Gun* (Robert Alton), *The Barkleys of Broadway* (Robert Alton and Fred Astaire), *An American in Paris* (Gene Kelly), *On the Town* (Gene Kelly), *Les Girls* (Jack Cole), *Kiss Me Kate* (Hermes Pan), *Small Town Girl* (Busby Berkeley), *Take Me Out to the Ball Game* (Gene Kelly), *Seven Brides for Seven Brothers* (Michael Kidd), *Show Boat* (Robert Alton), *Skirts Ahoy* (Nick Castle), and many other films.

Mr. Romero's own choreographic credits include several popular films of the 1960s through the 1980s, among them *Gigi, Jailhouse Rock, I'll Cry Tomorrow, The Four Horsemen of the Apolcalypse, The Prodigal, Love at First Bite, The Outriders, Speedway, The Stripper, Heidi's Song, Inside Straight,* and *The Frisco Kid.*

In 2001 Mr. Romero was honored with Jazz Dance LA Foundation's Lifetime Achievement Award.

anna sokolow

Anna Sokolow distinguished herself as a rebel for the human spirit and the art form. Fiercely devoted to the original intent of modern dance—self-expression through movement—she choreographed works that were passionate commentaries directed at breaking down inhibitions in a quest for truthful and organic movement and performance integrity. Ms. Sokolow's influence was far-reaching, whether in teaching movement to actors in the Actor's Studio or in choreographing Broadway shows, such as *Opus 63* and *Hair.*

Ms. Sokolow received her dance training at the legendary Neighborhood Playhouse, where she studied with Martha Graham and Louis Horst before joining the Martha Graham Dance Company as a teenager. She left the Graham company in 1938 and formed her own company. Ms. Sokolow had strong ties to Mexico and Israel, where she taught and helped both countries form their first modern dance performance groups. (Ballet Bellas Artes and the Inbal Dance Theater). More than seventy-five companies worldwide have performed her dances. Many of Ms. Sokolow's works are moody and highly dramatic and deal with social issues. Among her most noted works are *Homage to Garcia Lorca* (1941), *The Little Foxes* (1949), *Lyric Suite* (1953), *Rooms* (1961), *Steps of Silence* (1968), and *Two Preludes* (1987).

Ms. Sokolow received numerous honors and awards, including the American-Israel Cultural Foundation Tarbut Medal, Brandeis University's Creative Arts Medal, Dance Magazine Award (in 1938 and 1961), and honorary doctorates from Ohio State University and Boston Conservatory.

Anna Sokolow died in 2000 at the age of ninety.

gus solomons jr.

Gus Solomons Jr. has long been at the forefront of postmodern dance, first as a dancer in the 1960s and later as a choreographer with his company, Gus Solomons Jr. Dance Company.

Mr. Solomons' early dance training was in ballet and modern dance (Mary Wigman's technique) in his native Boston. After graduating with a bachelor's degree in architecture from MIT, he studied and performed in the companies of Donald McKayle, Pearl Lang, Martha Graham, Merce Cunningham, and others.

For his own company he choreographed *City/Motion/Space/Game* (1968), *Con/Text* (1986), *Site Line* (1989), *Opus Pocus* (1991), *Red Squalls I* (1992) and *Red Squalls II* (1997), and many other works. He cofounded the performance group Paradigm in 1998 with Carmen de Lavallade and Dudley Williams, for which he both choreographs and dances.

Mr. Solomons is a highly sought-after teacher, having served on the faculty of New York University's Tisch School of the Arts and as dean of the California Institute for the Arts. He has taught in schools throughout the United States, Argentina, Russia, and France. He is a highly respected writer and reviewer and has written extensively on the subject of dance for the *Village Voice*, *Dance Magazine*, *Ballet Review*, and the *Chronicle of Higher Education*. Among the awards he has received are the 2000 Bessie Award for Sustained Achievement in Chore-

ography and the Robert Muh Alumni Achievement Award from MIT.

elizabeth streb

Ms. Streb received her dance education at the State University of New York at Brockport, where she studied the techniques of Merce Cunningham, Doris Humphrey, and Charles Weidman. She attributes the development of her action-oriented choreography to her experiences with downhill skiing and motorcycle racing. Ms. Streb is best known for extreme-action choreography and acrobatic-like work. Since founding her company, STREB, in 1985, she has taken her daredevil high-impact performance pieces on tour to Australia, Europe, Asia, and extensively across the United States. Her work has been featured in the media and has appeared on ABC *World News Tonight*, CBS *Sunday Morning*, and *The Late Show with David Letterman*, as well as on other shows.

Her signature works include *Amphibian* (1985), *In the Blink of an Eye* (1987), *Mass* (1990), *Action Heroes* (2001), and *Pop Action* (2003). Her short series works include *Airlines*, *Airwaves*, *Fall Line*, *Freeflight*, *Pole Vaults*, *Ringside*, and *Runaway*.

Ms. Streb is the recipient of fellowships from the Guggenheim Foundation and the National Endowment for the Arts. She has also been honored with a Bessie Award, a MacArthur Foundation Fellowship for Lifetime Achievement, and a position as Dean's Special Scholar at the State University of New York at Brockport.

susan stroman

Susan Stroman is one of the most well-respected and sought-after choreographers of Broadway, the concert stage, and on television.

The former Broadway dancer has been creating her highly successful works for more than a decade. Her award-winning shows include *Crazy for You* (1992), *Show Boat* (1995), *Big* (1996), *Steel Pier* (1997), *Oklahoma!* (1998), *Contact* (1999), *The Music Man* (2000), and *The Producers* (2001). Her Off-Broadway credits include *Flora, the Red Menace*, while her choreographic work for the New York Opera includes *Don Giovanni, A Little Night Music*, and *110 in the Shade*. She choreographed *Blossom Got Kissed* for the New York City Ballet to celebrate its fiftieth anniversary, and the Martha Graham Dance Company commissioned her to create *But Not for Me*.

Ms. Stroman has been equally prolific on the small screen, choreographing numerous award-winning television specials, including *An Evening with the Boston Pops, A Tribute to Leonard Bernstein*, and *Sondheim: A Celebration at Carnegie Hall* for PBS. She has also choreographed the annual spectacular event *A Christmas Carol* for Madison Square Garden, as well as the 1999 dance film *Center Stage*.

Ms. Stroman is the recipient of numerous Tony Awards, the Outer Critics Circle Award, Drama Desk Awards, Emmy nominations, an American Choreography Award, and the Laurence Olivier Award for Choreography. Paul Taylor modestly refers to himself as a "reporter" whose job it is to observe and record his impressions. Yet audiences and critics regard him as the reigning master of modern dance.

paul taylor

Mr. Taylor, who grew up in Washington, DC, studied art until he discovered dance in the late 1940s. He attended Juilliard and as early as 1954 began choreographing his own dances. By 1955 he was a highly acclaimed soloist in the Martha Graham Dance Company, and he remained with the company well into the 1960s. His creative output spans almost half a century, with such signature works as *3 Epitaphs* (1956), *Aureole* (1962), *Esplanade* (1978), *Cloven Kingdom* (1976), *Arden Court* (1981), *Last Look* (1985), *Roses* (1985), *Speaking in Tongues* (1988), *Company B* (1991), *Piazzolla Caldera* (1997), and *Promethean Fire* (2002).

Since 1960 the Paul Taylor Dance Company has performed in more than 450 cities in more than sixty countries. Mr. Taylor has received dozens of awards, including the National Medal of Arts presented by President Clinton in 1993, the 1992 Kennedy Honors, and the Algur H. Meadows Award for Excellence in the Arts. In 1969 Mr. Taylor was knighted by the French government as Chevalier de L'Ordes des Arts et des Letters. He was also the subject of the Oscar-nominated film *Dancemaker*.

glen tetley

Glen Tetley received his early training with dance pioneer Hanya Holm in the mid-1940s. He danced in her company and later in the companies of Martha Graham, Doris Humphrey and Charles Weidman, José Limón, and Pearl Lang. Mr. Tetley was a founding member of the Joffrey Ballet during the 1950s and a principal soloist with the American Ballet Theater.

By 1962 Mr. Tetley was choreographing his own dances. He traveled to Europe, where he flourished as a ballet choreographer and artistic director. He served as artistic director to the Netherlands Dance Theater and the Stuttgart Ballet, in addition to working with numerous other companies, including the Royal Danish Ballet, Royal Swedish Ballet, National Ballet of Norway, and Paris Opera Ballet.

Mr. Tetley has choreographed more than seventy ballets, including *Pierrot Lunaire* (1962), *Embrace Tiger Return to Mountain* (1968), *Voluntaries* (1976), *The Tempest* (1979), *Alice* (1986), *Orpheus* (1987), and *Tagore* (1989).

In 1981 Mr. Tetley received the Queen Elizabeth II Coronation Award from the Royal Academy of Dancing. His televised version of *Firebird*, performed by the Royal Danish Ballet, won the 1982 Prix d'Italia RAI Prize and the Edinburgh Festival presented him with the Tennant-Caledonian Award for *Murder Hope of Women*. He has been awarded the Order of Merit by the king of Norway. In the United States, the state of Ohio presented him with the Ohioana Career Medal for his outstanding achievement, and New York University honored him with its Alumni Achievement Award.

helgi tomasson

Helgi Tomasson became artistic director of the San Francisco Ballet in 1985, raising the company's profile from that of a regional troupe to a national treasure praised for its rich repertoire and skilled dancers. Born in Reykjavik, Iceland, Tomasson began his ballet training at the National Theater's affiliated school and then continued at the Pantomime Theater in Copenhagen's Tivoli Gardens. He was discovered there by Jerome Robbins, who arranged for him to study in America at the School of American Ballet. Tomasson began his professional dancing career with the Joffrey Ballet and then danced with the Harkness Ballet before joining the New York City Ballet as a principal dancer.

Mr. Tomasson won the silver medal in the First International Ballet Competition in Moscow. He is one of the foremost interpreters of works of George Balanchine and Jerome Robbins, both of whom created roles expressly for him. He choreographed his first ballet in 1980 and has continued to create such highly acclaimed works as *Intimate Voices* (1987), *Swan Lake* (1988), *Sleeping Beauty* (1990), *Romeo and Juliet* (1994), *Silver Ladders* (1998), *Bartok Divertimento* (2002), and *Don Quixote* (2003).

Mr. Tomasson is the recipient of many distinguished awards, including the Golden Plate Award (1992) and the Isadora Duncan Special Award. In May 2001 he was honored with the rank of Officier in the French Order of Arts and Letters. He holds honorary doctorates from Juilliard and the Dominican College of San Rafael.

tommy tune

Tommy Tune has been the creative force behind many of Broadway's biggest hits. He is the only person in history to win Tony Awards in each of the categories of dancer, singer, choreographer, and director and to win awards two years in a row.

Born in Texas, the six-foot-six dancer/choreographer began his training in tap, acrobatics, and ballet at the age of five. He made his Broadway debut in 1965 in *Baker Street* and later appeared in *A Joyful Noise* (1967) and *How Now, Dow Jones* (1968).

In 1973 he danced in Michael Bennett's *Seesaw*, which won him his first Tony Award. His successful career continued as a director and choreographer in *The Club* (1976), *The Best Little Whorehouse in Texas* (1976), *The Will Rogers Follies* (1978, 1991), *A Day in Hollywood, a Night in the Ukraine* (1980), *Nine* (1982), *My One and Only* (1983), and *Grand Hotel* (1989).

Mr. Tune is the recipient of nine Tony Awards, eight Drama Desk Awards, two Obie Awards, two Astaire Awards (1990 and 1991), Dance Magazine's Lifetime Achievement Award, the 1990 Drama League Musical Theater Award, the George Abbot Award for Lifetime Achievement, and many other honors.

doug varone

Doug Varone began his performance career dancing in the company of José Limón, then moved to the Lar Lubovitch Dance Company. Since founding his own company, Doug Varone and Dancers, in 1986, he has performed with his troupe in more than fifty-three cities in nearly thirty states, as well as in Europe, South America, Asia, and Canada. He is best known for his many concert stage pieces, among them *Rise* (1993), *Aperture* (1994), *Possession* (1994), *Home* (1998), *Bel Canto* (1998), *Sleeping with Giants* (1999), and *12 Intimate Dances* (2000). Mr. Varone has also worked extensively in theater, television, and film. In 1994 he choreographed the dance and underwater sequences for *The Planets*, which aired on the A&E Network. In 1997 he made his Broadway debut with *Triumph of Love*; that year he also choreographed and staged works for the Minnesota Opera and the New York City Opera.

Mr. Varone's honors include several NEA Fellowships and a Guggenheim Fellowship, the Choo-San Goh Award, Metropolitan Life's Emerging Artist Award, and a Bessie for Sustained Achievement in Choreography. He has also been nominated for an International Emmy Award and a Cable ACE Award.

edward villella

Edward Villella was America's first male dance superstar. He originated many roles while he was a principal dancer in the New York City Ballet, among them *Tarantella*, the "Rubies" section of *Jewels*, the role of Oberon in *A Midsummer Night's Dream*, and, perhaps his most famous role, in the 1960 revival of Balanchine's 1929 masterpiece, *Prodigal Son*. Mr. Villella danced for President Kennedy's inaugural and for Presidents Johnson, Nixon, and Ford.

In 1985 he founded the Miami City Ballet. In addition to directing and choreographing for the company, he serves as advisor and artist in residence for many artistic and cultural institutions, including Florida Atlantic University and George Mason University in Virginia. He serves on the board of trustees of the School of American Ballet, is past chairman of New York City's Commission for Cultural Affairs, and is a former member of the NEA's Dance Advisory Panel, as well as the National Council on the Arts.

The recipient of numerous honors, including the 1997 Medal of Arts and the National Arts and Letters Award for Lifetime Achievement, Mr. Villella is one of several who have been named "America's Irreplaceable Dance Treasures" by the Dance Heritage Coalition. He has also been named a Kennedy Center honoree and is an inductee into the Florida Artists Hall of Fame, He is the recipient of honorary doctorates from Yale University, the University of North Carolina, and the College of Charleston. In 1997 he won an Emmy for his CBS production of *Harlequinade*.

christopher wheeldon

Christopher Wheeldon began his training at the age of eight in Yeovil, Somerset, England. Four years later, he was admitted into the Royal Ballet School. In 1991, at the age of eighteen, he became a member of the Royal Ballet and performed the works of such great ballet choreographers as Frederick Ashton, Kenneth McMillan, and George Balanchine. That same year he won the Gold Medal at the Prix de Lausanne Competition.

In 1993 he became a member of the New York City Ballet and five years later was promoted to the rank of soloist. Mr. Wheeldon retired from dancing in

the spring of 2000 to concentrate on his choreography work and a year later was appointed the company's first resident choreographer. In addition to choreographing work for the New York City Ballet, he has created works for the Boston Ballet, the Royal Ballet, the San Francisco Ballet, and the Colorado Ballet.

His choreographic works include *Slavonic Dances* (1997), *Firebird* (1999), *Sea Pictures* (2000), *Mercurial Manoeuvres* (2000), *Polyphonia* (2001), and *Variations Serieuses* (2002). Mr. Wheeldon made his Broadway debut in 2002, choreographing the stage version of *Sweet Smell of Success*.

He has been honored with the Mae L. Wien Award from the School of American Ballet and Lincoln Center's Martin E. Segal Award.

onna white

Onna White has enjoyed a successful dance career on the concert stage, on Broadway, and in feature films. She has been credited with creating some of the finest musical numbers at the end of the golden age of the movie musical.

Born in Canada and raised in Powell River, British Columbia, she moved to San Francisco in 1939 and shortly thereafter was admitted to the San Francisco Ballet, where she would perform leading classical roles. She made her Broadway debut in 1947 in *Finian's Rainbow* and appeared in *Hold It* (1948), *Regina* (1949), *Arms and the Girl* (1950), and *Silk Stockings* (1955).

Ms. White began her choreographic career assisting Michael Kidd while also dancing in *Guys and Dolls* (1950). In addition to restaging Kidd's *Guys and Dolls* and *Finian's Rainbow*, she choreo-

graphed *Carmen Jones* and *Fanny* (1956), *The Music Man* (1957), *Half a Sixpence* (1965), *Mame* (1966), *Gigi* (1973), *Goodtime Charley* (1975), and *A Little Night Music* (1990).

Ms. White was nominated eight times for Tony Awards. She received the Drama-Logue Award for *A Little Night Music* and the Gypsy Lifetime Achievement Award from the Professional Dancer's Society in 1991. She is also the proud recipient of an honorary Oscar given to her in 1968 for her choreography of the Oscar-winning film *Oliver*.

Editor's Note

Since the original printing of *Masters of Movement* in 2004, some of the profiled artists have died.

Onna White, April 8, 2005, age 83

Fayard Nicholas, January 24, 2006, age 91

Glen Tetley, January 26, 2006, age 80

Katherine Dunham, May 21, 2006, age 96

Sophie Maslow, June 25, 2006, age 95

acknowledgments

I am most appreciative to Caroline Newman and Don Fehr of Smithsonian Books for their recognition of this work as an important historical document and educational resource. Not only did they embrace *Masters of Movement* with enormous enthusiasm but they, along with Carolyn Gleason, Emily Sollie, Joanne Reams, Jan McInroy, and Kate McConnell, helped produce this beautifully crafted work. To them I extend special thanks.

To the artists presented in this work who entrusted me with their personal and professional stories and opened their homes, studios, stage doors, and above all their hearts, I am forever grateful. I would like to extend a special thanks to all the agents, managers, assistants, and staff who helped me schedule appointments, assisted in the shoots, served me coffee and juice, and even helped carry my gear.

I am often asked how I was able to assemble such a large body of work. The answer is that it took six years and the love of a wonderful husband. Betzalel "Bitzy" Eichenbaum has been my guiding light. He showed me by example that strength of character, sprinkled with generous portions of chutzpah, can make any dream a reality. His love, dedication, and financial support made this book possible.

To my three beautiful children, Ariella, Jeremy, and Talia—thank you for your patience, understanding, and love.

I am forever grateful to my brother, Aron Hirt-Manheimer, who from day one shared this unique journey with me. His steadfast commitment, personal and professional support, and love helped drive this work. A master editor, Aron taught me how to stage my vision and dance my words with imagery, intimacy, and intelligence. Then he moved in with the grace and finesse of Fred Astaire and stylishly smoothed the rough edges. Our collaboration has been among the most rewarding and meaningful experiences of my life.

I extend a special thanks to Clive Barnes for his kindness, literary contribution, and friendship.

There are many other people who also deserve thanks and recognition for their support of and contributions to this work: Russell Adams of Schulman's Photo Lab in Los Angeles, Zina Bethune, Carole Bidnick, Larry Billman of the Academy of Dance on Film, Beverly Blossom, Doug Caldwell, Connie Chin of Jacob's Pillow Dance Festival, Lisa Zeno Churgin, Pamela Cooper, Marguerite Derricks, Elsie Dunin and Joanne Kealiinohomoku of Cross Cultural Dance Resource, Sarah Eichenbaum, Sarah Elgart, Laura Faure of the Bates Dance Festival. J. R. Glover of Jacob's Pillow Dance Festival, Judy Hirt-Manheimer, Geoffrey Holder, Anne Holliday of the Stowitts Museum, Seth Joel, Kim Kaffrey of the Dance Art Museum of the Americas, Barbara Kaplan, Mary Ann Kellogg, Marcea Lane of Marcea Sportswear, Diana Leidel, Molly Malloy, Julie McDonald and Tony Selznik of McDonald-Selznik and Associates, Sean McLeod of the New York Institute of Dance and Education, Mary Miller, Madeline Nichols of the New York Library for the Performing Arts, Norton Owen of Jacob's Pillow Dance Festival, Amy Paston, Rudy Perez, Richard Philp, Lily Kharazzi, Stephanie Riven and Kathryn Adamchick of the Center of Creative Arts, Francis Roach, Bea Rovner, Howard Schatz, Allegra Fuller Snyder—Professor Emerita of Dance and Dance Ethnology at UCLA, Ted Spiegel, Donna Sternberg, Emma Lou Thomas—Professor Emerita of Dance History at UCLA, Ann Vashon, and Lula Washington.

BIBLIOGRAPHY

Acocella, Joan. *Mark Morris*. New York: Noonday Press, 1993.

Ailey, Alvin. *Revelations*. Secaucus, NJ: Carol Publishing Group, 1995.

Atkins, Cholly, and Jacqui Malone. *Class Act*. New York: Columbia University Press, 2001.

Billman, Larry. *Film Choreographers and Dance Directors*. Jefferson, NC: McFarland, 1997.

Bremser, Martha. *Fifty Contemporary Choreographers*. New York: Routledge, 1999.

Brown, Jean Morrison. *The Vision of Modern Dance*. Hightstown, NJ: Princeton Book Company, 1979.

Clarke, Mary. *The Encyclopedia of Dance and Ballet*. New York: G. P. Putnam, 1977.

Cohen, Selma Jeanne. *Doris Humphrey*. Pennington, NJ: Princeton Book Company, 1972.

——. *International Encyclopedia of Dance*. New York: Oxford University Press, 1998.

de Mille, Agnes. *Martha: The Life and Work of Martha Graham*. New York: Random House, 1956.

Desmond, Jane C. *Meaning in Motion*. Durham, NC: Duke University Press, 1997.

Dunning, Jennifer. *Alvin Ailey*. New York: Addison-Wesley, 1996.

Easton, Carol. *No Intermissions: The Life of Agnes de Mille*. Cambridge, MA: Da Capo Press, 1996.

Emery, Lynne Fauley. *Black Dance from 1619 to Today*. Hightstown, NJ: Dance Horizons, 1972.

Greco, José. *The Gypsy in My Soul*. New York: Doubleday, 1977.

Halprin, Anna. *Moving towards Life*. Hanover, NH: Wesleyan University Press/University Press of New England.

Hill, Constance Valis. *Brotherhood in Rhythm: The Jazz Tap Dancing of the Nicholas Brothers*. New York: Oxford University Press, 2000.

Jamison, Judith. *Dancing Spirit*. New York: Doubleday, 1993.

Jones, Bill T. *Last Night on Earth*. New York: Pantheon, 1995.

Jowitt, Deborah. *Meredith Monk*. Baltimore: Johns Hopkins University Press, 1997.

Lawrence, Greg. *Dance with Demons: The Life of Jerome Robbins*. New York: G. P. Putnam, 2001.

Limón, José. *An Unfinished Memoir*. Middletown, CT: Wesleyan University Press, 1998.

Louis, Murray. *Murray Louis: On Dance*. Chicago: A Cappella Books, 1992.

Luigi. *Luigi's Jazz Warm Up*. Hightstown, NJ: Princeton Book Company, 1977.

Martin, John. *Introduction to the Dance*. New York: A. S. Barnes, 1933. Reprint, New York: Brooklyn Dance Horizons, 1965.

McKayle, Donald. *Transcending Boundaries: My Dancing Life*. New York: Routledge, 2002.

Mitchell, Jack. *Alvin Ailey American Dance Theater*. Kansas City: A Donna Martin Book, 1993.

Morgan, Barbara. *Martha Graham*. New York: Duell, Sloan, and Pearce, 1941.

Needham, Maureen. *I See America Dancing*. Chicago: University of Illinois Press, 2002.

Sontag, Susan. *On Photography*. New York: Picador, 1973.

Taper, Bernard. *Balanchine*. Berkeley: University of California Press, 1987.

Tracey, Robert. *Goddess: Martha Graham's Dancers Remember*. New York: Proscenium Publishers, 1997.

Tune, Tommy. *Footnotes*. New York: Simon and Schuster, 1997.

Villella, Edward. *Prodigal Son*. New York: Simon and Schuster, 1992.

Warren, Larry. *Anna Sokolow*. Pennington, NJ: Princeton Book Company, 1991.

INDEX

7 New Dances 175
890 Broadway 25, 137

Affairs of Dobie Gillis, The 167
Agnon 187
Ailey, Alvin 6–7, 31, 34, 78, 118–119,
   123, 125, 178–179, 183, 222,
A Little Night Music 93
Alvin Ailey American Dance Theater
   2, 90, 117–119, 177–179, 227
Allen, Debbie 77–79, 246
Alton, Robert 115, 166–167
American Ballet Theater 43, 115, 215
American Choreography Awards 81,
   161, 225
An American in Paris 115, 166
Annie Get Your Gun 47, 115
Andrews, Julie 71, 82–83, 99
Ann–Margaret 50
Anthony, Mary 145–147, 221, 246
Apollo Theater 42, 163
Arenal, Julie 170
Argentinita 105
A Rockette's Tail 177
Ashston, Frederick 34, 186
Astaire, Fred 10, 115, 142, 166–167, 235
Atkins, Cholly 161–163, 246

Babes in Arms 11
Balanchine, George 11, 17–19, 26, 34,
   146, 186–187
Baldwin, James 182
Ballet Caravan 45–46
Ballet Rambert 215
Ballet Theater 46
Band Wagon, The 45, 115
Barkleys of Broadway, The 166
Barnes, Clive 54, 118
Barnett, Robby 57–59, 135

Baryshnikov, Mikhail 43
Basil, Toni 49–51, 170, 246
Baxter, Ivy 125
Beatty, Tally 183
Béjart, Maurice 123
Belafonte, Julie 85
Bennett, Michael 14, 70, 98
Berger, Rita 202
Berkeley, Busby 166
Billy Budd 191
Billy the Kid 46
Birdcage, The 47, 74
Birch, Patricia 93–95, 246–247
Blues in the Jungle 182
Blues Suite 178
Breaux, Marc 81–83, 247
Brown, Ronald K. 221–223, 247
Bujones, Fernando 50
Bye Bye, Birdie 39
Byrd, Donald 205–207, 247

Cabaret 97–98
Campbell, Don 50
Can Can 46
Candide 93
Carmen Jones 38
Caron, Leslie 115
Carnegie Hall 51
Castle, Nick 10–11, 166
Caton, Edward 114
Charisse, Cyd 115
Charisse, Nanette 209
Chase, Alison 57–59, 135
Chase, Lucia 45, 115, 215
Chattanooga Choo Choo 11
Chicago 14, 47, 70, 99
Cinderella 191
City Center 38
Clark, Russell 161, 233–235, 247

Clarke, Martha 58, 135
Coco Coco 14
Cole, Jack 14, 166, 209, 211
Coles, Honi 43, 163
Collins, Janet 5
Contact 21–23, 47
Corbett, Lynne Taylor 177–179, 248
Cotton Club, The 11, 42
Cunningham, Merce 14, 90–91, 93–94,
   125
Cry 118–119

Dale, Grover 189–191, 248
Damn Yankees 99, 210
Dance of the Horsemen 107
Dancer in the Dark 75
Dances at a Gathering 19, 187
Daniele, Graciela 13–15, 47
Da Pron, Louis 114
Davis Jr., Sammy 43
de Lavallade, Carmen 5–7, 91, 248
de Mille, Agnes 14–15, 45, 70, 94
Denishawn 91
Dion, Celine 194–195
Dirty Dancing 171, 235
Donen, Stanley 71
Dragone, Franco 194–195
Dreamgirls 175
Dubrovska, Felia 214
Dudley, Jane 146
Duncan, Isadora 101, 142
Dunham, Katherine 78–79, 81, 85–87,
   119, 202, 222, 248

Ebsen, Buddy 10
EFX 109, 111
Ellen, Vera 115
Embattled Garden 215
Episodes 187

Eros 226
Esplanade 175
Eugene Loring's Dance Players 46
Evita 75
Expression of a Man 90
Ezralow, Daniel 134, 225–227, 249

Fagan, Garth 125–127, 249
Fame 79
Fancy Free 47
Facciuto, Eugene. *See* Luigi
Feld, Eliot 25–27, 249
Finian's Rainbow 38, 46
Flashdance 235
Fokine, Michel 45, 114
Follies 14
Fosse 69
Fosse, Bob 14, 70, 78, 98, 167, 210–211
Fromm, Eric 87
Fonteyn, Margot 78
From Me to You in About Half the Time
   121

Garland, Judy 115
Garrison, Miranda 171
Gennaro, Peter 209, 211
Gentlemen Prefer Blondes 163
Girl from Kalamazoo, The 11
Giselle 58
Glover, Savion 71
Graf, Steffi 43
Graham, Martha 14, 23, 31, 34, 63, 79,
   91, 93–94, 102, 125–127,
   142–143–146, 174–175, 178, 211,
   214, 222, 226
Grease 93, 95, 170
Greco, José 105–107, 249
Green Bird 226
Greenwillow 191

Guys and Dolls 38, 45–47, 81

Hair 169–170

Hale, Teddy 42

Half a Sixpence 191

Halprin, Anna 229–231, 250

Haney, Carol 166

Happy Hunting 115

Harris, Rennie 157–159, 250

Hawkins, Eric 143

H' Doubler, Margaret 229

Here's Where I Belong 14

Hello Dolly 37, 46–47

Herskovits, Melville 87

Higher Ground 122

Hines, Gregory 41–43, 71, 195, 250

Hinkson, Mary 125

Holm, Hanya 83, 142, 146, 214

Horst, Louis 102, 142, 146, 175

Horton, Lester 5–6, 119, 178

Humphrey, Doris 82, 142, 146, 153

*Introduction, Theme, Variation
    Polonaise, Op. 65* 34

Ito, Michio 114

I Want to Be a Dancing Man 166

Jacob's Pillow Dance Festival 81

Jackson, Michael 74

Jagger, Mick 51

Jailhouse Rock 167

Jamison, Judith 117–119, 179

Jerome Robbins' Broadway 191

Joffrey Ballet 34, 214–215, 227

Joffrey, Robert 214–215

Johnson, Alan 209–211, 251

Jones, Bill T. 149–151

Judson Group, The 175

Kaye, Nora 215

Kajiwara, Mari 118, 125

Kelly, Gene 43, 75, 113, 115, 166–167,
    170–171

Kidd, Michael 38, 45–47, 70, 75, 81–82,
    115, 166, 190, 251

King, Alonzo 197–199, 251

King, King, and King 166

Kirstein, Lincoln 18, 45

Kiss Me Kate 214

Laban, Rudolf 142

Layton, Joe 191

Le Tang, Henry 42–43

La Fille Mal Gardée 186

Lewitzky, Bella 6, 29–31, 251–252

Lil' Abner 82, 190

Lilac Garden 215

Limón, José 125,143, 146, 153, 217, 222

Lion King, The 125–127

Lockers, The 50–51

Loring, Eugene 46, 114, 115

Louis, Murray 90, 141–143, 252

Lubovitch, Lar 137–139, 217, 252

Luigi (Eugene Facciuto) 113–115

Lyric Suite 162

Madonna 74

Mame 37

Mandala 227

Maracci, Carmelita 6

Martin, John 105, 142, 215

Marshall, Rob 47, 97–99

Martins, Peter 186–187

Mary Poppins 82

Maslow, Sophie 101–103, 146, 253

Massine, Leonide 45

Mattox, Matt 14, 209

McBride, Patricia 19

McKayle, Donald 1–3, 78, 85, 253

Michaels, Mia 193–195, 253

Midler, Bette 51

Miller, Norma 79

Miranda, Carmen 49

Momix 135

Monk, Meredith 129–131, 253

Morris, Mark 65–67, 253–254

Music Man, The 21, 23, 39

Neighborhood Playhouse 101

Neither 219

New York City Ballet 23, 34, 127,
186–187, 210

Nicholas, Fayard 9–11, 254

Nicks, Walter 85

Nijinsky, Vaslav 142

Nijinska, Bronislava 114

Nikolais, Alwin 141–143

Nureyev, Rudolf 143

Obukhov, Anatoly 214

O' Conner, Donald 115

Oklahoma! 14, 23

Ortega, Kenny 169–171, 254

Oliver 37, 39

On Stage 46

On the Town 115, 213

Pacific Overtures 93

Pan, Hermes 115, 166, 235

Panaieff, Michel 114

Parade 93

Paradigm 7, 91

Parsons, David 53–55, 226, 254

Passion Distanced 127

Paterson, Vincent 73–75, 254–255

Pendleton, Moses 58, 133–135,
    226–227, 255

Peters, Michael 74

Pierrot Lunaire 215

Pillar of Fire 215

Pilobolus 57–59, 255

Polyphonia 187

Presley, Elvis 50

Platova, Helene 214

Pomare, Eleo 181–183, 255

Prayers from the Edge 177–179

Primus, Pearl 1, 125

Producers, The 21–23, 210

Promises, Promises 14

Pulcinella 19

Radio City Music Hall 14

Ragtime 47

Ragni, Gerome 169

Rainbow 'Round My Shoulder 2

Redfield, Robert 87

Reinking, Ann 69–71, 255

Revelations 178

Rhoden, Dwight 121–123, 256

Richardson, Desmond 121–123

Rivera, Chita 38, 190

Robbins, Jerome 14, 17–19, 26, 34, 45,
    47, 63, 78, 94, 98, 187, 190–191, 214

Robinson Parker, Cleo 85, 201–203, 256

Rome and Jewels 157–159

Romero and Juliet 158, 213

Romero, Alex 115, 165–167, 256

Rooms 62

Ross, Herbert 75

Royal Ballet School 186–187

San Francisco Ballet 34, 38, 185, 187

School of American Ballet 34, 81, 93

Seven Brides for Seven Brothers 45–47,
    166

Shaw, Frieda Marie Richter 38

Show Boat 166

Sims, Sandman 43

Singin' in the Rain 115

Sing, Sing, Sing 166

Sleeping Beauty 155, 199

Small Town Girl 166

Smooth Criminal 74

Sokolow, Anna 61–63, 101, 146,
    256–257

Solo 122

Solomons, Jr., Gus 7, 89–91, 257

Sound of Music 82–83

Stravinsky, Igor 18

Stompin' at the Savoy 79

Stormy Weather 10

Streb, Elizabeth 153–155, 257

Stroman, Susan 21–23, 47, 258

Stuart, Muriel 45

Sullivan, Ed 50, 105–106

Swan Lake 51, 183, 186

Swing 177, 179

Swayze, Patrick 171

Sweet Charity 77

Take Me Out to the Ball Game 166

Taylor, June 115, 190
Taylor, Paul 54, 173–175, 257
Tetley, Glen 82, 213–215, 257–258
They Are Playing Our Song 93
Thompson, Clive 125
Threnody 147
Thriller 74
Tomasson, Helgi 33–35, 258
Toni Basil's Follies Bizarre 170
Tracy, Michael 57–59, 135
Traviata 106
Travolta, John 95
Trisler, Joyce 6
Truitte, James 6
Tudor, Anthony 26, 45, 213
Tune, Tommy 71, 109–111, 258
Turner, Tina 51

Unsinkable Molly Brown, The 191

Van Dyke, Dick 39, 73
Variations Serieuses 187
Varone, Doug 217–219, 258
Verdon, Gwen 70
Vereen, Ben 71
Village I Knew, The 103
Villella, Edward 17–19, 258–259
Vilzak, Anatole 45
Vladimoroff, Pierre 214
von Trier, Lars 75

Watermill 19
Webber, Andrew Lloyd 75
West Side Story 14, 27, 50–51, 77–78,
    93–94, 158, 210–211
What Makes Sammy Run? 14
Wheeldon, Christopher 185–187, 259
Will Rogers Follies, The 111
Weidman, Charles 82–83, 142, 146,
    153
White, Onna 37–39, 115, 259
Wigman, Mary 143
Williams, Dudley 7, 89, 91, 118, 125
Williams, Livinia 125
Williams, Robin 74, 134

Williams, Stanley 18–19
Winters, David 50
Wolken, Jonathan 57–59, 135
Wood, David 226
Wood, Dee Dee 81–83, 247
Wood, Donna 118
Wood, Marni 226

Xanadu 170–171

Yarborough, Sarah 118
Yates, Reginald 85
Young Frankenstein 211

Zane, Arnie 149
Zoot Suit 193